Conservative orators from Baldwin to Cameron

Manchester University Press

**New
Perspectives
on the Right**

Series editor
Richard Hayton

The study of conservative politics, broadly defined, is of enduring scholarly interest and importance, and is also of great significance beyond the academy. In spite of this, for a variety of reasons the study of conservatism and conservative politics was traditionally regarded as something of a poor relation in comparison to the intellectual interest in 'the Left'. In the British context this changed with the emergence of Thatcherism, which prompted a greater critical focus on the Conservative Party and its ideology, and a revitalisation of Conservative historiography. *New Perspectives on the Right* aims to build on this legacy by establishing a series identity for work in this field. It will publish the best and most innovative titles drawn from the fields of sociology, history, cultural studies and political science and hopes to stimulate debate and interest across disciplinary boundaries. *New Perspectives* is not limited in its historical coverage or geographical scope, but is united by its concern to critically interrogate and better understand the history, development, intellectual basis and impact of the Right. Nor is the series restricted by its methodological approach: it will encourage original research from a plurality of perspectives. Consequently, the series will act as a voice and forum for work by scholars engaging with the politics of the Right in new and imaginative ways.

Reconstructing conservatism? The Conservative Party in opposition, 1997–2010

Richard Hayton

Conservative orators from Baldwin to Cameron

Edited by
Richard Hayton and Andrew S. Crines

Manchester University Press

Published by Manchester University Press
Altrincham Street, Manchester M1 7JA

British Library Cataloguing-in-Publication Data
A catalogue record for this book is available from the British Library

Library of Congress Cataloging-in-Publication Data applied for

ISBN 978 07190 9724 9 hardback

First published 2015

The publisher has no responsibility for the persistence or accuracy of URLs for any external or third-party internet websites referred to in this book, and does not guarantee that any content on such websites is, or will remain, accurate or appropriate.

Typeset by Out of House Publishing
Printed in Great Britain by
CPI Group (UK) Ltd, Croydon CR0 4YY

Contents

Contributors

Judi Atkins is a Lecturer in Politics at the University of Coventry, and the author of *Justifying New Labour Policy* (Palgrave Macmillan, 2011).

Tim Bale is the Chair of Politics at Queen Mary University of London and is the author of *The Conservative Party from Thatcher to Cameron* and *The Conservatives since 1945: The Drivers of Party Change* (Oxford University Press, 2013), amongst others.

Mark Bennister is Senior Lecturer in Politics at Canterbury Christ Church University, and specialises in the study of political leadership. He is the author of *Prime Ministers in Power: Political Leadership in Britain and Australia* (Palgrave Macmillan, 2012).

Andrew S. Crines is a Research Fellow in Rhetoric and British Politics at the University of Leeds. He has published in leading academic journals such as *British Politics, Political Quarterly, Representation* and *Politics*. He tweets at @AndrewCrines.

Katharine Dommett is a Lecturer in the Public Understanding of Politics and deputy director of the Crick Centre at the University of Sheffield. She has published in leading academic journals such as *British Politics* and *Political Quarterly*.

Peter Dorey is a professor of British politics at Cardiff University. He is the author of a range of books focused on British politics such as *British Conservatism: The Politics and Philosophy of Inequality* (I.B Tauris, 2011) and sits on the editorial board of the *British Politics* journal.

Brendan Evans is Emeritus Professor of British Politics at the University of Huddersfield. He is the author of *Thatcherism and British Politics: 1975–1999* (Sutton Publishing, 2000) and, with Andrew Taylor, the co-author of *From Salisbury* *to Major: Continuity and Change in Conservative Politics* (Manchester University Press, 1996).

Mark Garnett is Senior Lecturer in Politics at Lancaster University. Amongst numerous other publications he has authored acclaimed biographies including *Keith Joseph: A Life* (Acumen Press, 2001), *Splendid! Splendid! The Authorised Biography of Willie Whitelaw* (Jonathan Cape, 2002) and *Alport: A Study in Loyalty* (Acumen Press, 1999).

Richard Hayton is Lecturer in Politics at the University of Leeds, and the author of *Reconstructing Conservatism? The Conservative Party in Opposition, 1997–2010* (Manchester University Press, 2012). He is also Convenor of the Political Studies Association specialist group for the study of conservatism and Conservative politics. He tweets at @Richard_Hayton.

Timothy Heppell is Associate Professor of British Politics at the University of Leeds and the sole author of four books including, most recently, *The Tories from Winston Churchill to David Cameron* (Bloomsbury, 2014).

Thomas McMeeking is a PhD student in the School of Politics and International Studies at the University of Leeds.

Philip Norton, Baron Norton of Louth, is a Conservative Peer and a leading expert on Parliament, the constitution, and the Conservative Party. He is also Professor of Government at the University of Hull and the author of numerous books, including most recently *The Voice of the Backbenchers* (Conservative History Group, 2013).

Andrew Taylor is a professor of British politics at the University of Sheffield and is the author of a number of books including, most recently, *State Failure* (Palgrave Macmillan, 2013).

Kevin Theakston is a professor of British government at the University of Leeds. He is also the author of *Winston Churchill and the British Constitution* (Politicos, 2004), *After Number 10: Former Prime Ministers in British Politics* (Palgrave Macmillan, 2010) and, more recently, *Winston Churchill* (Shire Books, 2012).

Acknowledgements

This edited book grew out of a conference on Conservative oratory organised under the auspices of the PSA Conservatives and Conservatism Specialist Group. That event was held at the University of Huddersfield in November 2012, and we are grateful to that institution for supporting it. We would like to thank all the contributors for taking part in the conference and for working with us to bring this project to fruition. We would particularly like to thank Tony Mason for supporting this idea from its inception, and owe a debt of gratitude also to the anonymous reviewers for their thoughtful comments and timely feedback.

Richard Hayton and Andrew S. Crines

Abbreviations

BBC — British Broadcasting Corporation
CND — Campaign for Nuclear Disarmament
CPS — Centre for Policy Studies
DSS — Department of Social Security
ERM — Exchange Rate Mechanism
IEA — Institute of Economic Affairs
NHS — National Health Service
PCP — Parliamentary Conservative Party
PMQs — Prime Minister's Questions

Introduction

Analysing oratory in Conservative Party politics

Richard Hayton and Andrew S. Crines

Introduction

The history of the Conservative Party has more often than not been framed around its leaders. The recent chronicle of the party by Robin Harris (2011), for example, proceeds through a series of chapters – 'Peel's Party', 'Disraeli's Party', 'Salisbury's Party' and so on – where there is no doubt what, or rather who, had come to define Conservative politics in any particular era. Only very occasionally is this narrative punctured by an event so cataclysmic or profound in its consequences that it is deemed worthy of a chapter in its own right, for example 'Suez', '1922' or 'Appeasement' (Harris, 2011). In adopting this approach Harris is not out of step with the rich tradition of Conservative historiography (Hayton, 2012a: 6–9), nor indeed with much of the political science literature which has also had a lot to say about the party's leading figures, epitomised perhaps by the title of Tim Bale's (2010) work, *The Conservative Party from Thatcher to Cameron*. Political scientists have also had a great deal to say about the leadership election and ejection procedures operated by the party, not least due to the Conservatives' reputation in recent decades for ruthlessly despatching failed or fading leaders. Even in relation to the most profound and widely discussed ideological shift on the right in recent decades, namely the rise and transformative effect of Thatcherism, much of the debate (and perhaps also the very essence of Thatcherism itself) is concerned with the role of one foremost individual.

In short, and in contrast to Labour which has its origins in an external mass movement, the Conservative Party has always been a top-down, elitist one. In the modern era the leader has always been the central figure in the party, and the 'statecraft' pursued by Conservative leaders has been seen as key to the party's successes and failures (Bulpitt, 1986). Given this, and given the importance of communication to political leadership, it is perhaps surprising that this is the first volume to seek explicitly to analyse oratory and rhetoric in Conservative Party politics. Prominent Conservative orators, whose words have had resonance in British politics and society more widely, soon spring to mind – Churchill, Powell and Thatcher to name just three. Some scholars concerned with the characteristics of effective leadership have noted the importance of communication skills, without necessarily exploring the nature of these systematically. For example, Theakston (2007) and Heppell (2012) have both applied the Greenstein model of leadership, previously utilised to evaluate the individual attributes of American presidential officeholders, to the British case. More generally as discussed below, the academic study of political communication (particularly in relation to rhetoric) is an area which has seen a notable upsurge in scholarly interest in recent years (see for example and for a wider discussion, Atkins *et al.*, 2014). Directly in relation to Conservative politics, Hayton and McEnhill (2014) have recently analysed the rhetoric of Coalition government ministers in relation to one specific policy area, welfare. A clear gap in the literature therefore exists for this book, which sits alongside a sister volume (Crines and Hayton, 2014) on Labour oratory.

This book consequently examines the use and impact of oratory in Conservative Party politics through the use of twelve individual case studies, each focused on a leading figure in the party in the post-war era. Each of these has been selected because of the prominence of the individual in the party's history, and/or because of their reputation as a speaker. A majority of the chosen figures are consequently individuals who have held the office of party leader (Stanley Baldwin, Winston Churchill, Harold Macmillan, Margaret Thatcher, John Major, William Hague and David Cameron). The others (Iain Macleod, Enoch Powell, Keith Joseph, Michael Heseltine and Boris Johnson) have all played a significant role in shaping debates about contemporary conservatism, or earned a reputation as charismatic communicators of the Conservative message.

As with the companion volume on oratory in Labour politics, each chapter reflects on how the figure under examination deployed their oratorical skills in relation to three key audiences: (i) the Parliamentary Party; (ii) the wider party membership; and (iii) the electorate. These audiences relate to three important oratorical arenas, namely (i) Parliament; (ii) party conference; (iii) public and media engagement (the electoral arena). The book argues that powerful oratory and persuasive rhetoric have been key features of Conservative politics in the modern era, and vital to the political success of many of the party's leading politicians.

Conservative Party politics and leadership in historical context

As noted above, the British Conservative Party has been the subject of a rich historiography, with defining works by the likes of John Ramsden (1978; 1995; 1996; 1998), Richard Shannon (1992; 1996), Robert Blake (1970; 1998) and Stuart Ball (1998; 2013).[1] One criticism that has been levelled against some of this work (notably Ramsden's) is that it pays insufficient attention to the role of ideology in the party (Addison, 1999; Garnett, 2013). In part this reflects the tendency to write the history of the party as a chronicle of the actions of its leadership elite. A corrective to this emerged in a revitalised political science literature that accompanied the arrival of Margaret Thatcher in Downing Street, with defining works on Thatcherism by the likes of Stuart Hall and Martin Jacques (1983), and Andrew Gamble (1988). Inspired as it was by Gramscian Marxism, this work represented a shift 'towards more structurally inclined modes of explanation, in contrast to the agency-focused historical narratives that preceded them' (Hayton, 2012a: 10). Yet the story of the Conservative Party is not one, in Addison's phrase, that should be told as one 'of doctrine or men' (1999: 289). Rather it is one of ideology, women and men, with the interplay between ideas and agency being at the crux of most of the defining moments in the party's past. Oratory and rhetoric mark an interesting analytical juncture as it is so often how a particular agenda or ideas are communicated that is crucial to their eventual success or failure.

The figures in this book span the history of the modern Conservative Party, which can be effectively dated from the famous Carlton Club meeting of 1922 (Clark, 1998). The first of the orators featured in this volume, Stanley Baldwin, was one of the leading Cabinet rebels who spoke against the continuation of the Coalition with Prime Minister David Lloyd George's Liberals, bringing about the end of that government and Austen Chamberlain's party leadership. While Ball plausibly argues that 'the impact of Baldwin's speech, well-worded though it was, has been overstated due to his later prominence' (2013: 475) the episode does stand as an illustration of the fact that verbal communication, and the ability to win over an audience, are essential elements of a successful political career. The speeches at the Carlton Club did not determine the eventual outcome, but 'reinforced the existing flow of opinion' (Ball, 2013). The speakers in favour of maintenance of the status quo 'were ineffective, and at best – as in Balfour's case – listened to with polite impatience' (Ball, 2013). Bonar Law's speech, in contrast, 'was crucial in offering an alternative direction under a credible leader' (Ball, 2013). Following the collapse of Lloyd George's government Bonar Law was subsequently invited to become prime minister, but when he was soon after struck down with ill health it would be Baldwin who would go on to articulate a new vision of conservatism. As Andrew Taylor has argued:

> New Conservatism was used to reposition the Conservative party on the class dimension and the result was the Conservative landslide of 1924, which structured British politics for the next fifty years. Baldwin institutionalized a class-based two-party system and thereby secured Conservative hegemony. (Taylor, 2005: 463)

In the post-war era, Conservative Party politics was dominated by the One Nation tradition. This combined the language of patriotism so successfully employed by Baldwin to build an electoral base drawing on elements of working class (as well as middle and upper class) support, with acceptance of the main tenets of the post-war settlement laid down by the Attlee government. While Churchill's influence on the trajectory of post-war conservatism was limited, his reputation as the supreme British orator of the twentieth century had already been secured during his leadership of the nation in the Second World War. The ageing hero did, however, lead his party back to power in 1951, which marked the commencement of another period of electoral dominance for the party. The thirteen years in office that followed saw four Conservative leaders hold the office of prime minister, but it was the premiership of Harold Macmillan that came to epitomise the One Nation era.[2] In an era of increasing affluence, the Conservative Party was able to harness popular capitalism and patriotism, steering (to borrow the title of a 1938 pamphlet Macmillan had penned) a 'Middle Way' between socialism and untrammelled free markets. Keynesian economic management and state planning were utilised to address collective problems such as a shortage of adequate housing, while the long post-war boom gave credence to Macmillan's 1957 boast that 'most of our people have never had it so good' (quoted in Blake, 1985: 281).

Rising prosperity throughout the Macmillan era helped mask some of the more deep-rooted underlying problems with the UK economy, which would reach crisis point in the 1970s. Two more of the orators featured in this volume, Iain Macleod and Enoch Powell, would be associated with opposing sides of the debate in the party about how to respond to these economic challenges. They were, however, as one in their refusal to serve under Macmillan's chosen successor, Lord Home, who was parachuted into the Commons as plain Sir Alec Douglas-Home. In a withering article in the *Spectator*, Macleod noted that: 'We are now proposing to admit that after twelve years of Tory Government no one amongst the 363 members of the party in the House of Commons was acceptable as Prime Minister' (quoted in Harris, 2011: 450). The episode would act as a 'catalyst' for the democratisation of the leadership selection process, through the introduction of parliamentary ballots (Heppell, 2008a: 14).

Following the narrow general election defeat of 1964 and the resignation of Douglas-Home the following year, the first beneficiary of the new rules for electing the party leader would be Edward Heath. In securing victory over the initial favourite, Reginald Maudling, Heath would be the first in what would become a notable trend of candidates who came from behind to defeat the initial frontrunner in Conservative leadership elections. Heath was a modernising leader, who 'would have to manage the conflict between progressives in the one-nation mould who believed that the Conservatives should remain situated in the centre ground and those on the right who wanted to pursue a more free market strategy' (Heppell, 2014: 39). Ultimately he failed to devise an effective statecraft strategy, as he vacillated between these two alternative visions. At first his government promised and pursued a radical strategy. Blake noted that:

> It had come in on a programme of libertarianism, lower direct taxation, reduction of trade union power, support for law and order, selectivity in social services and minimal state intervention in industry ... This can be seen in retrospect as a highly 'Thatcherite' strategy. (Blake, 1985: 312)

Bale similarly stresses the government's initial ambition, but notes that within two years it 'had buckled in the face of strike action' (2012: 152). The conventional narrative of the Heath premiership – that it was 'proto-Thatcherite' but then abandoned this approach 'when the going got tough from 1971 onwards' – is contested by Richard Wade (2013: 105). He argues that 'the macroeconomic ideas which influenced Conservative policy making remained remarkably consistent' in the Heath era, and that these were essentially neo-Keynesian (2013). However, the rapidly changing economic context necessitated 'drastic changes in policy' to try and realise these ideas (Wade, 2013). Nonetheless there is no doubt that the perception of failed policy U-turns was important for the likes of Keith Joseph (Chapter 6) in advocating a free market monetarist alternative, and for clearing the ground in the party for Thatcherism. As Wade notes, the subsequent 'collapse of neo-Keynesianism in the Conservative Party was total' (2013: 104).

The remarkable and enduring transformative effect of the Thatcher era is one (as noted above) that has been widely documented, so need not detain us overly here. However, for the purposes of this volume it is worth briefly highlighting how Thatcher came to redefine the way that leadership in the Conservative Party, and indeed more widely, is understood and assessed. Each of Thatcher's successors as party leader came to be judged against her, largely unfavourably. Thatcher's tenure in Downing Street was also pivotal in the emergence of the 'presidentialisation' of the premiership thesis in Britain (Foley, 2000). Although the extent to which the British prime ministership has truly become presidentialised remains the subject of extensive academic debate (Webb and Poguntke, 2013) it is clear that over the past four decades the office of prime minister has become a more powerful one (Dowding, 2013).

In spite of her evident unpopularity with the public by the time of her removal from office in 1990, presiding as she was at that time over a government increasingly split over the European issue (which prompted the resignation of Cabinet heavyweights Nigel Lawson and Geoffrey Howe), the fact that Mrs Thatcher never suffered a general election defeat helped ensure her legend within the party. As Heppell noted:

> Thatcherism had created misplaced expectations among some Conservatives. Their guilt over the manner of her removal contributed towards a revisionist account of the Thatcher years. They began to mythologize Thatcherism … [which] was viewed by them as coherent and the golden age of Conservative politics. (Heppell, 2014: 95)

This inevitably created difficulties for her immediate successor, John Major. Thatcher's success in curbing the power of the trade unions and in pursuing a wider programme of economic liberalisation had settled intraparty debate in favour of an essentially neo-liberal view of the appropriate role of the state. This fault line was replaced, however, by a widening rift over the issue of European integration, which would erupt into parliamentary warfare in the early 1990s. Major played an important personal role in negotiating the Maastricht Treaty (Bale, 2012: 279–80) and the traumatic passage of the treaty's ratification bill served to brutally expose the deep divisions in the Conservative Party (Baker *et al.*, 1994). When combined with the calamitous exit of pound sterling from the Exchange Rate Mechanism in

September 1992 (also a policy in which Major had invested much personal political capital), the issue of Europe came to symbolise the collapse of Conservative statecraft and the loss of a reputation for governing competence.

The inescapable election defeat that followed brought to an end the longest period of single-party government in twentieth-century British history. What followed for the Conservatives was the lengthiest period of opposition they had endured since the Carlton Club meeting of 1922. This period has been analysed by amongst others Bale (2010), Dorey *et al.* (2011) and Hayton (2012a). The Conservative leaders that followed Major – William Hague, Iain Duncan Smith, Michael Howard and David Cameron – each faced essentially the same challenge, namely how to construct and expound a post-Thatcherite narrative with resonance beyond the bounds of the party's core support. Through the rhetoric of modernisation Cameron found a partial answer, but it proved insufficient to propel his party to outright victory at the 2010 general election. The Conservative leader was, however, able to successfully negotiate a Coalition agreement with the Liberal Democrats and return his party to power, and through effective statecraft dominate the government's agenda (Hayton, 2014). Whether Cameron can bring about a longer term reassertion of his party's electoral dominance of British politics remains to be seen, and key questions about the nature and viability of post-Thatcherite conservatism remain unanswered. Yet the Conservatives today remain a leader-focused party, so it will be up to Cameron or his successors to devise and articulate the party's strategy to meet these challenges.

The study of oratory and rhetoric in British politics

The art of oratory is a relatively under-scrutinised element of political communication within the existing body of academic literature. This is rather surprising given the clear importance of effective speechmaking in understanding political leadership and the broader advancement of ideological positions. However, the study of rhetoric has benefitted from something of an upsurge of interest amongst a relatively small but dedicated group of analysts of British politics in recent years. These significant contributions stem primarily from Richard Toye (2011; 2013), Alan Finlayson (2003; 2004; 2007), James Martin (2013; 2014), Judi Atkins (2011), Jonathan Charteris-Black (2011) and Max Atkinson (1984; 2004). As this section briefly reviews, collectively these have shed new light upon the nature of political rhetoric and how it is used by leading actors in British party politics.

Toye's (2013a) concise summation of the value of rhetoric emphasises the enduring relevance of classical approaches for better understanding how contemporary politicians communicate. He first reminds the reader that rhetoric needs 'to be taken seriously, not least as the progenitors of a very modern notion: that the art of communication can be taught and that it is a marketable skill' (2013a: 7). Toye continues by drawing attention to the longevity of the study of rhetoric and reminding the reader that it was classically developed by the Sophists – Protagoras, Gorgias,

Prodicus, Hippias, and Thrasymachus (2013a). It was these early philosophers who first conceptualised rhetoric as an influential technique. In terms of how conservative speakers have historically employed the rhetorical art, Toye notes 'Conservatives, for their part, turned to history and familial metaphors to justify royal authority' (2013a: 26). More broadly they 'succeeded in wresting the discourse of patriotism from the radicals and reformers who had previously wielded it as a weapon against governmental corruption' (2013a: 27). For Toye, the art of conservative oratory is a patriotic defence of national institutions such as the monarchy in opposition to radical reformers, both historical and contemporary.

Toye also rightly notes that successful persuasion requires, as Aristotle discerned, the use of three modes of rhetoric. 'The first kind depends on the personal character of the speaker; the second on putting the audience into a certain frame of mind; the third on the proof, or apparent proof, provided by the words of the speech itself' (Aristotle, 2004b). For analytical purposes these are condensed into *ethos*, *pathos* and *logos* (appeals to character, emotion and logic). These valuable devices enable analysts to deconstruct how an orator is communicating with their respective audience, and for Toye they represent a remarkable means of dealing 'systematically with the problem of rhetoric, and the categorisation [Aristotle] devised was to have a long influence' in the continuing study of communication (2013a: 14). Of course how an orator employs these devices in their delivery may prove more influential with one audience than another. Indeed, expectations shift between supporters, opponents and the public. Also Toye is correct in arguing that the political and social context is significant. This is because 'rhetoric is a social phenomenon, and its reception depends on the norms in operation in the society in which it is delivered' (2013a: 109). It must also be noted that 'however good the effect on the immediate listeners, it is impossible to tell how a speech will travel' (2013a). This note of caution rightly suggests that a written speech can, and often is, reinterpreted after its initial delivery, thereby producing changes of emphasis in the political message.

It is also worth noting that in the United States the study of rhetoric is considerably more advanced than in the British academy. In part this is because the presidential personalisation of politics in the United States led to a greater analytical emphasis upon the communication skills of individuals. Indeed, 'the emphasis, in reality and in political science, on acutely personalised leadership itself (from Frankin D. Roosevelt onwards) as an agency of political change' (Gaffney and Lahel, 2013: 484) has driven the American study of rhetoric. Thus, scholars such as Toye have embraced both the classical approaches and gained inspiration from the more developed study in the United States.

Finlayson (2006) uses the study of rhetoric to draw attention to its creative power in persuading an audience of an argument. He astutely argues that 'rhetoric is a creative activity in which a political actor seeks to develop arguments and put them to an audience in a way that they will be encouraged to pursue a particular course of action' (Finlayson, 2006: 544). This also connects with the linguistic creation of reality in constructing ideological messages that a particular audience may find persuasive (Atkins and Finlayson, 2013). Moreover, Finlayson and Martin rightly argue that 'political rhetoric offers a rich seam for those seeking both to interpret and explain the interplay of tradition, innovation, ideology, action, performance, strategy and rationality in British politics' (2008: 446). Thus distinctive interpretations of political rhetoric, tied to the advancement of various ideological perspectives, can emerge within the analytical discourses. Finlayson also rightly notes that 'ideologies provide actors with a series of locally established "commonplace" arguments which must be adapted to the demands of the situation' (2012: 758). This is particularly important given that the expectations of the audience, the particular ideological values of the orator, and a broader appreciation of what is politically expedient are significant issues which a political actor needs to consider when texturing their arguments.

Furthermore the orator may employ metaphors and anecdotes as devices that communicate short narratives to their audience. These draw the experiences of members of the public into the political discourse. Such 'witnesses', as noted by Aristotle, are designed to elicit credibility for the message an orator is striving to convey. Given a broader shift in audience expectations towards narratives, these experiences can be used to emotionalise a particular argument. Indeed, Atkins and Finlayson note that the use 'of anecdote[s] in political speech has recently become more extensive' within British politics (2013: 161). For example when outlining his vision of the 'Big Society' in 2010, Cameron used witnesses in a speech to Conservative supporters. He argued:

> I went to a brilliant social enterprise in Liverpool called 'Home By Mersey Strides'. It gets former prisoners, the homeless and the long-term unemployed to repair and assemble damaged flat-pack furniture and then sells it to students and the local community. Started in November it already employs forty people. But at the moment, the amazing work of this enterprise in Liverpool is confined to just one location. This is exactly the sort of thing we need to spread across the country. (Cameron, 2010)

This enables the orator to use more pathos-driven arguments to justify a particular political agenda, thereby avoiding the complexities of more empirical or logos-driven argument. This shift towards a greater use of 'witnesses' is attributed by Atkins and Finlayson to 'a populist shift in the "rhetorical culture" of contemporary British politics' (2013: 162). This enables an orator to claim a greater degree of authority as the narrative carries 'force because of its presumed reality: the source confers authority, and the actuality of the events enables a conclusion about reality to be drawn' (2012: 164). Indeed, as Leader of the Opposition William Hague invited his audience to 'Come with me to the Rother Valley, to the heart of South Yorkshire. Come and meet the people I grew up with ... who had no choice but to live from one week's pay packet to the next' (Hague, 2000b). Through this kind of rhetorical technique, the orator is hoping to enhance their ethos by the implicit virtue of their appreciation of the linguistically constructed 'real world'.

For Charteris-Black such metaphorical devices are a key element of effective speechmaking because of their importance in persuading an audience of their argument. He argues that 'voters make decisions based on their judgements of the honesty, morality, and integrity of politicians' (2011: 1). Rhetoric is the means through which audiences gauge the values of the speaker, and therefore acts as a positive and informing force that elites use to drive forward their case. The consequence of this is the tone of the argument used by an orator will affect how the political process functions, the overall quality of the democratic process, and how it is perceived by the audience/electorate. To that end 'rhetoricians such as Aristotle and Quintilian recognised that different contexts required different methods of persuasion: influencing political decisions would not require the same methods as arguing legal cases or commemorating fallen heroes' (2011: 7). For Charteris-Black 'metaphors are very effective' in that process 'because they provide cognitively accessible ways of communicating politics through drawing on ways of thinking by analogy' (2011: 321). The use of metaphors is an important weapon in the oratorical armoury because they help a speaker to communicate complex ideas in a way that allows the audience to engage with the argument, thereby gaining and securing their attention. This is a vital element of successful oration given that, as Max Atkinson argues, 'the speaker who proves himself to be incapable of holding the attention of live audiences stands little chance of winning their approval' (Atkinson, 1984: 9). Atkinson also rightly suggests that an orator can use other techniques to measure the immediate success or otherwise of their speech. Indeed, 'depending on whether they are greeted by frequent bursts of applause, heckling or complete silence, they will be deemed to have had a rapturous, hostile or indifferent reception' (1984: 13). Succinctly, silence descends when an orator fails to communicate effectively.

A successful orator may also have the ability to draw out specific audience reactions to particular arguments. Atkinson (1984) argues that techniques such as the 'claptrap' can be used to elicit support through careful timing and phraseology. 'Claptraps' are delicately crafted sentences to which the audience is expected to respond with applause. As Atkinson contends, an orator:

> has to communicate with his audience in much the same way as a conductor communicates with an orchestra or choir. A single movement of the hand, arm, head, lips or eyes is unlikely to be enough to get musicians to come in on time … but if he waves his baton, nods his head, and mouths the word 'now', synchronizing them all to occur at the same time, the chances of everyone spotting at least one of them are greatly increased. In the same way an effective claptrap must provide audience members with a number of signals which make it quite clear both that they should applaud and when they should start doing so. (1984: 48)

For the Conservative orator these can be patriotic reminders, highlighting economic success, celebrating the outcome of military action, or condemning the social democratic ideologies of their opponents. To ensure their greater success an orator can also emphasise specific words or phrases using carefully crafted delivery in order to draw out the intended reaction from the audience.

Finally Dennis Glover highlights the value of such rhetorical techniques by arguing that 'the best orators are those who understand the needs of their audience and employ the right combination of logic, character, and emotion to convince, charm and sway' (2011: 56). Knowing one's audience is, for Glover, vital before attempting to employ a rhetorical device. This is particularly damaging if a particular speech is given to the wrong audience: 'the sudden disappearance of a forum can spell the end for a faltering politician. Like the sand rushing through an hourglass, an audience making for the exits usually signals that a leader's time is up' (2011: 63). Ineffective speeches can be highly costly, particularly if, as happened to the former Conservative leader Iain Duncan Smith, the 'quiet man' is never afforded the opportunity to turn up the volume due to an unexpected *coup d'état* (Hayton, 2012b). Glover argues such an unfortunate outcome can be avoided by correctly using the classical devices outlined earlier. Success can be garnered by those who 'combined the rules of rhetorical style – ethos, pathos, and logos' (2011: 74). Such devices are used interdependently by successful orators; however, for the purposes of analysis they can be distinguished from each other.

Moreover, Glover is in agreement with Atkinson that words and phrases can be changed in their delivery, which the classical philosophers differentiated into *tropes* (changes to an accepted meaning of a word) and *schemes* (rearranging the delivery of words to make them more appealing) (2011: 91). Their contemporary relevance can be appreciated in their continued use by political elites. As an example, the electorate may witness politicians using *tropes* and *schemes* 'every day when we watch the evening news: using the same word with double meaning; employing overstatement and understatement; asking a question and sometimes answering it; balancing a statement with its opposite; using the same words but in a different order; and repeating words, clauses and sounds' (2011: 95). These classical rhetorical devices remain central to modern political speech. Indeed, 'watch a good or even moderate speaker in a political meeting or on television and you will notice that the applause tends to follow the use of these rhetorical devices' (2011). The personal, political and delivery style of the speaker informs their method of communication and broader relationship with the audience, thereby suggesting that an examination of their oratory, which is connected to growing field of rhetorical investigation, is of equally significant importance.

Structure of the book

The twelve chapters that follow this introduction are individual case studies of leading Conservative orators in the post-1922 party, namely Stanley Baldwin, Winston Churchill, Harold Macmillan, Iain Macleod, Enoch Powell, Keith Joseph, Margaret Thatcher, Michael Heseltine, John Major, William Hague, Boris Johnson and David

Cameron. As noted earlier, seven of these figures reached the apex of the party to hold the office of leader, while the others all played a notable part in debates about the Conservatives' policies, ideology and strategic direction. Indeed, the five featured orators who did not go on to head the party were all at various times spoken of as possible future party leaders. At the time of writing one of them, Boris Johnson, is still widely expect to contest the post at some future date. Powell (in 1965) and Heseltine (in 1990) were both candidates in leadership elections, and but for his premature passing Macleod may well have been a serious contender in 1975 (Chapter 4). Joseph's prospects at that election were 'spectacularly destroyed' (Harris, 2011: 479) before the contest officially began by a deeply misguided speech that led him to be 'denounced by social commentators as a mad eugenicist' (Heppell, 2008a: 58). Thatcher consequently decided to enter the leadership race, illustrating how a single speech can occasionally have profound and unforeseen political consequences.

In Chapter 1, Andrew Taylor argues that Stanley Baldwin used his considerable talents as an orator to give voice to a new conservatism which would resonate with the electorate in the democratic era. Baldwin devised a rhetorical strategy based on the sophisticated use of commonplaces to structure his appeal and reach across geographical and class boundaries. After the Second World War, the Conservatives needed to rediscover a broad-based appeal sufficient to challenge Attlee's Labour Party. The wartime oratory of Winston Churchill has been widely discussed and analysed elsewhere (for example Toye, 2013b) but in the second chapter of this volume Kevin Theakston considers the rhetoric of Winston Churchill in the post-war period, particularly in relation to domestic and party issues. Chapter 3, by Brendan Evans, considers how Harold Macmillan was able use his oratory to cultivate an ethos which appealed to a mass electorate, embodying the notion of One Nation conservatism. In Chapter 4, Mark Garnett profiles another One Nation Tory who was lauded and remembered for his oratorical skills, Iain Macleod. He argues that his subject was able to exploit ethos, pathos and logos to great effect, winning him plaudits from, amongst others, the subject of the following chapter, Enoch Powell.

As political contemporaries Macleod and Powell worked alongside each other as young men in the Conservative Research Department. As Philip Norton discusses in Chapter 5, however, their politics developed in very different directions. As probably the most powerful Conservative orator of the post-war era, Powell gained notoriety for his inflammatory rhetoric about immigration, leading to his exclusion from the party elite and his eventual departure from the party completely. Norton argues that the force of Powell's words came not as is commonly assumed primarily from appeals to the emotions of his audience, but was founded on ethos and logos.

The subject of the following chapter, Keith Joseph, shared some of Powell's politics, and both figures were recognised by Thatcher as key intellectual influences on her thinking. In terms of oratorical effect, however, the contrast could hardly be greater. As Mark Garnett demonstrates in Chapter 6, Joseph was the weakest orator featured in this collection by some measure, so is a curious case study of a figure with significant political influence in spite of (rather than because of) his aptitude as a communicator. Margaret Thatcher, discussed by Peter Dorey in Chapter 7, was also not a natural orator but developed into a skilful and commanding one. She combined her ethos as 'the grocer's daughter' with populist emotional appeals, which were also underpinned by a formidable capacity for rational argument.

Perhaps surprisingly given the loyalty of the party membership to Thatcher, Michael Heseltine's status as one of her leading critics did not prevent him establishing his status as darling of the Conservative Party conference. As Mark Bennister explores in Chapter 8, Heseltine's flamboyant oratory from the conference platform could greatly enthuse his audience, and helped mask the ideological and policy differences he had with the Thatcherites. It could not, however, secure him the leadership when Thatcher fell, which passed instead to John Major, who is analysed by Timothy Heppell and Thomas McMeeking in Chapter 9. They suggest that Major's 'most notable oratorical flourishes' occurred in relation to the intraparty disputes that dogged his premiership, particularly over the European issue, reinforcing the image of the Conservatives as deeply divided.

Major's successor as party leader, William Hague, proved incapable of reversing the Conservatives' fortunes following the landslide election defeat in 1997, taking his party to a second landslide loss in 2001. In spite of this ignominious record, Hague retained popular standing within Conservative Party ranks, not least because of his oratorical skill. As Judi Atkins discusses in Chapter 10, however, his considerable talent as a debater, regularly exhibited in the Commons, had limited relevance to the wider electorate with whom he struggled to establish a fruitful connection. By contrast Boris Johnson, reviewed by Katharine Dommett in Chapter 11, has cultivated a reputation as something of a political outsider and used this, along with considerable humour, to appeal directly to the mass electorate. Finally in Chapter 12, Tim Bale appraises the oratorical skills of the first Conservative prime minister of the twenty-first century, David Cameron. As Bale notes, Cameron's proficiency as a communicator was undoubtedly of considerable importance in his ascent to the party leadership, and he has demonstrably exploited these skills with considerable effect in pursuit of his political objectives.

Conclusion

The role of political agency is of course central to the history of all political parties. Nonetheless in the case of the Conservative Party the prime role played by the leading elite is especially dominant. In analysing the oratory and rhetoric of twelve leading individuals from twentieth-century Conservative politics this book aims to contribute a new perspective on the party's history. In addition, and in conjunction with the volume on oratory in Labour politics, we hope that it will also help raise the profile of this area of academic enquiry, and add a new dimension to the burgeoning literature on rhetoric in British politics through the focus on oratory.

Notes

1 For a broader review see Hayton (2012a: chapter 1).
2 Apart from Churchill (until 1955) and Macmillan (1957–63), the other officeholders were the ill-fated Anthony Eden (1955–57) brought down by the Suez Crisis, and Alec Douglas-Home (1963–64) who narrowly lost the 1964 general election.

1

The oratory of Stanley Baldwin

Andrew Taylor

Introduction

Stanley Baldwin (1867–1947) was MP for Bewdley (1908–37), leader of the Conservative Party (1923–37) and prime minister three times (May 1923–January 1924; November 1924–June 1929; June 1935–May 1937). He was at the apex of British politics in a tempestuous and formative period making his oratory an important aspect of modern politics. Baldwin spoke frequently, formally and informally, on a vast range of political and non-political topics, and to a diverse range of audiences (Williamson, 1999: 153–4). The scale and scope of this oratorical and rhetorical effort can be sensed from the 137 examples in four (well selling) volumes of speeches: *On England* (1926), *Our Inheritance* (1928), *Torch of Freedom* (1935) and *Service of Our Lives* (1937). Baldwin refused to retreat into the ritual pessimism of democracy's critics (although he was critical) who argued that more voters meant an inevitably worse politics. Rather, he believed a fractious democracy could be educated and that its diversity disguised deep strength and resilience. 'By the outbreak of the Second World War', LeMahieu argues, 'Britain was still a nation profoundly divided by class. Yet an emerging common culture provided shared frame of reference among widely divergent groups. Individuals ... could find common ground' (1988: 4). This chapter explores Baldwin's contribution to creating that common ground.

Rather than focusing on a single arena such as the House of Commons, or even a particular speech this chapter focuses on the mid-1920s which is, I believe, a critical period in the formation of modern British politics (Taylor, 2005). Permeating Baldwin's speeches is disquiet at the consequences of the First World War and its disruption of economic, social and political patterns of behaviour. In 1928 J. C. C. Davidson, Baldwin's confidant and party chairman, told Baldwin:

> Before the War it was possible with a limited and highly expert electorate to put forward Party programmes of a restricted & well defined character, but nowadays I am quite sure that while not departing from the principles of our Party we must endeavour to gain the confidence not only of our own supporters but of the mugwump vote. (HLRO, 1928)

Dislocation created and stimulated new forces – an enlarged electorate, an assertive trade union movement, and an electorally expanding Labour Party – and after 1918 politicians experimented with responses such as coalition, fusion and repression. All failed.

Rhetoric and Conservative strategy

Conservative dominance was not pre-ordained; class was now the dominant political cleavage but how Conservatives responded was yet to be finalised. Political space was not yet fixed so it could be manipulated and constructed. In the 1920s the Conservatives were potential losers, possible futures included a multi-party system, coalition politics, perhaps even a majority Labour government and Baldwin's first response, protection in 1923, cost the Conservatives the election, reunited the Liberals, and put Labour in office. Labour's rise and industrial militancy was paralleled by the rise of a suburban, lower-middle-class conservatism, fuelled by a deep post-war crisis that was profoundly hostile to the working class, and especially the organised working class, which saw the Conservatives as their sole defence (McKibbin, 1998: 50–62). The danger of the country pulling apart into antagonistic social groups was real and posed a possibly fatal strategic problem for the Conservatives who had to retain their core vote and attract large numbers of new voters and ex-Liberals. If anti-socialism, detestation of trade unions, anti-communism and so on, were reasons for *not* voting Labour, what were the reasons *for* voting Conservative? Baldwin was convinced an anti-Labour/anti-socialist majority existed; his task was to make it a *Conservative* majority.

Stimulated by defeat in 1923 Baldwin announced in February 1924 a re-think of organisation, policy and propaganda aimed squarely at the new democracy, especially the working-class and women. The rhetoric was central (Cowling, 1971: 407). The result was a re-cast One Nation appeal expressed in the *Aims and Principles* (May 1924) statement and published in June as *Looking Ahead*. The difference between the 1923 and 1924 manifestos shows the extent of the repositioning on anti-socialism and moderate social reform with the intention of the Conservative Party becoming a mass national party (Ramsden, 1978: 188–215). This was the fundamental objective of Baldwin's rhetoric.

This chapter is based on nine speeches by Baldwin. These speeches were delivered in a three-year period critical for the modern Conservative Party and they cover elements central to Baldwin's thinking and the scale of the problems – mass democracy, the rise of the Labour Party and industrial militancy – are reflected in the range of audiences addressed. Some of the speeches (notably 'England' and 'Peace in Industry') are often cited as quintessential statements of Baldwinism, others (for example, 'Service' and 'Freedom') address norms Baldwin considered fundamental, whilst others (for example, 'Political Education' and 'Democracy and its Task') articulate aspects of Conservative strategy. Baldwin's rhetoric is frequently presented

Table 1 The speeches

Source	Date	Audience
England	6 May 1924	Royal Society of St. George
Peace in Industry	6 March 1925	House of Commons
Service	13 March 1925	Leeds Luncheon Club
Truth and Politics	6 November 1925	Edinburgh University
The Citizen and the General Strike	12 June 1926	Chippenham public meeting
Freedom	16 June 1926	Junior Imperial League
Political Education	27 September 1926	Philip Stott College
Democracy and its Task	4 March 1927	Cambridge University Conservative Association
The Industrial Situation in England	3 August 1927	Canadian Club, Ottawa

as a panegyric to a lost, rural, socially cohesive world; although this rural myth declined in significance in Baldwin's oratory it played an important role in pathos and ethos, defining Baldwin's image and cross-class appeal. Baldwin held ideas in his mind for long periods and frequently tried them out on different audiences to judge their effects (Barnes and Nicholson, 1988: 398). Table 1 gives the speeches by date and the audience to which it was addressed.

To analyse the speeches I employed NVivo, a computer software program designed for quantitative research. Reading Baldwin's speeches in this period one quickly becomes aware of repeated themes and ideas irrespective of the specific audience which suggests an underlying structure and purpose. This opens the possibility of a more systematic analysis that can explore the ideational and conceptual structure of the speeches (data, or in NVivo, sources) and model how these ideas and concepts interrelate. Coding is the basis of the analysis (Bazeley, 2007: 66), reducing data (the speeches) to codes that represent general categories as well as overarching themes that produce patterns of association. Coding takes the form of nodes (see Appendix for the definition of the nodes) that cover nineteen concepts, themes and attributes present in the nine speeches. Thus, 'Englishness' is present in all nine and with thirty-four references/uses. Each node represents a theme in Baldwin's speeches. Table 2 shows the nodes used and number of references. NVivo does not substitute for interpretation and analysis. The coding and their application to the speeches are my own; NVivo is used to 'unpick' Baldwin's rhetorical strategy.

Rhetorically Baldwin had two objectives: first, to offer a diagnosis of the current instability; and second, offer a solution that was intelligible, plausible and grounded in a narrative that was recognised by, and acceptable to, his audiences. He sought

Table 2 The coding

Source	Nodes used	References made
Peace in Industry	12	63
The Industrial Situation in England	10	41
Service	10	10
The Citizen and the General Strike	9	30
England	9	29
Democracy and its Task	8	26
Freedom	9	19
Political Education	8	15
Truth and Politics	5	12

to mobilise public sentiment to create a public opinion that saw the Conservative Party as the best and only guarantor of good governance. Baldwin was a late-Victorian, entering politics when 'public opinion' meant that of the middle- and upper-classes but after 1906, and especially after 1914, public opinion broadened. Creating a public opinion required Baldwin to articulate sentiments identified as common to all classes and then construct an image and appeal around which a cross-class integrative political strategy intended to preserve the existing distribution of wealth and power with as few concessions as possible, could be mobilised. The real test of rhetoric is its persuasiveness which depended, in turn, on its plausibility and the perceived trustworthiness, or *propriety*, of the rhetorician. The 'New Conservatism' was a public doctrine appropriate to the new matrix of political forces and utilised a rhetorical strategy that relied on the repeated articulation of core themes expressing immutable national values that connected democracy to conservatism and vice versa. This rhetorical effort was all the more difficult because Baldwin was 'a Tory PM, surrounded with a Tory Cabinet, moving in Tory circles' (Jones, 1969a: 167).

Studies of rhetoric, classical or contemporary, often focus on the single speech (for example, Wills, 1992 and Pauley, 2007) but a campaign of persuasion (or political education) rests on a clear and believable definition of the problem, the articulation of a persuasive solution and repetition of a few core themes. The foundation is defining the problem. Baldwin's definition went something like this. The pre-1914 world had gone, democracy could not be rolled-back and the Conservative Party was the only viable defence of the status quo. To tame mass democracy the party itself had to be tamed. This pointed to a rhetoric using language, imagery and sentiments that evoked a common remembered past but which re-moulded and manipulated language, imagery and sentiment to fit the post-1918 context. Baldwin's rhetoric was pushed by the past but pulled by the future and he developed arguments that are outside political time and space to explain why things are as they are and pointing a way forward by exploiting attributes already recognised by auditors as defining 'us' (and therefore 'them') in the service of change. This strategy appealed to his auditors' emotions (pathos) and stressed the speaker's straight-dealing (ethos) to establish trust, as such logos (reason and logic) were less significant. Stylistically Baldwin's rhetoric exploits the familiar to convince auditors his proffered solution is appropriate and viable, that the rhetorician (and by extension the Conservative Party) is best placed to carry it out, and that the auditors can trust Baldwin and the Conservatives. He does this by painting a picture of how auditors see themselves and by so doing shape their conduct. A simple way to visualise this is to use NVivo to create a tag cloud of the words used in the nine speeches (Figure 1).

This will not bear a great deal of analytical weight (a key assumption is that frequency is a proxy for significance) but Figure 1 sheds light on the speeches' conceptual and linguistic architecture and elucidates their strategic purpose. The structure and appeal is manifestly integrative, with an emphasis on a sentiment of common 'belonging'. Interestingly, neither in this partial nor the full concordance is Conservative or conservatism counted; nor is Labour or socialism. This reflects case selection (there are, for example, no election speeches) but it does point to a broad appeal directed at the median voter that is 'non-partisan', perhaps even 'above' politics. What audience Baldwin was aiming at in these speeches? Without opinion polling or audience research we must rely on impressions but I would refer you to Noël Coward's 1939 play (and David Lean's 1944 film), *This Happy Breed*, that follows the fortunes of the property-owning, hard-working, law-abiding, politically quiescent, upwardly mobile, lower-middle-class/working-class Gibbons family in the south London suburbs between June 1919 and June 1939 (Chapman, 1998: 242–4 and Aldgate and Richards, 1994: 210–13. See also, Jeffrey, 1989: 198–216). The Gibbonses, an urban not rural family, strike me as emblematic of the audience Baldwin was aiming to attract in these speeches. On the eve of the 1935 election Baldwin was told 'of a Labour family in Ladywood who were brought right over to our side by listening to you', so 'If you can put those simple issues across to the working man and his family as they sit by their firesides tonight all over provincial England, I believe you [note, not "we"] shall have a great victory' (Baldwin, 1935a). The next section moves away from strategy to consider Baldwin's style.

Definition, construction and delivery

Style, as Aristotle noted, 'is a technical matter' (Aristotle, 2004a: 217). In 'Rhetoric' Baldwin declared: 'I have never been a rhetorician or an orator' (1926: 94). This is, of course, a classic oratorical device, suggesting rhetoric is the antithesis of honest plain-speaking and one of the most difficult oratorical skills is to appear honest and because believe between british business century

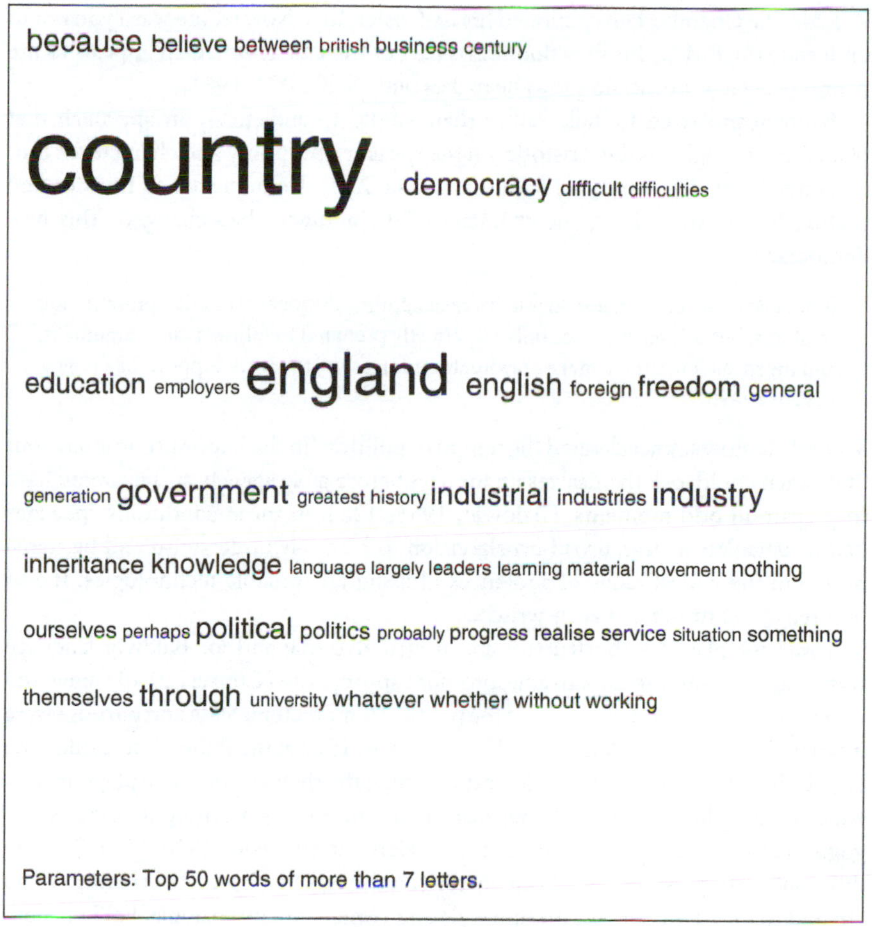

country democracy difficult difficulties

education employers england english foreign freedom general

generation government greatest history industrial industries industry

inheritance knowledge language largely leaders learning material movement nothing

ourselves perhaps political politics probably progress realise service situation something

themselves through university whatever whether without working

Parameters: Top 50 words of more than 7 letters.

Figure 1 All speeches cloud.

plain-speaking while indulging in sophisticated rhetoric. Observers identified this skill in Baldwin (Jones, 1954: 155–6; Rhodes James, 1969: 171), who dismissed 'that appalling two penny-ha'penny' gift of fluency ... which stirs the emotions of the ignorant mob and sets it moving' (Baldwin, 1926: 96) and he feared language's consequences in a democracy. Baldwin agreed with Aristotle that 'words mean something' (2004a: 235) and in a democracy, language's consequences could be devastating: 'the wrong words may raise issues not settled by dropping pieces of paper in a ballot box but by dropping bombs on cities' (1926: 95).

Perhaps with himself in mind Baldwin contended 'it is not necessarily the man most fluent of speech to whom we should entrust the destinies of the country' (1926:

97). Neville Chamberlain cautioned his half-sister, Ida, 'Now let me warn you not to underrate the PM ... his very dullness is part of the character which appeals to the country ... He is not so simple as he makes out' (Self, 2000: 193).

Baldwin preferred to 'talk' rather than 'speak' to audiences, an approach that placed great weight, as did Aristotle, on the speaker's propriety and character as fundamental to an effective style (Aristotle, 2004a: 228). Democracy had transformed oratory in two ways. First, the character of the audience had changed. This new democracy

> is not dishonest in itself, nor does it desire or approve dishonesty or misrepresentation in others, but it is an audience only imperfectly prepared to follow a close argument, and the speaker wishes to make a favourable impression, to secure support for a policy. (1926: 89–90)

Second, democracy accelerated the tempo of politics: 'In the happy pre-war days our Statesmen could lock themselves up for days before a big speech, and now you have to prepare in odd moments' (Baldwin, 1955: 122). In these conditions speeches had to articulate a clear, broad-brush, vision to be easily understood and be transmitted to the widest range of audiences utilising all available technologies. It also pointed to the need for speech-writers.

Language played a constructive and destructive role and for Baldwin language was a tool to neutralise the extreme, promote appropriate (Conservative) values and resist democracy's tendency to raise the political temperature. Style and purpose were intimately connected (Williamson, 1999: 155). In 1923 at the Philip Stott College he urged 'a healthy distrust of rhetoric' and shunning the rhetorician ('who plays on half-educated people') as the most dangerous figure in politics, warning that the demagogue had always beaten the 'sane and sober element' (Baldwin, 1926: 155). Baldwin does not distinguish oratory from rhetoric, although he deprecates rhetoric as an attempt to fool it is clear that for him style and content are inseparable. Baldwin condemned street-corner leftists and communists, Lloyd George and Churchill equally. 'I cannot', he told Tom Jones, 'rival L.G. at that sort of speech – full of clever thrusts, innuendos, malicious half-truths. To L.G. and Winston it is all part of a game' (Jones, 1954: 227). So how were Baldwin's speeches constructed and delivered?

Baldwin made extensive use of speech-writers; given the demands of democratic politics this was inevitable. *Whitehall Diary* is replete with references to speech-writing. Prime ministerial speeches were 'inevitably [a] patchwork' of departmental briefs that Jones 'stitched together, adding an introduction and conclusion' (Jones, 1954: 254, 303). Baldwin was not, however, a mouthpiece; he had his own ideas ('notions') and often gave only the sketchiest of indications ('His entire instructions to me ... would hardly have made half a dozen sentences' (Jones, 1969b: 4)) to his speechwriters. Sometimes Jones asked Baldwin for 'half a sheet of notepaper [with] the sort of ideas he wanted worked up'; when given a draft Baldwin would work on it putting in 'a good deal of himself' and Jones estimated one major speech was about two-thirds Baldwin 'and all the best parts of it were the PM's own' (Jones, 1969b: 2).

Baldwin was also urged not to 'think of his "briefs" at all but to trust to the moment for words and phrases' (Jones, 1969a: 312). Baldwin claimed 'I can't do like Winston … put it all down for days in advance, and commit it to memory' (Jones, 1969b: 181) but he nonetheless prepared very carefully, particularly so for radio broadcasts (D. Taylor, 2002: 81–2). Jones described Baldwin 'eviscerating' a draft speech, adding his own ideas, re-writing and polishing right up to delivery (Jones, 1969b: 152, 180), which perhaps explains why his notes were sometimes messy ('more squalid than a young Labour candidate would dare to produce at a Wapping by-election'; Nicolson, 1966: 285). Jones told Baldwin his speeches were best when 'he took the material prepared for him, soaked himself it, and then poured it out freely' (Jones, 1969b: 2).

Davidson described Baldwin as having 'a superb speaking voice, although he had some very peculiar mannerisms which sometimes irritated his audience, even his pronunciation' (Rhodes James, 1969: 177). He was usually nervous before a speech and Harold Nicolson remarked on his 'odd nervous ticks' that

> He has an extraordinarily unpleasant habit of smelling his notes and licking the edges slightly as if they were the flap of an envelope. He scratches himself continuously … And a strange movement of the head, with half-closed eyes, like some tortoise half-awake smelling the air – blinking, snuffy, neurotic. (1966: 228)

Many of his peers did not regard him as a 'classic' Commons performer (Williamson, 1999: 77) but he did, nonetheless, deliver authoritative performances. Take, for example, the March 1925 speech on the MacQuisten Bill. Neville Chamberlain thought it a major triumph because 'it created the atmosphere he wanted' (Self, 2000: 275). Amery described it as 'simple, quiet, reminiscent about his own days as an employer and his old workmen, [he] carried the House away … It was by far the greatest political triumph S.B. has ever had' (Barnes and Nicholson, 1980: 400). Over ten years later Nicolson described Baldwin's speech on the Abdication thus:

> There is no moment when he overstates emotion or indulges in oratory … we have heard the best speech that we shall ever hear in our lives … No man has ever dominated the House as he dominated it tonight, and he knows it. (Nicolson, 1966: 285–6)

Baldwin was not a 'natural' orator but he did know what he wanted to achieve and worked hard to develop an appropriate 'voice' (Jones, 1969a: 181).

This style came into its own on the radio. Baldwin imagined himself speaking to two or three people around the sitting-room fire or kitchen table. He eagerly sought information on the nature of the audience; he believed the radio offered the best medium and acted accordingly (Jones, 1969b: 182). Radio also hid his 'nervous ticks' and the unpleasant habits complained of by Nicolson. As radio produces the best images, Baldwin used language to paint pictures in the listeners' minds of themselves and their relationship with the Conservative Party; in the 1930s newsreel expanded this by allowing him to present a visual image of himself (and by extension of the Conservative Party) and develop the sound-bite. It is worth mentioning at this point that as well as appearing honest, straightforward, sympathetic and likeable Baldwin's rhetoric had teeth. He could be vituperative when the occasion demanded, as with his speech on 18 March 1931 condemning the press lords during the St George's Westminster by-election.

Not all Baldwin's speeches were triumphs. Channon described a speech by Baldwin as 'slow, steady, uneloquent but convincing' and passing his notes to Mrs Baldwin commented 'Never let me see them again' (Rhodes James, 1967: 39). Amery described a House of Commons speech in November 1930 censuring the Labour government as 'a most rambling ineffective speech with absolutely no punch in it … S.B.'s speech had a profoundly depressing effect on our own people' (Barnes and Nicholson, 1988: 137). Baldwin may have regarded partisan audiences as less important for his purposes than public and non-political audiences and, though risky, in terms of his wider political strategy this attitude would make sense. Speeches to party audiences were sometimes criticised as insufficiently inspirational (Amery described Baldwin's 1923 party conference speech as good and well delivered but not calculated to produce 'bursts of enthusiasm' [Barnes and Nicholson, 1988: 420]) but Neville Chamberlain noted, 'you cant [sic] have it both ways. S.B.'s strength lies in his sympathy and thoughtfulness, not in polemics and its [sic] of no use to try and make him talk like someone else' (Self, 2000: 313). Baldwin's frequent 'non-political' speeches, many delivered as radio broadcasts, were 'worth a ton of politics' (Jones, 1969a: 160) and Chamberlain, for instance, describes a speech to the Royal Society as 'altogether delightful [,] witty and eloquent and a wide range of literary allusions which charmed the audience. He is inimitable on such an occasion' (Self, 2000: 432).

Discussing one of the collections of speeches Jones believed they expressed his '"typical Englishness" in "professedly non-party" tones but they are really about Stanley Baldwin – by the time you are through the book it is his character which emerges' (1954: 157). Classical writers on rhetoric such as Aristotle stress the importance of character and propriety coming through his words, thereby boosting a speech's persuasive power. Putting aside the inevitable ups and downs Baldwin's style reflects his conviction that in a democracy language could bring immediate rewards and damaging long-term consequences. His rhetorical strategy was long term and mass political education depended on the repetition of themes using the same tone and delivery 'so that ultimately the public … got hold of the idea' but this 'to a certain extent destroyed his style as an orator' (Rhodes James, 1969: 171). It does not seem to have damaged its effectiveness.

Content and structure

Caution is required when applying the precepts of classical rhetoric to the modern polity. Classical oratory was usually directed at an audience of a few hundred aristocratic men and was often *forensic* (delivered in a law court) rather than *deliberative* (to influence policy). The demands of mass democratic politics and the opportunities offered by new communication technologies enabled Baldwin to address bigger audiences than his predecessors with greater immediacy and this placed increased weight on the audience's awareness, and assessment, of the rhetorician's character. His rhetoric is difficult to classify. Baldwin obviously used ethos (the speaker's credibility and character to emphasise propriety) and *all* political rhetoric employs pathos (emotional appeals). Both the New Conservatism and the wider political education effort relied on logos (reasoning and constructing an argument) particularly employing symbols, myths and history. But the object was *enthymematic*, using generally accepted propositions to support his conclusions. Baldwin combined the deliberative with *epideictic* (celebratory, concerned with praise and blame) that relied heavily on 'topics', the *topoi*, or commonplaces. When addressing non-party/non-political audiences, his rhetoric was broadly *homiletic*. For these reasons Baldwin's rhetoric 'resembles a rough sketch, for the larger the crowd should be, the more remote is the inspection, so that precision is unnecessary' (Aristotle, 2004a: 243).

Baldwin's rhetorical strategy had two components: the problem and the solution. The structure of this rhetorical strategy and his diagnosis of the problems confronting the country had the war, which had disrupted society, economy and polity, at its centre. Mass democracy, industrial unrest and socialism were products of the war, which accelerated trends already embedded in industrial capitalism. Combined this meant the progressive (and accelerating) decline of a paternalistic and deferential industrial, political and social culture. The rise of 'big' capitalism was accompanied by the rise of 'big' labour, the threat of growing alienation and anomie was reflected in growing materialism and the pursuit of the novel and fashionable (including in politics), tendencies which the war had again accelerated. Baldwin's rhetoric is backward-looking, not reactionary. The lost-world Baldwin conjures was, of course, mythical (that he had lived in this world increased the plausibility of his analysis) but its power lay precisely in the myth and the image concocted and not the myth as a political project. Baldwin might regret the demise of his remembered world but he was not so foolish as to try and (re-)create it.

Baldwin's rhetoric draws heavily on a conception of an idealised traditional, social and industrial culture that emphasised paternalism, mutual respect and social conservatism. His purpose was to modernise this and transplant it into the post-war world to mitigate the dislocation by encouraging both sides of industry to adopt cooperation not confrontation in the interests of social and political peace. These new attitudes would underpin a new social and industrial order. Domestic politics in wartime showed division and discord, but in Baldwin's rhetoric the experience of the war could be presented positively: the war showed what could be achieved when the country united behind a common goal. This was reflected in his emphasis on the necessity for both sides of industry (and by extension, left and right in politics) to revivify cooperation and develop new forms of cooperation analogous to the now moribund paternalism and order of the traditional industrial culture. This new social, political and industrial order had to be as appropriate to this new context as the former (supposedly) was to its context. As this new order would not emerge spontaneously, this raises the question of how it was to be achieved.

The only available vehicle, for reasons already explained, was the Conservative Party. But it was a particular *type* of Conservative Party. Baldwin could, and did, draw heavily on the Disraelian One Nation tradition, originally developed to address the post-1867 urban industrial working class (Disraeli's 'angels in marble'). This had proved successful (Pugh, 1985) but now seemed dangerously lacking in political vitality in this new world. Despite this tradition there was a real possibility that the party might adopt a harsher 'exclusionary' approach, which explains the rhetorical visibility of 'country' and 'England' as all-embracing terms.

The political and cultural centre of this new conservatism were the nodes (see Appendix) 'Englishness', 'the image of England' and 'Baldwin's remembered world'. Combined these articulate the lost pre-1914 world but they also provide the organising frame for Baldwin's rhetoric, imparting political coherence to the type of conservatism Baldwin believed necessary and appropriate in post-war conditions. 'Englishness' is the essential integrative component but is given a particular twist by the 'image of England' and his 'remembered world'. It is these that give his rhetorical strategy its pathos. An appeal of this type was hardly original, so why was it felt to be so effective? These themes were insufficient in themselves as they relied on a rural conception of Englishness (ruralism became less visible in his speeches over time) that could be (and was) criticised as lacking relevance in an urban industrial society, so there had to be a deeper foundation of 'universals' that were the property of no party but which were widely recognised by voters of all classes. This foundational reflex was, for example, articulated by Davidson during the General Strike:

> if you could have moved about amongst the people it would have been borne in upon you that the heart of the people is absolutely sound & that the vast majority of the public & the vast majority of the strikers themselves are not only good citizens but very patriotic. (HLRO, 1926)

The strikers were part of the nation. This mentality would enable the Conservative Party to see itself, and be seen, as the embodiment of truly national values and therefore the party best trusted to govern in the national interest. The Conservative Party would be both a founder and buttress of the new order; it would also be its chief beneficiary thereby guaranteeing conservatism's hegemony and the survival of the new political dispensation.

An appeal of this type could easily be seen as mawkish and even attract derision but unlike Arthur Bryant, a Conservative propagandist, Baldwin did not pretend he was writing history (Roberts, 1994: 287–322). Baldwin largely avoided Bryant's saccharine celebratory guff (which nonetheless sold well) even though, like Bryant, 'English' was his major political signifier and this brings us to an important puzzle about Baldwin's rhetoric. How did 'English' avoid the charge of exclusion? How does a sectional term come to symbolise common and universal national traits? Baldwin's use of English as a synonym for British (Williamson, for example, has no separate index entry for 'Britishness', it is subsumed in 'Englishness') sounds incongruous to the modern ear but was, of course, common usage. A Mass Observation report found that 'England' tended to be used to convey feelings of intimacy, where as 'Britain' was a more formal term that overlapped with, but was distinguished from, England (MO, 1941: 5, 7). Baldwin's most 'developed' statement is 'Our National Character' broadcast on the BBC in September 1933 (Baldwin, 1937: 15–22). He did speak about Wales and Scotland, and the English overseas, praising their qualities, and Baldwin (who sometimes described himself as Welsh) was fully conscious of differences between the English. Assuming his use of English was neither arrogant nor derogatory what was its rhetorical purpose? Baldwin, like Orwell, used English as a talisman, or palimpsest, to argue that it was possible for differences to fade or be over-written in the face of external threats. This was, in effect, a common culture (Orwell, 1982: 41). The political value of this cannot be underestimated: a common culture

> could exist within the context of great diversity as a shared experience that transcended boundaries without eliminating them or even lessening their social significance. A common culture might be experienced differently by a wide variety of groups and yet retain its value as a mutually acknowledged frame of reference. (LeMahieu, 1988: 227)

Baldwin's rhetoric did not deny difference but argued that a common patriotism trumped any difference, up to and including class conflict. Patriotism might take different forms in different groups 'but it runs like a connecting thread through nearly all of them' (Orwell, 1982: 49). Baldwin's rhetoric was united by this thread and was designed to mobilise this connection and both the left and right imagined political communities bound by a common culture that need not be standard or uniform. As such this culture could not be entirely appropriated by any single political tradition. Baldwin sought to mobilise this culture in the Conservative interest. Like Disraeli, Baldwin was convinced (rightly) that the Conservative Party and its values could prosper in the new mass democracy. This brings us to the commonplaces, or *topoi*.

Topoi play a critical role in Baldwin's rhetoric. A commonplace represents knowledge shared by an audience as part of a community and *topoi* assumes a large common store of cultural capital and symbols that define and expands the moral virtue of audiences who see themselves as the embodiment of those virtues. Baldwin's employment of commonplaces emphasised virtue (*encomium*) and permeated his political and non-political speeches, all of which were delivered in a manner foregrounding Baldwin's character (Williamson, 1999: 337). Commonplaces were, therefore, Baldwin's fundamental rhetorical device.

To examine *topoi* I focused primarily, but not exclusively, on the famous 'England' speech (6 May 1924) which Wright refers to as the *ur-text* of an understanding of 'deep

England' common to both intellectuals and wider society (Wright, 1985: 82–3). The Mass Observation report cited earlier found the clearest images among all classes, urban or rural, were topographical: 'The feeling of the land, the soil of Britain under our feet, the firm basis for all our work and play and hopes and fears, is the foundation of most of these feelings' (MO, 1941: 9). The commonplaces identified (see the Appendix for definitions) were 'the rejection of foreign models', 'produces geniuses', 'kindness and sympathy for the underdog', 'grumble but remain cheerful', 'emotional stability in a crisis', 'efficiency not supreme virtue', 'diversified individualism' and 'anti-intellectualism'. The commonplaces defined the national character and provided the foundation on which the political superstructure was erected to respond to the country's problems. The commonplaces provided the linkage between national character and political action. Baldwin used the commonplaces to paint a picture, later captured by Mass Observation, as 'qualities of steadiness, calmness, good humour, green hedges, dusty lanes, freedom from fear, cottages and busy shopping streets' (MO, 1941: 14). His audiences recognised attributes that offered a foundation for the resolution of post-war discord and the creation of future stability.

Topoi are, therefore, an inventive starting point using culturally symbolic language stressing values that render the world understandable. Interpreting and organising experience through a 'new' discourse that not only makes sense of reality but indicates the way forward to a desired end state. These commonplaces were not exclusive to Conservatives, so to be effective they had to be 'above' politics and resonate throughout political and social life operating as powerful cultural signposts. For *topoi* to be effective they had to stimulate a widespread positive response, so they had to be beyond party. One way to illustrate their potential influence is to refer to their use in other political traditions. George Orwell is a good illustration of this. In his magnificent *The Lion and the Unicorn* (1941), and especially the first part, 'England Your England', Orwell used *Baldwinesque* language (or Baldwin used Orwellian language?), noting the English genius, its dislike of abstract thought (for example) and a continuity of identity that stretches into the future and the past which means 'the whole nation can suddenly draw together and act upon a species of instinct, really a code of conduct which is understood by almost everyone, though never formulated' (Orwell, 1982: 38, 39). A second manifestation is the wartime documentaries of Humphrey Jennings (such as 'London Can Take It' (1940), 'Words for Battle' (1941) and especially 'Listen to Britain' (1942)) that celebrate nationhood, national identity, history and culture, and which express admiration for the qualities (such a decency and moderation) of the ordinary man and woman who are the products of a common history. Baldwin and Orwell drew on a similarly conceived common culture and both stress the critical role of a new intermediate class (personified by the Gibbonses) after 1918. Orwell and Baldwin saw this culture and class as the social bedrock. Orwell described England as a country with the wrong members in charge and wanted to change it; Baldwin wanted to create a community of interest in which they remained in charge. Baldwin captured *topoi* for the Conservatives.

An interesting illustration of Baldwin's 'connectivity' is a letter written by David Kirkwood to Baldwin in 1939. Kirkwood, an industrial militant in the First World War, ILP-er and member of 'Red Clydeside' and, from 1922, Labour MP for Dumbarton Burghs, contrasted the cooperation of 1939 with the unrest of 1916–19, after arguing this change was in no small part due to Baldwin's rhetoric. Particularly symbolic, Kirkwood argued, was Baldwin's speech on the MacQuisten Bill. This private member's bill proposed to replace 'contracting-out' with 'contracting-in' with respect to trade union political funds. It was widely seen as a frontal assault on the Labour movement. Baldwin delivered a speech asking for the bill not to be proceeded with, a speech ending with the peroration 'Give peace in our time, O Lord' (Baldwin, 1926: 41–52). Kirkwood wrote that:

> It seemed to me … that in your speech you made flesh the feelings of us all, that the antagonism, the bitterness, the class rivalry were unworthy, and that understanding and amity were possible. You would not accept it from me, if I said that the speech caused the change. I prefer to say that it expressed the inarticulate feeling for a change and so materialised and ideal thought into living reading. (HLRO, 1939)

This, of course, ignores the 'disciplining' of Labour by the General Strike, mass unemployment and electoral defeat (and, of course, the surge in industrial unrest after 1941) but Kirkwood's letter does illustrate the 'universality' of Baldwin's appeal.

A common judgement of Baldwin was that his audiences, the overwhelming majority of who never had (and never would) meet him, believed 'there was no nonsense about him', identifying his 'extraordinary friendliness, candour, and liberality of mind' (CUL, 1938). Observing a working-class cinema audience in Wood Green, a correspondent noted that of the party leaders only Baldwin was applauded. He also reported a working man saying, 'What I likes about Baldwin 'e don't sling no mud' (Stannage, 1980: 77). Extreme partisanship 'in the ordinary voter's mind reek of party politics and fail to carry weight on that account', hence Baldwin talking 'to people sitting in their armchairs at home'. This meant 'the more personal, intimate and friendly these talks can be, the greater influence they will exercise' (Baldwin, 1935b). Baldwin's image was, of course, manufactured and carefully nurtured and, in the absence of opinion polls and audience research it is difficult to assess its effectiveness. There is, however, a wide range of contemporary testimony from politicians, party officials, newspapers, and so on that insists on his rhetoric's effectiveness and the evidence for this was so widespread it could not have been totally artificial or manufactured (Williamson, 1999: 87). As Orwell noted at the time, 'however much one may hate to admit it, it is almost certain the National Government represented the will of the mass of the people' (Orwell, 1982: 53). The commonplaces were fundamental in making the connection with the audience and articulating them in a strategy required a high degree of political skill.

Baldwin's diagnosis of contemporary politics stressed change and instability. To a far greater extent than before 1914 political space was oriented on a left–right dimension with socialism being a more fundamental threat than radical liberalism. Politics was in a state of flux. Previous approaches (such as Bonar Law's) hoped to isolate Labour or strangle it at birth, presenting socialism as an extension of bolshevism and fundamentally un-English. Baldwin's broad and a-historical conception of political space sought to isolate extremism (as with press barons and during the General Strike) and certainly engaged in powerful assaults on Labour and socialism in elections whilst eschewing violently exclusionary language. Thus:

> He managed to convey the impression that honest chaps though the Opposition might be they lacked tradition and experience ... and with a sob in his voice suggested that in these anxious times it might be wise for the country to give the Government he led another turn. (Rhodes James, 1969: 171)

Baldwin's conception of the national character emphasised evolution and universalism, which allowed him to present conflicts and difficulties as natural and recurring features of 'our Island story' and, whilst not decrying their seriousness, by locating them in the flow of history put them into perspective. Labour, socialism, democracy, industrial unrest were problems but also part of a tradition, in contrast to communism, which like Japanese knot-weed, was an alien and deeply threatening incursion. Baldwin's use of non-historical time allowed him to define contemporary political space broadly enough to envelop new and disturbing developments that could be, with some exceptions, transmuted given time and patience into legitimate parts of the national tradition. Over time, after their education, these new elements would be fully part of this tradition and be literally domesticated; exclusion would threaten that tradition and risk serious unrest.

Conclusion

Baldwin summed up his strategy thus: 'I have spent a large part of my public life trying to get the people of this country to sing in tune' (Jones, 1954: 490). The commonplaces, the core of Baldwin's rhetorical strategy, were critical in reconciling opposites – contemporary instability with deep socially conservative roots, a class-based industrial society with the rural, national myth, reconciling radicalism with conservatism – and in identifying common ground, narrowing difference, excluding political extremes and defining the centre.

Like a film Baldwin's rhetoric was subject to creative editing to produce a powerful associative montage of the familiar and unfamiliar to create new meanings. To do this he relied on *topoi*: 'a storehouse of unifying symbols and experiences which helped to define communities of intricate and often highly diverse functions ... powerful components of individual identity and social cohesion' (LeMahieu, 1988: 227–8). Baldwin appealed successfully to all classes and regions, blurred the dividing line between mass and elite, and encouraged the political convergence of left and right.

In January 1938 Chips Channon recorded that 'Baldwin has already faded into obscurity. His stock is low indeed, though history may make him out a great man, half Machiavelli, half Milton' (Rhodes James, 1967: 143). Baldwin had an essentially Whig interpretation of history and his rhetoric, rooted in a historical moment, represents a specific distillation of the national experience. An obvious weakness of oratory is its reliance on its creator. Neville Chamberlain, Baldwin's successor, could not, even if he wanted to, replicate Baldwin's oratory and, in any case, the context was changing. Nevertheless, that Baldwin was onto something can be seen in the appropriation of Baldwin's *topoi* by, *inter alia*, Orwell, Jennings and Priestley, and in Labour's 1945 victory.

When Baldwin retired in 1937 the Conservative Party, though electorally stronger in some areas than others, was palpably a national and cross-class party; its spatial mal-distribution and reliance on specific social groups being far less than Labour's. Baldwin's rhetoric eased the party's translation into mass democracy helping it cross class boundaries and, despite setbacks such as 1929, prosper. The resonance of the imagery on which Baldwin drew can still be felt. In the midst of the fratricidal blood-shed over Europe John Major declared that:

> Fifty years from now Britain will still be the country of long shadows on county grounds, warm beer, invincible green suburbs, dog lovers and pools fillers and – as George Orwell said – 'old maids bicycling to Holy Communion through the morning mist' … Britain will survive unamendable in all essentials. (Major, 1993)

This was a self-conscious and deliberate appeal to Baldwinite conservatism and an evocation of 'deep England' in a failed effort to bridge a profound divide. Can Baldwin's sentiments still evoke a response? Demonstrating this in the modern era is extremely difficult but anyone who saw Danny Boyle's London 2012 Olympic opening ceremony caught an echo, perhaps, of elements of Baldwin's remembered world.

2

The oratory of Winston Churchill

Kevin Theakston

Introduction

Winston Churchill has to be ranked as one of the greatest political orators, his war-time oratory regularly featuring in collections of the 'great speeches of history' and his style and rhetorical methods often used as the basis of 'how to' advice for budding speechmakers and business executives anxious to project the 'language of leadership' (Glover, 2011; Humes, 1991). He had a feel for words and great artistry in their use – 'he gets the last ounce out of the English language', it was once said (Hore-Belisha, 1953: 271) – but also worked extremely hard at his speechmaking (Cannadine, 2002; Humes, 1980; Weidhorn, 1987). Churchill was not a natural or spontaneous speaker but he made himself into a great orator – he studied the ora-tors of the past and actually wrote about the subject – and always relied on detailed preparation, being dependent upon full and carefully worked-out scripts that even included stage directions ('pause'). Though he developed skills in repartee, his lim-ited powers of improvisation meant that his oratory could be rather inflexible and he could give the impression of speaking at his audience (particularly in Parliament) rather than properly debating. However, one of his great strengths as an orator was that 'he could speak in both an arcane, heroic style and a plain everyday style', being able to utilise both an ornate, sometimes even anachronistic, vocabulary and also strong, short and simple words and colourful images to make his points (Rubin, 2003: 46–54). And a key aspect of Churchill's oratory was the performance elem-ent: his physical presence, his 'richness of gesture', his sense of timing, his voice, and his manner of delivery (Fairlie, 1953; Weidhorn, 1987: 23–6). The written words alone were not enough. It has been suggested: 'Churchill's speeches, even if deliv-ered verbatim by someone else, couldn't have had the same effect on audiences' (Montalbo, 1990: 13).

The length and intensity of Churchill's political career, however, poses a special challenge for the analysis of his oratory. He was an MP for over sixty years, changed parties twice, engaged with most of the big political issues and controversies of the time, and his collected speeches fill eight fat volumes totalling nearly 9,000 pages and over four million words. During the Second World War, it was famously said, he mobilised the English language and sent it into battle. His showmanship, rhetoric and charisma projected and inspired confidence and determination. That was the period of his greatest and most successful oratory (Charteris-Black, 2011: 53), and some of his famous phrases from that period became part of the national vocabulary and the collective historical memory. This chapter, however, focuses just on Churchill as Conservative leader in opposition and then back in government as prime minister between 1945 and 1955, a critical period in defining the post-war trajectory of British conservatism. It deals mainly with his oratory on domestic and party issues rather than the grand themes of world affairs and foreign policy that have hitherto received more attention. The chapter shows that whereas as Leader of the Opposition his preferred approach was to mount thunderous, slashing and strongly worded attacks on the mistakes and failings of the Labour government, his tone on return to office as prime minister was more restrained and consensual. Analysis of his speeches and of how his oratory worked casts light on how Churchill accommodated to the changed political landscape after 1945, won back power again in 1951, and approached the problems of governing in the 1950s.

Oratory as Leader of the Opposition, 1945–51

The Churchill speeches that are most remembered after 1945 are those he delivered on the international stage, warning about the 'Iron Curtain' and the Soviet threat, and calling for European unity. He often seemed more comfortable in, and better fitted for, the role of world statesman than for the hard grind of domestic politics and party leadership at home in the UK, as Leader of the Opposition, a role he discharged in a semi-detached and rather erratic fashion (Theakston, 2012). It is striking that between 1945 and 1947 he took part in none of the parliamentary debates over the Labour government's key nationalisation, social insurance or health service measures (Addison, 1992: 390). Policy re-thinking and renewal in opposition after 1945 owed little, if anything, to Churchill and his speeches largely avoided policy detail and promises. His strength was in the making of powerful, fighting speeches that went down well on his own side at least, and he always liked a good House of Commons ding-dong argument, though some Tories felt that he was liable to go over the top (Ball, 1999: 494, 498, 517, 528, 530, 535; Catterall, 2003: 26, 36, 52; Nicolson, 1968: 114). Hoffman (1964: 222) put it well:

> A brilliantly delivered harangue of the Government's policy by Winston Churchill might have – and often did have – the desired effect on the Press Gallery, but within the narrower parliamentary context, the speech might be regarded, even by some of his own party, as a wild, unreasonable, and perhaps embarrassing display, whose only contribution was to unite a divided government party.

At times also Churchill's set piece parliamentary speeches could be too ponderous, lengthy and stylised to be effective. The more pedestrian Attlee – dry, astringent, precise, unemotional, matter-of-fact – could sometimes cut him down to size and score tactical debating victories.

Churchill's speech in Parliament in September 1949 on the devaluation of the pound was one of his most effective in this period and illustrates well the political themes he developed as opposition leader and his style of argumentation (Rhodes James, 1974a: 7844–57). Conservative MP and diarist 'Chips' Channon actually considered it 'one of his very greatest speeches ... to a crowded and anxious house ... a stupendous performance, highly audible, polished, unanswerable, and damning. He held the House entranced for over an hour ... the speech was ... a clarion call to rally the nation' (Rhodes James, 1967: 535). Churchill ranged across arguments based on 'the brutal fact[s]' and rival political ideologies (logos), more populist and emotive appeals (pathos), and denigration of his opponents' motives and trustworthiness and reminders of his own character and record (ethos). Describing devaluation as 'a serious disaster', he attacked the government's 'mismanagement' of the country's finances 'in the these last four lavish years', a period of 'continued drift and slide downhill', with high public spending and crushing taxation burdening the public and stifling production and economic initiative. A mass of controls gave the government 'that power of interference on the daily life of the country which is a characteristic of Socialism'. There was 'prejudice against profit earners' and the government had 'thrust upon the nation ... the evils of nationalisation', which was 'being proved every day more clearly to be a costly failure'. Cutting through the technicalities and statistics, Churchill vividly summed up the impact of devaluation:

> It can only mean that we are forced to give much more of our life energy, that is to say toil, sweat, physical fatigue, craftsmanship, ingenuity, enterprise and good management, to buy the same quantity of indispensable products outside this country as we had before. We have to do more work and draw more upon our spirits and our carcasses to win back the same amount of food, raw materials and other goods without which we cannot carry on ... The devaluation of the pound sterling draws a further draft in life blood and ... energy not only from the wage-earning masses but from all that constitutes the productive fertility of Britain.

Stafford Cripps had given Churchill a secret personal briefing before devaluation had been announced, at which he had wept and complimented the Labour Chancellor on his wisdom and bravery but said that, of course, he would have to make political capital out of it (Addison, 1992: 402; Hennessy, 1992: 376). Indeed, in a devastating personal attack on his opponent's integrity, Churchill 'went for the jugular' (Bryant, 1997: 432), vehemently accusing Cripps of inconsistency, incompetence and dishonesty. He went on to cite his own personal history of involvement with the great Liberal social reforms before 1914, as Chancellor in the 1920s extending pensions, and as head of the wartime coalition which had planned for many of the social services reforms enacted after 1945. He rejected accusations that he was 'callous about unemployment or the welfare of the people' and claimed he had actually shown 'services rendered to the working classes' greater than those that could be claimed by his Labour opponents.

And throughout his speech on devaluation Churchill was suggesting that the government was playing 'the party game', was motivated by 'party spite', 'malice' and 'party doctrines' (referring to 'the fallacy of Socialism ... which ... can only be enforced upon nations in its entirety in the wholesale fashion of Communism'), whereas the Conservatives 'put country before party'. 'Personally', he said, 'I do not think that a large part of the British people are lower than vermin [a reference to an infamous remark by Aneurin Bevan]. I think that the British nation is good all through'. His argument was that the parties were far apart and that Labour was dividing the country with its 'extreme plans' and measures: 'there is a great gulf of thought and conviction between us' and there were 'more fundamental divergencies at every grade and in every part of our society than have been known in our lifetime'. It was, in all, a powerful, attacking and combative performance and 'a superb, rollicking electioneering speech, roaming freely ... over the whole field of socialist iniquity', only a brilliant debating response from Bevan firing up Labour MPs and saving the day for a government that was on the back foot and reeling (Campbell, 1997: 208–9).

Once described as 'the greatest living British humorist' (Herbert, 1953: 295) and as possessing a 'devastating wit' (Shrapnel, 1978: 21), Churchill certainly understood the political uses of jokes and witticisms (Weidhorn, 1987: 81–106). When the new Minister for Fuel and Power, Hugh Gaitskell, advocated a policy of fewer baths to save on fuel, Churchill retorted that ministers had 'no need to wonder why they are getting increasingly into bad odour' and asked the Speaker if he would allow the word 'lousy' as a parliamentary expression, 'provided, of course, that it was not intended in a contemptuous sense but purely as one of factual narration' (Rhodes James, 1974a: 7548). He offered mock sympathy to Herbert Morrison, faced by Labour rivals, in a parody of Tennyson: 'Crippses to the right of him, Daltons to the left of him, / Bevans behind him, volleyed and thundered ... / What tho' the soldiers knew / Someone had blunder'd ... / Then they came back, but not the four hundred' (Rhodes James, 1974a: 7571). In the middle of a speech attacking the government for squandering the nation's resources, a Labour MP shouted that he should sell his racehorse (which was then having a winning streak), Churchill winning huge gales of laughter in the Commons by quickly firing back: 'I could sell him for a great deal more than I had bought him for but I am trying to rise above the profit motive' (Herbert, 1953: 301; Rhodes James, 1974a: 7846). He gently mocked 'official Socialist jargon': 'You must not use the word "poor"; they are described as the "lower income group"', with 'houses and homes ... in future to be called "accommodation units". I don't know how we are to sing our old song "Home Sweet Home". "Accommodation Unit, Sweet Accommodation Unit, there's no place like our Accommodation Unit"' (Rhodes James, 1974b: 7927). But the humour could have a vicious edge, as when he laid into Bevan after the latter's 'lower than vermin' outburst in 1948, saying that:

We speak of the Minister of Health, but ought we not rather to say the Minister of Disease, for is not morbid hatred a form of mental disease, moral disease, and indeed a highly infectious form? Indeed I can think of no better step to signalise the inauguration of the National Health Service than that a person who so obviously needs psychiatrical attention should be among the first of its patients. (Rhodes James, 1974a: 7679)

Whether used to charm, attack, deflate or divert, Churchill's humour was a key part of his persuasive armoury, representing a form of pathos (by stirring emotions to laughter) but also helping to bolster his ethos (by getting the audience on his side).

When speaking at public rallies and Conservative Party meetings, Tory MP Cuthbert Headlam thought Churchill 'always overstates his case – but our rank and file like this – from him at any rate' (Ball, 1999: 535). Ramsden (1995: 110) says the party had no other speaker to match him when it came to 'enliven[ing] the ... party faithful'. At party conferences and rallies in this period he typically used three sorts of ethos appeals. First, there were the allusions to his record of wartime leadership and opposition to appeasement in the 1930s: 'It may perhaps be that you give me some indulgence for leading you in some other matters which have not turned out so badly' (Rhodes James, 1974a: 7254); 'Sometimes in the past I have not been wrong' (Rhodes James, 1974a: 7386); 'I warned the nation before the war, and my advice was not taken. I warn them now' (Rhodes James, 1974a: 7529). And references to the war – '1940 – that breathless moment in our existence' (Rhodes James, 1974a: 7254) – arguably linked his personal leadership credibility with feelings of patriotism and collective historical memories (pathos). Second, he would refer to his long record as a minister in earlier governments (Liberal, Conservative and coalition administrations) to rebuff arguments that the Conservatives were not concerned about unemployment, social problems or welfare (Rhodes James, 1974a: 7389, 7530). And third, he signalled personal determination – to keep 'carrying the flag as long as I have the necessary strength and energy' (Rhodes James, 1974a: 7387) – as a way of spurring on the party, with echoes of his wartime oratory when he insisted that the Conservatives would recover power provided they did not 'fail or falter or flag' (Rhodes James, 1974a: 7255).

In terms of pathos-type appeals, Churchill would often appeal to patriotism and paint Labour as extreme 'sectarians' who had 'led our people so far astray' (Rhodes James, 1974a: 7255). At a party gathering in November 1945 he framed the issue as:

'The People versus the Socialists.' On the one hand will be the spirit of our people ... the ancient, glorious British people, who had carried our name so high and our arms so far in this formidable world. On the other side will be the Socialist doctrinaires with all their pervasive propaganda, with all their bitter class hatred, with all their love of tyrannising ... with all their hordes of officials and bureaucracy. (Rhodes James, 1974a: 7260)

The division at the next election, he said in 1946, would be 'between those who wholeheartedly sing "The Red Flag" and those who rejoice to sing "Land of Hope and Glory"' (Rhodes James, 1974a: 7390). This was pretty mild compared to the attacks he sometimes made on 'this evil Socialist rule' (Rhodes James, 1974b: 8000) and the 'totalitarian' tendencies he sometimes claimed to detect in the government's policies and aims (Rhodes James, 1974a: 7531; Rhodes James, 1974b: 8002). At the 1949 party conference he cleverly used a wartime reference to paint Labour as divisive and driven by party and class spite. Recalling 'the days of Dunkirk', he pointed out that:

> We did not think then about party scores. We did not divide the men we rescued from the beaches into those we cared about and those for whom, to quote a Ministerial utterance, we did not care a tinker's curse. The rescuing ships that set out from Britain did not regard a large part of the wearied and hard-pressed army we were bringing back to safety, and as it proved in the end to victory – we did not regard them as 'lower than vermin'. (Rhodes James, 1974a: 7863)

Drawing sharp lines between the parties in this way served to rally and fire up the Tory activists who, it is said, simply 'idolised' him (Addison, 1992: 397).

Churchill would also speak to his party in terms of logos-type arguments, claims and assertions though not usually getting bogged down with excessive detail. There were nice swipes at 'the gloomy State vultures of nationalisation' hovering above the country's industries, replacing the profit motive with 'the loss motive' (Rhodes James, 1974a: 7256). Socialist regulations meant that ordinary people were being 'harassed, harried, hampered, tied down and stifled' (Rhodes James, 1974a: 7255). Reviewing the Labour government's failures on the housing front, he summed up by saying of socialism that 'in its revolt against the unequal sharing of blessings it glories in the equal sharing of miseries' (Rhodes James, 1974a: 7311). Denouncing the government's 'ineptitude … inefficiency and … blunders' in 1946, he used *anaphora* to hammer home his points:

> Look around you. Look at the taxes. Look at the unbridled expenditure … Look at the queues … Look at the restrictions and repressions on every form of enterprise … Look at the ever-growing bureaucracy … Look at food … Look at the housing of the people … Look at coal. (Rhodes James, 1974a: 7384)

Churchill framed his appeals to the electorate in his political broadcasts and election addresses using broadly similar rhetorical techniques and approaches. In terms of ethos he would sometimes allude to his war and pre-war record ('I have given you my warnings in the past, and they were not listened to'; 'We went through a lot in those days together. Let us make sure we do not throw away, by the follies of peace, what we have gained in the agonies of war'; 'One gets quite tired of saying things which are first mocked at and then adopted, sometimes, alas, too late' (Rhodes James, 1974a: 7192; 1974b: 7929, 8259)). At other times he stressed his social reform credentials ('I am the oldest living champion of [Social] Insurance in the House of Commons'; 'My friend Mr. Lloyd George'; 'We did not christen it [the welfare state] but it was our political child' (Rhodes James, 1974a: 7187; 1974b: 7926)). And in the 1951 general election, with Labour attempting to paint him as a threat to peace ('whose finger on the trigger?'), he argued that a Third World War was not inevitable and that 'the main reason I remain in public life is my hope to ward it off and prevent it' (Rhodes James, 1974b: 8258).

At times, it must be said, his language could seem archaic – as in the reference to 'the cottage home to which the warrior will return' in a 1945 broadcast (Rhodes James, 1974a: 7174). On other occasions there were deliberate echoes of his war-time oratory, such as in his swipe at the Labour government in a 1949 speech: 'Never before in the history of human government has such great havoc been wrought by such small men' (Rhodes James, 1974a: 7832). And he remained ver-bally inventive, as in his description of the 'Socialist dream' in 1950 as 'no longer *Utopia* but *Queuetopia*' (Rhodes James, 1974b: 7912) and his depiction of the Labour government's reliance on the big US loan – 'these large annual dollops of dollars from capitalist America': 'They seek the dollars; they beg the dollars; they bluster for the dollars; they gobble the dollars' (Rhodes James, 1974b: 7929–30). When Attlee complained that it was contradictory for Churchill to attack the gov-ernment for both extravagance and austerity, he shot back: 'Has he never heard of having to pay a very high price for a very poor meal?' (Rhodes James, 1974b: 7954).

The 1945 election broadcast that backfired so damagingly because of the ill-judged smear about a Labour government needing to create 'some form of *Gestapo*' or 'political police' illustrates in other respects some characteristic Churchillian combinations of logos and pathos (Rhodes James, 1974a: 7169–74; Toye, 2010). Thus he argued against the socialist view of the state as a threat to property, free-dom, individualism and liberty: under socialism the 'formidable machine' of the state would be 'the arch-employer, the arch-planner, the arch-administrator and ruler, and the arch-caucus boss'. It would involve a vast bureaucracy of 'civil servants, no longer servants and no longer civil', interfering in every detail of ordinary life. These arguments were linked to patriotic sentiment, in that he depicted socialism as an alien 'continental conception' and declared that 'Here in old England, in Great Britain ... in this glorious Island, the cradle and citadel of free democracy through-out the world, we do not like to be regimented and ordered about and have every aspect of our lives prescribed for us'. And then, resorting to metaphor, as he had done so often in his wartime speeches (Charteris-Black, 2011: 52–78), he conceded that while socialist-style conditions may have been necessary in wartime 'to save our country', it was now time to 'quit the gloomy caverns of war and march out into the breezy fields, where the sun is shining and where all may walk joyfully in its warm and golden rays'.

In his 1950 election broadcasts he was still making highly aggressive attacks on socialism and 'the idea of an all-powerful State which owns everything, which plans everything, which distributes everything', and on the 'Socialist policy of equalising misery and organising scarcity' (Rhodes James, 1974b: 7904–5). But with a return to government finally within sight, in October 1951, he struck a different and more moderate note in his election broadcast. The country now needed, he said, 'a period of several years of solid stable administration by a Government not seeking to rub party dogma into everybody else'. The National Health Service (NHS) and other post-war social reforms had been based on 'common policy. It was British policy, not party policy ... four-fifths of the social legislation since the war was the agreed policy of all parties when I was Prime Minister with a large Conservative majority' (Rhodes James, 1974b: 8254–5). He used a neat analogy to explain the difference between the socialist and conservative outlooks: 'We are for the ladder. Let all try their best to climb. They are for the queue. Let each wait in his place till his turn comes.' But there was reassurance for anyone who might slip off the ladder: 'We shall have a good net and the finest social ambulance service in the world' (Rhodes James, 1974b: 8256).

Churchill's oratory as prime minister, 1951–55

Churchill's oratory as prime minister after 1951 was in general much more consensual in tone and content than had been the case when he was fighting to regain office and taking up an adversarial stance as leader of the opposition. His unique personal prestige as a world statesman and his institutional status as prime minister meant that he had an automatic authority in the eyes of the audiences he was addressing. But he faced two particular challenges in terms of projecting and maintaining his credibility or ethos. The first was his great age (seventy-seven when he took office again, the oldest prime minister of the twentieth century), meaning that the issue of the succession and how long he could go on as prime minister was constantly in the minds of his colleagues, insiders and close observers. As Jenkins (2001: 846) put it:

> The major milestones in his political year were occasions when he would endeavour to show the Cabinet or the Americans, the Conservative Conference or the House of Commons, that he was fit to carry on. It was not so much what he said on these occasions, although he maintained his habit of meticulous preparation and sometimes produced speeches in which wit and vision were uniquely blended, as the fact that he was able to keep on his feet, and retain the resonance of his voice, long enough to say it at all.

Churchill, then, needed successful oratorical performances – he needed to 'put on a great show' as prime minister (Jenkins, 1994: 492) – to demonstrate that 'he still had the capacity and the will to govern' (Montague Browne, 1995: 177) and to stave off pressure for his retirement. Speeches that misfired could seriously damage his political capital and hasten the end of his leadership, his misjudged and muddled speech in April 1954 in a bad-tempered and ineptly handled debate on the hydrogen bomb, and one with some highly partisan exchanges, being a case in point (Catterall, 2003: 304–5; Gilbert, 1988: 965–70; Moran, 1968: 562–6). The second challenge he faced was to overcome Labour's 'warmonger' campaign (which he felt had done him and the Conservatives 'great harm' and which he blamed for the slender majority of only seventeen seats in 1951 (Rhodes James, 1974b: 8289, 8317, 8412)). Hence Churchill's presentation of himself less as the great war-leader and more as a would-be international peacemaker, seeking a high-level summit meeting with the Americans and the Russians to try to defuse Cold War tensions and avert the horrors of a nuclear holocaust. Churchill's oratory on this issue was mostly framed in terms of pathos (appealing to emotions and values), backed up by logos (reasoning about the international situation), but also had an ethos dimension as he sought to define and communicate his political character and justify his continuation in office.

Speaking as prime minister in the House of Commons some of Churchill's oratory was based on logos or presentation of evidence to make his case: 'it is necessary to present the facts clearly to the nation in order that they may realise where we stand ... I am only reciting facts' (Rhodes James, 1974b: 8295). This might be the case in relation to setting out the government's inheritance and the situation it faced in terms of the balance of payments, the financial position, coal supplies, transport or housing when it came to power in order to show the scale of the problems faced and make claims about the progress the government had made. Similarly when speaking about foreign policy, defence and international issues, there would be a large element of evidence, information and reasoning in the presentation of the arguments and analysis. But, as Woodrow Wyatt (1958: 203) observed, 'if his speeches could not avoid the use of many figures and technicalities there were always breaks in them designed to restore the attention of the House to a high pitch should it have grown a little bored'. For instance, 'to relieve the gloom of the [defence] manpower statistics', he threw in a joke about making a Latin quotation which he then proceeded to translate, for the benefit, he said, with a humorous and barbed thrust at the Labour intellectuals he always despised, 'of our Winchester friends'. In the same speech, in a nice piece of *antimetabole*, he linked two of the government's objectives: 'solvency is valueless without security, and security is impossible to achieve without solvency' (Rhodes James, 1974b: 8459). He would use the same sort of trick to liven up otherwise routine party speeches: 'Bankruptcy banished by Butler' being a clever alliteration at a Conservative Women's meeting in 1954, for instance (Rhodes James, 1974b: 8570).

Arguably the main thrust of Churchill's parliamentary oratory was about projecting an ethos as a national leader, someone not simply trying to foster the interests of his party but to 'lead, inspire and unite his countrymen' (Seldon, 1981: 36). One of his main ways of doing this was by emphasising what united rather than divided the parties and the public. Thus in his first major speech to the House of Commons after being elected prime minister again he said:

> We meet together here with an apparent gulf between us as great as I have known in fifty years of House of Commons life. What the nation needs is several years of quiet, steady administration, if only to allow Socialist legislation to reach its full fruition. What the House needs is a period of tolerant and constructive debating on the merits of the questions before us without nearly every speech on either side being distorted by the passions of one Election or the preparations for another … Controversy there must be on some of the issues before us, but this will be a small part of the work and interests we have in common.

If the nation continued 'deeply and painfully divided … split in half in class and ideological strife', with the opposing parties 'more or less evenly balanced', with closely-fought elections and narrow majorities, and an atmosphere of 'fierce, bitter, exciting class and party war', the results would be deeply damaging to the country's economic and international position (Rhodes James, 1974b: 8289–90).

Churchill's speech in the House of Commons on 3 November 1953, during the debate on the Address at the opening of the new session, provides an example of persuasion through pathos, with an emphasis on shared values and identity and on collective problems and challenges (Rhodes James, 1974b: 8497–505). Although he devoted a chunk of his speech to controversial policy subjects – touching on the government's proposals for dealing with housing repairs, rents and landlords, and also on plans for the system of agricultural marketing and subsidies after the end of food rationing and controls – he struck a consensual and reasonable note, quoting from the Scottish socialist politician and former wartime minister Tom Johnston to try and suggest that housing be treated as a non-partisan issue. His general theme on the domestic front was again to play down political divisions and conflict. 'It may sometimes be necessary for governments to undo each other's work, but this should be an exception and not the rule', he said in a key passage.

> We are, of course, opposed, for instance, to nationalisation of industry … We abhor the fallacy, for such it is, of nationalisation for nationalisation's sake. But where we are preserving it, as in the coal mines, the railways, air traffic, gas and electricity, we have done and are doing our utmost to make a success of it, even though this may some- what mar the symmetry of party recrimination.

'Having rows for the sake of having rows between politicians might be good from time to time', he ventured, 'but it is not a good habit of political life'. The country was not as divided as some tried to make out, he argued. Fourteen million people voted Tory and about another fourteen million voted socialist: 'It is not really possible to assume that one of these fourteen million masses of voters possess all the virtues and the wisdom and the other lot are dupes or fools, or even knaves or crooks.' It seemed to him 'nonsense for party politicians to draw such harsh contrasts between them'. 'We have to help our respective parties, but we also have to make sure that we help our country and its people', he concluded, humorously ruling out the idea of a coali- tion, however, as that 'would be carrying good will too far'.

At times in the speech it seemed that he was, as Moran (1968: 520) put it, 'brooding on the future of the world' – what Churchill himself, with his usual verbal inventiveness, called this 'quivering, convulsive, and bewildered world'. There had been a row with Anthony Eden and the Foreign Office over the section where he wanted to talk about a possible change of policy and outlook in the post-Stalin Soviet Union and about his proposal for a heads of government summit meeting, and these remarks were accordingly toned down and heavily qualified (Moran, 1968: 515, 520–1). But the main rhetorical impact (again using pathos) came with Churchill's musings on the 'fearful scientific discoveries' involved in the development of the hydrogen bomb and the dangers of atomic warfare that 'cast their shadow on every thoughtful mind'. 'I have sometimes the odd thought', he said, 'that the annihilating character of these agencies may bring an utterly unforeseeable security to mankind. When I was a schoolboy I was not good at arithmetic, but I have heard it said that certain mathematical quantities when they pass through infinity change their signs from plus to minus – or the other way round [*laughter*] ... It may be that this rule may have a novel application and that when the advance of destructive weapons enables everyone to kill everybody else nobody will want to kill anyone at all'.

Churchill concluded the speech with a stirring and emotional passage in which he said that if nuclear weapons made another world war and 'the dread of mass destruction' perhaps now more remote, the resources set free offered the human race the alternative of 'the swiftest expansion of material well-being that has ever been within their reach, or even within their dreams. By material well-being I mean not only abundance but a degree of leisure for the masses such as has never before been possible in our mortal struggle for life ... We, and all nations, stand at this hour in human history, before the portals of supreme catastrophe and of measureless reward. My faith is that in God's mercy we shall choose aright'.

Harold Macmillan thought that this was a 'really remarkable' speech and that Churchill had proved himself 'complete master of himself and of the House' (Catterall, 2003: 272). 'Chips' Channon believed Churchill had made 'one of the speeches of his lifetime. Brilliant, full of cunning and charm, of wit and thrusts, he poured out his Macaulay-like phrases to a stilled and awed house. It was an Olympian spectacle. A supreme performance which we shall never see again from him or anyone else' (Rhodes James, 1967: 479). The speech in fact 'went down well on all sides of the House' (Jenkins, 2001: 871), and afterwards Lord Moran talked to a Labour MP who was in tears, murmuring 'He is a very great man ... The country needs him' (Moran, 1968: 521).

'We are one country', Churchill had declared in a speech at Harrow School in December 1951 (Rhodes James, 1974b: 8314), and this was also a dominant theme in the prime-ministerial broadcasts he made to the public. Some of his appeals in these broadcasts (Rhodes James, 1974b: 8314–18, 8368–72) were built around what he presented as 'what we found on taking over', the state of the national finances, the balance of payments and the reserves being sketched in to justify the need to 'put our house in order'. Although he cited facts and figures, he was quick to move into metaphor as a way of encapsulating the nation's problems. Thus the country was likened to a train running downhill at high speed on the wrong track: it could not be instantly stopped without the train being 'wrecked and the passengers mangled'; rather, the brakes had to be applied, the situation brought under control and then the engine put in reverse to get onto the right line – something which would take the government several years, so patience would be needed (Rhodes James, 1974b: 8315). Or the country was like a 'swimmer who cannot keep his head above water long enough to get a new breath' and 'we are swimming against the stream trying to keep level with a bush on the bank'. 'A truly national effort', he said, 'is needed to make headway', based on 'three or four years of steady, calm and resolute Government at home and abroad' (Rhodes James, 1974b: 8370). He then appealed to a spirit of national unity: 'This is not the time for party brawling.' There had to be a halt to what had been two years (1950–51) of party divisions and electioneering: 'It can't go on if we are to go on.' The differences between the parties were not so great as observers might think, who only listened 'to our abuse of one another', he insisted. 'There are underlying unities throughout the whole British nation. These unities are far greater than our differences … we all sink or swim together.' On domestic policy, the social services, foreign affairs and defence, he believed, 'nine-tenths of the British people agree on nine-tenths of what has been done and is being done and is going to go on being done'. These pathos appeals, with Churchill using the language of 'this island' and 'our people', were reiterated with an allusion to wartime threats and unities – 'what we have to face now is a peril of a different kind to 1940' – serving to underline his character and credibility (or ethos) as a national and not just a party leader.

Churchill was a master of display or *epideictic* rhetoric, speaking to history and for the nation, as seen to brilliant effect in this period in his tributes on the death of King George VI in February 1952 in the House of Commons and in a broadcast (Rhodes James, 1974b: 8336–42). Jenkins (2001: 860) describes them as 'among his finest *éloges*' and 'Chips' Channon thought his Commons speech was 'sublime, so simple and eloquent with his Macaulay phrases pouring out. The attentive House was electrified' (Rhodes James, 1967: 564). In just 1,700 words in Parliament, Churchill evoked the continuities of British history, the central place of the monarchy in national life, the deaths of previous monarchs, the unity of the British Commonwealth and Empire, and the country's surmounting of the terrible challenges and threats of the twentieth century: 'we salute his memory because we all walked the stony, uphill road with him and he with us.' In his radio broadcast, his eulogy included a memorable and moving passage about how the king 'walked with death as if death were a companion, an acquaintance whom he recognized and did not fear. In the end death came as a friend'. Few political leaders could match Churchill's skill in this branch of oratory, based as it was on a deep sincerity of thought and feeling, and in a way being very revealing of his character and personality.

In Churchill's party conference speeches in this period the attacks on Labour were more humorous and mocking than venomous. In 1953, for instance, he explained how he had watched the Labour frontbench reaction to the government's budget:

> From where I sat I had a fine view of the faces of our Socialist opponents and could watch their expressions as the story was unfolded. It was quite painful to see their looks of gloom and sorrow when any fact was stated which was favourable to our country and its prospects They frowned and scowled and hung their heads until I thought some of them were going to break into tears. However, we are far from being out of the wood yet, and when warnings were given by the Chancellor of the disappointments that had occurred or dangers that lie ahead, it was wonderful to see how quickly they cheered up. Their eyes twinkled, their faces were covered with grins not only of mirth but of mockery. However, on the whole they had a bad time and there was much more for them to bemoan and bewail than for them to jibe and jeer at. (Rhodes James, 1974b: 8468)

Conciliatory remarks would also be directed from the conference platform at the trade unions, consistent with his political aim of getting on with them – rather than taking them on. As Addison notes (1992: 412), 'they had supported rearmament, collaborated in the war effort, and championed the Cold War. In Churchill's view they formed a patriotic estate of the realm'. 'We owe a great deal to the trade unions', he asserted in 1952 (Rhodes James, 1974b: 8417). 'I regard the trade unions as one of the outstanding institutions of our country', he said a year later (Rhodes James, 1974b: 8466).

He would use logos-type arguments to make the point that 'Socialist predictions' and 'prophecies' of what the results of a Conservative government would be had been falsified (Rhodes James, 1974b: 8412–13, 8466). And he would trumpet Conservative achievements: 'We let the traders trade and we let the builders build. Our aim has been freedom, not control. The ration book has gone down the drain with the identity card. Two-thirds of the wartime regulations we inherited have been scrapped ... Form-filling has ceased to be our national pastime.' 'This year', he declared in 1954 in a neat piece of *epiphora* (end repetition), 'our countrymen and women ate more, earned more, spent more, saved more than has ever happened before in all our records' (Rhodes James, 1974b: 8594). 'The facts cannot be challenged', he asserted, saying the government should be 'judged ... by results' (Rhodes James, 1974b: 8593). He would not deny the 'immense doctrinal differences' between Conservatives and 'Socialists', and the 'rivalry and partisanship' between the parties. But, as in his parliamentary speeches and public broadcasts, so in his party speeches at this time he would often try to speak as a national leader and rally his followers through appeals to consensual values and interests. There was a need for 'a definite period of stability, confidence, and recuperation [to] be granted to this overburdened island after all she has done for others and all we have gone through ourselves' (Rhodes James, 1974b: 8469). Rather than 'class hatred or doctrinal pedantry', the country 'stand[s] in need of a breathing space. This is not a time for violent ideological conventions'. The political parties and the masses of voters lined up behind them 'have a great deal in common' (Rhodes James, 1974b: 8595).

It is worth looking in some detail at one of Churchill's Conservative Party conference speeches in particular – the one he delivered at Margate on 10 October 1953 – because there was a huge amount at stake and it was one of the most crucial speeches of his second premiership. This was because it was a test of whether he would be able to continue as prime minister following the stroke that had almost killed him three months earlier. That had been concealed from the media and the public but rumours about his illness had been swirling around the party, and the succession question had been preoccupying senior ministers, most of whom wanted him to quit (Seldon, 1981: 44). Was the nearly seventy-nine-year-old Churchill finished or was he fit to go on? 'Never before', Churchill admitted, 'has so much depended on a single bloody speech' (Moran, 1968: 503). He had not spoken in public for five months ('the first time in my political life that I have kept quiet for so long', he quipped (Rhodes James, 1974b: 8496)), and put considerable effort into working on and preparing for the ordeal. He practised his speech in front of a looking-glass, had a full dress-rehearsal to see if he could actually stand for fifty minutes (the idea of delivering the speech while sitting on a high stool having been rejected), knocked back the usual Churchill-style 'very light luncheon' ('a dozen oysters, two mouthfuls of steak and half a glass of champagne'), had a throat spray administered by his throat surgeon, and then swallowed a special pep-pill given to him by his personal doctor, Lord Moran (Moran, 1968: 501–4) before setting forth.

One of Churchill's Cabinet ministers, Oliver Lyttelton, once noted how he often began 'and of course on purpose, with a few rather stumbling sentences; his audience was surprised that the phrases did not seem to run easily off his tongue. The tempo was slow and hesitant. Then gradually the Grand Swell and the Vox Humana were pulled out and the full glory of his words began to roll forth' (Chandos, 1962: 183). And indeed the Margate speech (Rhodes James, 1974b: 8489–97) started quietly and low-key, on a 'peripheral' subject (British Guiana) (Jenkins, 2001: 870). Churchill then set out to 'take stock of our position', as he put it, two years after taking office. There were eleven separate tributes to named Cabinet ministers, 'which, while fence-building and maybe well deserved', comments Jenkins (2001: 870), 'were not the stuff of which high oratory is made.' For a party conference speech, it was 'relatively unpartisan. While he mentioned Attlee five times he did so with more respect than venom, and his jokes about the "Socialists" were good-humoured' (Jenkins, 2001: 870). Commiserations were offered to Labour's leader for 'having to put up with a lot of trouble', Labour's own conference being described as a 'confused and incoherent spectacle'. While Attlee was commended for his 'sensible statements on foreign policy', the 'Bevanite faction' was attacked for its 'irresponsible' attitude of 'carping and sneering at the United States and … hostility to the new Germany'.

Swipes at 'the inherent fallacy of Socialism as a philosophy' and at Labour's 'class warfare' approach and its 'exploitation of jealousy and envy', with nationalisation described as a 'fallacy' and a 'failure' rather than as 'the Eldorado of the workingman', and as 'an utter flop', were designed to appeal to the Tory grassroots through evoking their collective dislike of their political opponents. Trade unions were described as playing 'an important part in our national life', however, Churchill praising their 'useful work' in 'restraining the featherheads, crackpots, vote-catchers, and office-seekers from putting the folly they talk into action'.

The use of pathos could also be seen in the identification of the Conservatives not with 'class interests' or 'faction' and 'party triumphs', but with serving the British people, 'the nation', and 'the world-wide Commonwealth and Empire'. Conservative policies, Churchill insisted, were 'sensible and practical'; 'we have tried very hard', he said, 'to make our administration loyal, sober, flexible, and thrifty'. He made it clear that he stood for 'the progressive Conservatism of Tory democracy'. Using a classic mix of the three-part list (*tricolon*) and *anaphora* he declared:

> We stand for the free and flexible working of the laws of supply and demand. We stand for compassion and aid for those who, whether through age, illness, or misfortune, cannot keep pace with the march of society. We stand for the restoration of buying and selling between individual importers and exporters in different countries.

'We are for private enterprise', he continued, 'with all its ingenuity, thrift, and contrivance'.

The speech was fairly light in terms of logos-type appeals to evidence of policy detail or achievement. 'Two years ago we were sliding into bankruptcy and now at least we may claim solvency', he said. The target of building 300,000 houses a year had been met. The steel and transport industries had been 'liberated just in time' (in other words, denationalised) but the coal industry and the railways had to remain nationalised. Food rationing was one of Churchill's main domestic concerns (Seldon, 1981: 210), and while meat was not finally derationed until July 1954 he took pride in the increasing consumption in a rather humorous part of the speech. 'I am always very chary about loading a speech with percentages' he began. 'I like the simplest forms of statement.' Mocking 'those professional intellectuals who revel in decimals and polysyllables', he declared that 'personally I like short words and vulgar fractions'. 'Here is the plain vulgar fact', he stated before going on to misquote the figures for meat consumption in the first two years of the Conservative government. Instead of 400,000, he said the public had eaten 4,000 tons more meat than under Labour (Moran, 1968: 506). When corrected by somebody at his side his response won more applause and laughter: 'How lucky it was that I did not complicate it with percentages. I will give you the figure again – I like the taste of it' (*The Times*, 1953a).

Over a quarter of the speech was devoted to foreign affairs and the world scene. Here the points were sometimes framed in terms of pathos – the need of 'getting through this awful period of anxiety without a world catastrophe' and 'finding a secure foundation for world peace', the way in which 'we have lived through half a century of the most terrible events which have ever ravaged the human race', and the international dangers hanging 'so heavily on the daily lives of every one of us'. But he also put forward basic arguments about the facts of Western defence and NATO, and the necessity for the American alliance and a rearmed West Germany in the face of the Soviet threat. This shaded into an ethos appeal, based on his personal history: 'You must not mind my putting these things plainly to you because I have had a life of experience in the matter.' And he then used the speech to reiterate his personal policy of seeking a high-level summit meeting to tackle Cold War tensions – 'let us not try to see whether there is not something better for us than tearing and blasting each other to pieces, which we can certainly do' – though he did not disguise that the Americans were doubtful about this idea.

All this was inevitably tied up with Churchill's own political future. He used the speech to say there would be no general election that year or next. His remarks that 'We have to do our duty ... We have to do our work, our job. We have to do it or try to do it with all our lives and strength' could be interpreted as a signal that he was intending to remain at the helm for some time yet (*The Times*, 1953a). His peroration was 'quietly phrased' (Jenkins, 2001: 870) but used to suggest he was staying in politics because he felt he could play a part and had big things to do on the world stage:

> If I stay on for the time being bearing the burden at my age it is not because of love for power or office. I have had an ample share of both. If I stay it is because I have a feeling that I may through things that have happened have an influence on what I care about above all else, the building of a sure and lasting peace.

The speech was widely seen as a triumph: 'a tribute not only to his powers of recovery, but to his determination to continue in office' (Gilbert, 1988: 895). To his audience 'he seemed (as he was) an old man, but a very brilliant and commanding old man' (Grigg, 1977: 12). 'The old fighter and sage was back', noted *The Times* (1953b), with his characteristic 'flashes of wit, the love of the resounding phrase, the zest for the party tussle'. 'The way he speaks, his little tricks and mannerisms, bring back to them the war and all they owe to him', Moran (1968: 507) commented about the reaction of the Tory party faithful. Harold Macmillan called it a 'magnificent' performance 'in the best Churchillian vein. The asides and impromptus were as good as ever' (Catterall, 2003: 269). At one point, Churchill paused to take a sip from a glass of water that was passed to him. There were roars of laughter as he chuckled and said, 'I don't often do that ... when making a speech' (*The Times*, 1953a). Followed up by an equally commanding performance in the House of Commons three weeks later, Churchill had succeeded in asserting his authority and his command of the party, holding on to the premiership for another year and a half, and seeing off those who were longing for him to step down.

Conclusion

Of Churchill's great wartime speeches it has been said that:

> He succeeded because he combined the rules of rhetorical style, ethos, pathos and logos, with an historian's sense of historical moment, and because he employed *topoi* from the storehouse of English history and drama that had such a deep hold on the English psyche that they were almost guaranteed to create the desired response from the audience. (Glover, 2011: 74)

He set the oratorical standards or the benchmark against which the rhetoric of subsequent leaders in crisis situations is measured (Charteris-Black, 2011: 52).

After 1945 he had to deploy his oratory in a different context and for different purposes. The verdicts on Churchill's post-war oratory are mixed. His parliamentary speeches as leader of the opposition were often not highly rated by either side (Rhodes James, 1993: 515). While they could be entertaining, they could also be vituperative, vague and not always convincing (Cannadine, 2002: 108). To some extent it was 'good clean political chaff' and hyperbole of the sort of he had had thrown at him in the past, and that he had thrown himself: 'Though he may really believe that Britain is going down the drain and that the Socialists are handmaidens of the devil, he is half of the time winking at us and joining us in admiration of his wit and rhetoric' (Weidhorn, 1974: 180). Moreover, his opposition rhetoric may have distracted attention away from the point that he actually led the Conservative Party from a centre ground position, something that became more obvious back in office again after 1951.

As prime minister between 1951 and 1955, 'of necessity his rhetoric was less inspirational and more emollient' than it had been during the war and it is said that 'the words no longer flowed as easily or majestically as they once had' (Cannadine, 2002: 109). However, he could draw on all the 'artfulness and artifice' honed over a lifetime of public speaking (Chandos, 1962: 183) and, at his best, the old maestro's performances could still impress his different audiences, other politicians and close observers (Fairlie, 1953; Wyatt, 1958: 194–215). Whatever his other limitations and failings as prime minister for the second time in the 1950s, Churchill remained capable of formidable oratory and stylised public performance pretty much until the final curtain.

3

The oratory of Harold Macmillan

Brendan Evans

Harold Macmillan's oratory is inextricably linked to his persona. His personality, style, oratory and rhetoric were each inter-connected and comprised his political craft. He was a self-conscious orator who critically analysed what he referred to as both the 'matter and manner' of his speeches. His education would have included Aristotle's theories with its concepts of ethos, pathos and logos.

Macmillan's personality: image and reality

Macmillan sedulously cultivated his speaking style as an extension of his political personality. The image that he developed is linked to the ethos on which he traded. Many have referred to Macmillan's acting and his insouciance. He acquired this 'protective theatrical façade' (Sampson, 1967: 10) of 'Baliol nonchalance' and a languid style while at Oxford (Coote, 1965: 35). Edward Heath claimed to have 'watched Macmillan cultivate the image of an Edwardian gentleman' (Heath, 1998: 44) and he implies conscious image building in his reference to Macmillan's 'deceptively laid back manner' (Heath, 1998: 130). A decade later Macmillan had transformed himself from his late 1940s appearance, complete with 'pince-nez' and 'disarrayed teeth' and looking like 'a bizarre Edwardian academic', to become a 'dapper television personality' (Horne, 1989: 144–6) dressed in Savile Row suits and with a clipped moustache and newly fixed teeth. Lawrence argues that politicians relish playing a part (Lawrence, 2009: 3). In exploiting his cultivated persona Macmillan used logos, particularly in serious speeches concerned with his ministerial and governmental roles. Yet even on such official occasions he relied heavily upon deploying his considerable ethos.

Much of his ethos resulted from his skilful exploitation of his formal roles in government between 1951 and 1963. He also drew heavily on his intellectual credentials as a publisher, and as the author of highly regarded political tracts in the inter-war years. In later years he used the status of his advancing age and experience to evoke his wartime valour in the trenches, his experience of mass unemployment as MP for Stockton in the inter-war years, his claim to a unique appreciation of the sweep of twentieth-century international history and the respect that he claimed was accorded to him by contemporary international statesmen such as Presidents Eisenhower, Kennedy and De Gaulle. Under the guise of this ethos Macmillan was able to launch into crude pathos in vitriolic attacks. On at least one occasion he was able to combine the ethos of citing learned allusions with an emotional appeal to pathos, as when he described socialism as a political panacea that was 'already "old hat" when Aristophanes was ridiculing Socrates' (Sampson, 1967: 161). He considered that the political capital which his ethos secured him permitted him to indulge in demotic colloquialisms to gain an emotional connection with the British electorate when as Foreign Secretary on returning from the Geneva Conference in 1954 he informed the country that, 'there ain't gonna be no war' (Hughes, 1962: x).

Macmillan's ethos interacted with his persona in the 'unflappable' superiority which he projected. An episode which reveals this performance was his response to the resignations of his Chancellor of the Exchequer, Peter Thorneycroft, and two junior ministers, Enoch Powell and Nigel Birch, over economic policy. He dismissed the resignations as a 'little local difficulty', as if losing a couple of minor servants. His assumed nonchalance was such that he was able even to feign anxiety. This occurred when he was out of the country for six weeks after those resignations on a Commonwealth tour, and in a speech delivering a toast in Karachi, he said, 'as we grow older we are beginning to realise the importance of strict party discipline', however, 'I can claim that – I think so – that I am the first Prime Minister to visit Pakistan, and as it is now Sunday night, I do not think anything serious can happen tonight to deprive me of that toast' (Commonwealth Tour papers, 1958: 280). The throwaway 'I think so' and the faux anxiety were characteristic Macmillanisms. His humour was a reflection of his desire to avoid a rigid distinction between the 'serious' and the 'flippant' (Lord Carrington, 1998: in Horne, 1998: xxi) although Bevan thought his humour reeked of 'midnight oil' (House of Commons debs. Vol. 524, Col. 50).

Macmillan's humour was designed to reinforce his ethos, as he demonstrated at the twenty-fifth anniversary of BBC Television in 1963. He acted his script to perfection. Referring to his media portrayals he described returning from international meetings to face a barrage of camera lights, and with an exaggerated version of his world-weary voice, said the press would comment about 'weary Mac' of 'Mac looking old and haggard'. He then demonstrated his capacity to switch from flippancy to seriousness by returning to the Commons where he instantly 'slipped into high statesmanship and let off a speech on the Vassal tribunal which positively boomed with Gladstonian severity' (Evans, 1981: 420). His affected upper-class oratory was also apparent in his 'put down' of Mr Khrushchev at the United Nations on October 1960. In response to Khrushchev's interruption of his speech in which he took off his shoe to bang the table, Macmillan coolly called for a translation. This insouciance may not have amounted to much but it played well on international television screens, strengthened his image of a statesman and reinforced a Conservative propaganda hoarding of the time showing him 'Speaking for Britain'. He recorded his satisfaction in saying that the delegation 'seemed to like the manner of delivery, even if they did not all agree the matter' (Catterall, 2003: 317).

Yet this confident use of ethos was not the real man (Becket, 2006: 2). In reality, Macmillan was anxious about speeches (Catterall, 2003: 89) admitting 'I have hardly ever had to make an important speech, without feeling violently sick most of the day before' (Laing, 1972: 12). He was physically sick before delivering his 'Winds of Change' oration (Heffer, 2007: 213) and refused food before speeches as 'he was too tense to eat' (Boyd-Carpenter, 1980: 151). He felt that a gall bladder infection in 1953 resulted from the 'heavy labour' of preparing and delivering speeches (Catterall, 2003: 220). It was his image which mattered, however, and the public display of ethos enabled him to lapse authentically into pathos. His ethos and pathos proved to have a waning appeal. The changing context of British politics by the early 1960s, with its frantic emphasis on the need for modernisation, meant a waning of Macmillan's effectiveness, and his ethos and pathos even became the victim of cruel satire.

Macmillan's oratory: Parliament and MPs

Macmillan was sometimes conscious of the insignificance of House of Commons speeches, but more frequently considered them to have a positive political role. Parliament and MPs provided him with an arena similar to that discussed by Aristotle.

Despite his intermittent doubts as to its importance he always took the Commons seriously, regarding it as his main performance arena and he addressed MPs like a 'theatre audience' (Williams, 2009: 183). Labour's Bessie Braddock reminded him during a debate in 1954 that he was 'not on the stage now' (House of Commons debs. Vol. 533, Col. 328). He sometimes commented that it is difficult to build a political reputation in the Commons and wrote in 1953 that debates 'are no longer followed with the same interest as in the old days' (Catterall, 2003: 23). He regretted that parliamentary votes were not affected by oratory and suggested that debates should 'start by taking a vote, so that those of us who are interested in the subject could stay and continue the discussion afterwards' (House of Commons debs. Vol. 480, Col. 874). As a result of party discipline, 'on all great issues our speeches are declaratory exercises, like those of schoolboys. We scarcely know what their purpose is. Nobody reads the debates, the newspapers scarcely report them. The television ignores them' (Catterall, 2003: 386). He questioned whether parliamentary speeches communicated to an electorate 'bored by all this manoeuvring in the Commons which seem to them somewhat ridiculous' (Catterall, 2003: 203). Nor could the press compensate. He complained that 'sentences are taken out of context and printed in heavy type. The qualifying sentences are suppressed. Jokes are turned into serious points and vice versa' (Catterall, 2003: 477).

Yet his growing ability to dominate the Commons suggested a pride in his oratory and he 'acquired a mastery of the House which rippled centrifugally on the whole electorate' (Blake, 1980: 2). He advised a new MP that the Commons had to be studied closely:

> You have to know the man who is your questioner … Like a prep school, there are boys who are popular whom you must never slap down … then there are the unpopular, the tiresome, and the House enjoys their being slapped down. You must remember that, like a school, on the whole it dislikes the front bench (the masters) … often you can turn an enemy into a friend. Always keep your temper … and always have a good control of questions and supplementaries, in many ways this is the most anxious work; I would never have lunched out on question day. (Horne, 1989: 153–4)

At times Macmillan demonstrated his capacity for logos and thought it vital to be an 'homme serieux'. On such occasions he presented the Commons with detailed policy speeches and was concerned simply to have policy justifications placed on to the record (Catterall, 2003: 365). He self-consciously evaluated the effectiveness of his speeches and judged that in responding in the Commons to criticisms of his 'Night of the Long Knives' (when he dismissed a third of his Cabinet in July 1962), 'my reply was not at all good oratorically' (Macmillan, 1973: 108). In contrast, he considered his defence of the expulsion of Chief Enahoro to Nigeria 'the most effective speech I had ever made in the House of Commons' (Catterall, 2003: 532). In this speech, he posed rhetorical questions, which displayed an understanding of legal technicalities redolent of logos, to reveal the damage which he considered a refusal to return Enahoro would do to the Commonwealth as it would cast doubt on the integrity of the Nigerians (House of Commons debs. Vol. 675, Col. 1298). He relished this type of debate as there was a real opportunity 'to try to persuade the waverers', and thought he had given 'a rabble rousing wind up in the old style' (Catterall, 2003: 537–8).

Macmillan perceived a range of functions which parliamentary speeches could perform. These included exploiting the divisions on the Opposition benches and effective internal party management and electoral propaganda. In his early Commons speeches, however, he proved unsuccessful. His maiden speech was described as 'priggish' (Sampson, 1967: 24), 'ponderous' (Horne, 1989: 75) and consisting of 'lumbering wit' (Turner, 1994: 17). The speech attacked Philip Snowden, the Chancellor of the Exchequer's economic policy as 'a sort of horrible political cocktail, consisting partly of the dregs of the exploded economic views of Karl Marx, mixed up with a little flavour of Cobdenism, well iced by the late Chancellor of the Exchequer and with a little ginger from the Member for Gorbals' (House of Commons debs. Vol. 183, Col. 405). This was a 'weary' resort to anti-socialist drink metaphors that he deployed on other occasions (Sampson, 1967: 76–9). His oratory improved, and his favourite oratorical device after 1945 was that of pathos through the use of binaries, to bolster a Conservative group identity, by condemning Labour for being socialist. Like many leading Conservatives after Labour's election victory of 1945 he exaggerated both the ideological and electoral threat which Labour posed, informing the House in 1950 of the contrast between the 'freedom' for which he stood versus Labour's socialism, with its 'sinister combination of Marxist socialism and Russian Imperialism' (House of Commons debs. Vol. 478, Col. 1126).

Macmillan adopted the size of the majority at the end of debates as a measure of his oratory. These were the occasions when the party discipline system, which he sometimes criticised for undermining Parliament, broke down, as after the Suez debate of 1957 and the Profumo debate in 1963. Fourteen Conservative MPs abstained over Suez, when he had feared twenty abstentions, which would have been a repeat of the 'Norway syndrome' in 1940 when a reduced majority fatally compromised the authority of Neville Chamberlain's government (Evans and Taylor, 1996: 108).

It was this first major speech in the Commons after the Suez debacle in which he achieved dominance and entrenched his position as prime minister. The speech mattered for more than establishing his authority, as he was required by the needs of both his party and his country to employ rhetoric to conceal the direction in which he was leading his government, while trying to explain that change was necessary. Although he achieved this he was much criticised by later Conservatives for being 'the master of doing one thing while seeming to do another' (Cosgrave, 1989: 152). In foreign affairs he manipulated the retreat from Suez and a coming to terms with a diminished world role, a retreat from Africa and decolonisation, and the changing relationship between Britain and Europe. Fearing a government collapse in the febrile post-Suez atmosphere (Nutting, 1967: 167) with the Opposition in full cry from one side and the Suez group of right-wing rebels from the other, he defended the fiasco and the decisions of his discredited predecessor, Sir Anthony Eden, and reasserted Britain's status as a world power. Crucially, he argued that Eden had 'a fuller experience of world affairs than almost any man in the country', had acted 'from the highest patriotic motives' and received 'the unanimous support of the Government' (House of Commons debs. Vol. 570, Col. 425). He asserted that 'it is in the interests of this country not to represent the situation as an unequivocal success for Colonel Nasser' (House of Commons debs. Vol. 570, Col. 435). His peroration satisfied the party's right-wing with the comment that 'Britain is a great world power and we intend to remain so' (House of Commons debs. Vol. 570, Col. 436), although his actual policy announcement was Britain's humiliating acceptance of increased Egyptian tolls for British ships using the canal (House of Commons debs. Vol. 570, Col. 425–437). The speech saved his prime ministership and set the party on the course to recovery, but as there were limits to how far he could use oratory alone to deny Britain's decline in the world, he made a commitment which bedevilled the rest of his prime ministership: 'that this country should remain a nuclear power' (House of Commons debs. Vol. 570, Col. 437). Some suggest that Macmillan's speech succeeded in creating an atmosphere of national strength (Morgan, 2001: 159) while others argue he defended the Suez invasion to maintain national pride while presiding over decline and holding the various forces in his party in balance (Siedentop, 1979: 99–103).

Macmillan was content with fourteen dissentient votes after the Suez debate. At other times he considered that the peroration at the end of speeches required particular effort to minimise rebellions. He was aware of the risk, however, as in winding up a debate on the Middle East in 1950 he acknowledged that a seven-minute peroration of 'high-falutin stuff about war mongering was risky. But it came off. Had it crashed, it would have done so badly – like an aeroplane, not like a motor car' (Catterall, 2003: 91).

Macmillan sought to engage emotions. When his position was threatened, he sought ethos by resorting to promoting his own credentials. 'I am content to be judged by those with whom I've worked during fifty years of active life in the Army, in business, here in the House of Commons and in government' (House of Commons debs. Vol. 663, Col. 672). A rare instance of his misjudging the Commons occurred in his final months as prime minister, although he was unapologetic. Shortly after the death of Hugh Gaitskell, the Leader of the Opposition for most of Macmillan's time as prime minister, and with his stock low, he sought to 'rally the party and the country'. Following on from a television address on Gaitskell's death during which he had complained, perhaps in a bid for sympathy, of the fickleness and cruelty of political life (Macmillan, 1973: 394), he cited a quotation from Gaitskell, to embarrass Labour's new leader, Harold Wilson. There was then what Macmillan described 'a fake protest' on Gaitskell's behalf and he noted in his diary that 'the movement to beatify (as a preliminary to sanctification) is very strange' (Catterall, 2003: 589). His last debate as prime minister was when he was seeking to save himself after the Profumo affair. He resorted to pathos and a mournful tone when he said the affair had 'inflicted a deep wound' (House of Commons debs. Vol. 679, Col. 54) and combined pathos with a bid for ethos in comparing that week with 'the horrible and distasteful week of the Cuba crisis and I have been through some in peace and war' (House of Commons debs. Vol. 679. Col. 68). He concluded with his peroration which he described as 'the personal bit' (Catterall, 2003: 601).

If Aneurin Bevan was Labour's leading orator in the 1950s, Macmillan took a competitive delight in defeating him in the Commons. Once he accused Bevan of 'synthetic anger' and of 'lashing himself into a state of fury' (House of Commons debs. Vol. 524, Col. 429). He took pride in setting traps for Bevan. In the course of a debate on housing, for example, when Bevan challenged him about the undesirability of a phrase in a government circular which Macmillan had issued, he quoted back to Bevan the offending words, stating that they were identical to those which Bevan had used in a circular when he had been a minister. He concluded, 'I apologise for the plagiarism' (House of Commons debs. Vol. 494, Col. 2244). Macmillan's account of the exchange is that he allowed Bevan 'to work himself up into a great show of indignation. What could these words signify? They were a trap, a swindle etc' (Catterall, 2003: 121). He recorded that it was Bevan who had fallen into his trap, adding 'the great thing with Bevan is to stand up to him. Like all bullies he is easily put off' (Catterall, 2003: 158). His assessment was partial as on another occasion Bevan challenged the accuracy of Macmillan's quotations. When Macmillan stated that Bevan had claimed that the 'managers' of the steel industry had betrayed the nation, Bevan demonstrated that he had not used the word 'managers' (Hughes, 1962: 49).

Macmillan considered that his speeches to the backbench 1922 Committee were the most vital in advancing and safeguarding his position in the Conservative Party, Parliament and the country. Before 1963, the Conservatives remained a party of notables exemplified by the fact that the party leader was not even elected by Conservative MPs, but famously 'emerged'. The unique character of the 1922 Committee is captured by the fact that its meetings were sometimes held in the Savoy amid 'clouds of cigar smoke and fumes of brandy' (Williams, 2009: 433). Macmillan was acutely aware of the committee's importance in securing him the office of prime minister when he and his rival for the role, R. A. Butler, addressed it immediately after Britain's withdrawal from Suez. Butler was acting prime minister and favourite to succeed Eden but invited Macmillan to join him at a key meeting of the committee. While Butler spoke briefly, Macmillan exploited the opportunity in a thirty-five-minute tour de force, in which he associated Butler with appeasement in the 1930s. To seize this opportunity Macmillan laid down his marker to succeed Eden with 'a veritable political organ voluntary', 'pulling out every stop and striking every majestic chord in his well-practiced repertoire' (Howard, 1987: 241). His speech ended with 'a tremolo on his own advancing years', an obvious attempt to gain ethos as an elder statesman (Williams, 2009: 269). Enoch Powell described it as 'one of the most horrible things I remember in politics, seeing the way in which Harold Macmillan, with all the skill of an old actor-manager, succeeded in false footing RAB. The sheer devilry of it was disgusting' (Cosgrave, 1989: 150).

After the political tide had turned against Macmillan's second administration he revealed a manipulative capacity in his speeches to the Committee. In 1962, under fire for the 'night of the long knives', he regretted that 'you cannot say the truth in speeches', as he could not say that Selwyn Lloyd 'had lost his grip' (Catterall, 2003: 487). Five months later, threatening the Committee that he was 'happy to resign … if it would help', he noted that it was the only time that he had used that ploy (Catterall, 2003: 222). Four months later, in April 1963, he urged that the party should 'stick together and hold on' or Harold Wilson would form a government. He was satisfied that 'this lecture had a salutary effect'.

After an undistinguished start Macmillan mastered both the Commons and the 1922 Committee. In his early years in the Commons Lloyd George assisted him in improving both the 'manner' and the 'matter' of his speeches. He advised that Macmillan should combine body language with rhetoric, vary pace and pitch, use the whole arm rather than just his wrist or hands and speeches should not be essays with twenty-five points as one or two were sufficient. Lloyd George added that 'the art of speaking is to leave the audience a clear picture of what it is you want' (Horne, 1989: 78). In his years in office from 1951 to 1963 Macmillan rarely lapsed from his own concern to deliver speeches which were successful in both 'manner' and 'matter', and this was the arena in which he never lost his touch. In the House of Lords in the final year of his life his use of metaphor remained potent when he compared privatisation to a declining family selling off the 'Georgian silver', 'nice furniture' and the 'Canalettos' (Riddell, 1991: 87).

Macmillan and the Conservative Party

Macmillan rarely treated the Conservative Party to a distinct type of oratory and rhetoric and his private comments suggest that he devoted least attention to these performances. He learnt the importance of allowing pauses for applause (Macmillan Papers, 1963). Most frequently, and assuming the potency of the ethos which he conveyed, he deployed pathos in order to reinforce group solidarity. His main device was to emphasise his enmity towards Labour. In one speech in 1946, for example, he told members that socialist intellectuals were dragging Labour 'down the slippery slope to Communism' (Sampson, 1967: 76–9). A year later he informed them that 'Socialism led inevitably to totalitarianism. German socialism led to Nazism. Russian socialism led to Communism'. He discovered that this use of binaries succeeded, noting after one speech, 'the contrast between the policies of the two parties went very well. It was clear and simple and something which the audiences appreciated' (Macmillan Papers, 1963). In 1963 he observed that such binaries were better utilised in addressing the party, leaving the message about 'modernisation' for the national press (Macmillan Papers, 1963).

Although he disliked them Macmillan recognised that the annual party conferences mattered, and in Llandudno in 1961 he commented to a reporter that 'Gladstone and Disraeli never had to put up with this' (Thorpe, 2010: 324). He judged that conferences were important for two reasons. First, the reception which speakers received affected their overall standing in the party, and second there were occasions when the membership had to be persuaded to accept a divisive or unpopular policy.

For Macmillan the adulation at party conference mattered, for when he was Minister of Housing in the early 1950s he happily contrasted the good receptions that he began to achieve with his previous 'years of unpopularity' (Catterall, 2003: 189). For example, in 1950, when opposing an amendment proposing repressive measures against home-grown communists, and using faux self-deprecatory sentences, he succeeded in his aim of getting the amendment withdrawn. His diary entry recorded that 'I feel much more confident of my position in the party. I gather the press will be good and I was told later that my speech came across well in the broadcast' (Catterall, 2003: 23). At the 1952 conference he relished the 'tremendous reception' that his speech secured (Catterall, 2003: 189).

The 1962 conference mattered because the crucial and controversial issue of Britain's application to join the Common Market was on the agenda. This was an opportunity for an educative speech, featuring all the qualities of logos he could muster, but Macmillan's emphasis, and the best audience reception, was based on pathos in the form of ridiculing Gaitskell for Labour's indecisiveness on the issue. He cited a famous song, delivered with impeccable timing, 'She didn't say "yes"; she didn't say "no"; she didn't say "stay"; she didn't say "go"; she wanted to climb, but dreaded to fall; so she bided her time and clung to the wall' (Williams, 2009: 422).

Macmillan's effectiveness as an orator declined in the early 1960s, as some of his policies unravelled, as was apparent even when he addressed supporters. He was disappointed by his reception at a meeting of the Oxford University Conservative Association (OUCA) in February 1962, where he was compelled to abandon his speech owing to interruptions (Catterall, 2003: 446). Even the *Daily Telegraph* described one of his speeches at the time as revealing 'the mournful picture of a rather tired, silver haired gentleman with nothing to say and no particular interest in saying it well' (Hughes, 1962: 247).

Macmillan and public engagement

If all prime ministers are concerned with electability then this was a central pre-occupation for Macmillan such that his oratory, together with his economic policy preferences, was directed towards that end. Aristotle's theory of oratory long pre-dated modern ideas on electability; although logos, and more particularly ethos and pathos, remain relevant even on electronic media.

It was in this arena that Macmillan's penchant for metaphor and for demotic soundbites was most apparent (Jamieson, 1988: 91). This further illustrates that the politician and the real man were distinct, as personally he had advanced literary tastes and delivered parts of his speeches as the Chancellor of Oxford University in Latin (Sampson, 1967: 177). One example of his colourful use of metaphor was 'raining umbrellas', as a device to associate those who were lenient towards communism in the 1950s with Neville Chamberlain's policy of appeasement (Horne, 2008: 116; Turner, 1994: 136). Another was to journeys, as when he claimed the Cold War could be won 'step by step' 'on no ordinary journey' (Hughes, 1962: 71).

Anti-Labour rhetoric brimming with pathos was as evident in his public speeches as it was in meetings with Conservative supporters, when he described socialism as 'the product of a weak intellect and a diseased and rancorous attitude to life' (Catterall, 2003: 78). He also deployed similar sentiments on official occasions. He was concerned to arrest the spread of communism across the world and addressing Commonwealth dignitaries he contrasted the 'material crudities of a purely materialist philosophy' with 'the spiritual values of our civilisation' (Commonwealth Tour papers, 1958: 190).

Macmillan spoke at many public meetings, although sensing their declining importance, he considered them less important than 'door to door canvassing'. He reflected on his public performances, taking pride in occasions when he discarded his notes and spoke spontaneously which he thought audiences welcomed. This implied his impatience with logos and he refers to professional groups preferring informality as they had become 'sated with academic essays' (Macmillan, 1973: 56). His self-scrutiny led him to judge the oratory of others. He described Churchill's broadcasts as speeches, mocked the Labour MP Bill Blyton for addressing the Council of Europe as if it was the Durham Miners Gala, thought that while Clement Attlee spoke in a 'precise', 'cold' way he maintained 'a certain dignity'. He criticised Herbert Morrison as 'rousing the spirits of his party' but offering 'a poor intellectual performance' (Catterall, 2003: 8, 15, 18).

Macmillan dealt with hecklers at a time when political meetings had not yet become stage-managed for carefully selected audiences. He noted a failure and reflected 'beware of rhetorical questions! I was caught out by one. "What is the obstacle to progress"? "You are". This floored me' (Catterall, 2003: 456). Some situations were rowdy. In 1955 he confronted communist 'toughs', bussed in to challenge him on the issue of German rearmament (Catterall, 2003: 386). Five years later, he complained about 'a rowdy element of Empire Loyalists' who engaged in 'a rather stupid, repetitive kind of abuse' (Catterall, 2003: 332). When challenged by left-wingers in April 1962, after the Conservative candidate had come third in a by-election behind the Liberal, he took the opportunity to deploy flippancy, saying that he was not persuaded that 'one Liberal swallow heralds the advent of a neo-Asquithian summer' (Catterall, 2003: 376).

Macmillan spoke to seventy-four public meetings during his triumphant 1959 general election campaign. The audiences were large because in this first television election voters were enticed out to see the politicians in person (Lawrence, 2009: 167). His delivery was assisted by consuming vintage port for his vocal chords (Horne, 2008: 150). He exploited two main themes against the backdrop of affluence and an advertising campaign on the slogan 'Life's Better Under the Conservatives. Don't Let Labour Ruin It'. He argued that to 'build is the laborious task of years. To destroy can be the foolish act of a single day' (Butler and Rose, 1960: 66). Gaitskell gifted him a further theme when he made what appeared to be rash promises on taxation. Macmillan used mockery and rhetorical questioning. 'Will he sign the pledge for beer and other drinks? Will he promise not to put up petrol duty; the entertainment tax or the purchase tax? If not, why not?' (Butler and Rose, 1960: 66).

Oratory can be most effective when the speaker talks from total conviction. By 1962 both his view about Britain's future and his concern with his electoral prospects convinced Macmillan about the importance of Britain's application to join the Common Market. In a by-election meeting in Stockton in 1962, which might have been an opportunity to make an intellectual case based on logos, his speech was redolent of ethos linked to high politics and leadership.

> The Common Market presents us with a tremendous challenge – and a gigantic opportunity. The Government accepts the challenge. It has seized the opportunity. But, of course, we have set about our negotiations with care as well as confidence, with responsibility as well as resource. This is not child's play. This is high policy-and we know what we are doing. (Hutchinson, 1980: 83)

As prime minister Macmillan sought to differentiate partisan speeches, which were discussed with Conservative Central Office, from governmental speeches prepared in Downing Street. But when 'the going got rough' between 1962 and 1963 the line was crossed (Evans, 1981: 37). He sought to 'breathe his own personality' into prepared speeches by dictating sections and adding extempore passages during delivery and preferred speeches to be put into Psalm form, that is to say one hundred words of a large typeface on small pages (Evans, 1981: 40). Wyndham described how the speeches were prepared. George Christ of Conservative Central Office provided a draft which he, Macmillan and Wyndham modified in the Cabinet Room (Lord Egremont, 1968: 176). Macmillan's papers reveal the multiple revisions which took place and elaborate calculations about the delivery time (Macmillan Papers, 1960). Wyndham argued that such speeches with their plural contributions were less good than Macmillan's 'off the cuff' efforts, some of which were recorded and used as the basis for future speeches (Lord Egremont, 1968: 177).

There was obvious need for ethos and logos on certain official occasions such as his Commonwealth Conference speech, when Macmillan invoked age and experience in outlining world history, stating that it was 'tempting' for someone of his advanced age 'to do nothing'. He used logos to present a statistical case that Britain was an inadequate source of capital and markets for Commonwealth countries. Yet even in such speeches his enthusiasm for pathos intruded. He lyrically declaimed the Commonwealth's role in expressing 'the fundamental unity of the human race' (Macmillan, 1973: 529–30) and stirred the emotions when he regretted Britain's past neglect of Europe having led to 'a degree of destruction and misery unexampled in our history' (Macmillan, 1973: 530). He feared that without Britain, Europe could 'succumb to Soviet power which would then perhaps reach the straits of Dover' (Macmillan, 1973: 538).

Undoubtedly the public speech for which he is particularly remembered is 'the Winds of Change' delivered to the South African Parliament in 1960. The context was the combined impact of African nationalism and the continuing existence of apartheid in South Africa, still a Commonwealth country, in splitting the Conservative Party. Macmillan had appointed Iain Macleod as Colonial Secretary who accelerated the decolonisation programme which was creating tension in east and central Africa owing to the large number of British settlers there; and much of the Conservative Party was sympathetic to their interests. Macmillan had a complex attitude towards the pace of decolonisation, but in the Winds of Change speech he used many devices both to signal his support for African nationalism and his opposition to apartheid, while simultaneously pacifying those who disagreed with him in white Africa and on his own backbenches. His striking metaphor of the Winds of Change gave traction to the speech and it was his first public recognition of the legitimacy of the black African nationalist movement and of the growing impatience with apartheid (Heffer, 2007: 213–14). The speech has been characterised as 'the centre-piece of the final chapter in the history of Empire' (Griffiths, 1969: 232).

The Winds of Change speech is an example of achieving a disassociation between the present and the situation that the speaker advocates (Kingdom, 1984: 133). It set the policy framework for succeeding leaders. In his extensive analysis Myers (2000: 555–72) argues that Macmillan had to satisfy three audiences: those who were positive towards him but rejected his policy (white south Africans, white settlers and the Conservative right-wing), those who agreed with him but questioned his sincerity (black African leaders) and those who favoured both Macmillan and the policy but who needed to be rallied (moderates in the Conservative Party). His main method was to use qualitative arguments to appeal to those who opposed his policy and quantitative arguments to stress the inevitability of change. In qualitative language he praised the uniqueness, religiosity, literature and the pioneering spirit of the South African whites and by using analogy compared them with emerging black African nationalists. He implied a disassociation between the preferable, the vain hope that the status quo could be maintained, and the reality. He mollified those who did not want to hear that change was inexorable by stressing the contributions which white South Africans had made, and while supporting majority rule in Britain's colonies, he reassured settlers by suggesting that there were many ways it could be introduced. To gain ethos and pathos in appealing to the right-wing Conservatives he cited Edmund Burke's statement that 'we are fleeting phantoms on the great stage of history', but he also employed quantitative arguments to appeal to the 'realpolitik' tradition in Conservative foreign policy with non-moralistic assertions about the spread of nationalism, the role of world opinion and the need to resist communism. He described nationalism as a fact 'we must come to terms with' (Heffer, 2007: 215) and asserted that the African choice between West and East was in the balance. These 'realpolitik' parts of his speech, which he delivered deliberately with slow diction, were matched by idealistic appeals to other audiences about the merits of the cause, Christian principles and the rule of law. Since the speech was a mix of 'cold eyed realism' and idealism, it was not a logical construction, but was rather 'a musical rondo' to appeal to distinct audiences. His peroration was almost Churchillian, beginning with such phrases as 'Let us resolve' and 'Let us remember' which demonstrated *anaphora*, or the repetition of successive phrases to achieve an effect.

One contemporary argued that Macmillan 'spread the speech, unambiguous as it was, with so much butter that he fairly hypnotised the joint assembly that it implied support for them' (Myers, 2000: 568). Yet he reinforced his claim for ethos through consistency, when he cited a speech delivered by the British Foreign Secretary, Selwyn Lloyd, at the United Nations in 1959, which explicitly rejected the ideas of racial superiority. Yet while Macmillan's rhetoric was cleverly devised, and his grand diplomatic manner added an oratorical flourish, it could only minimise rather than conceal Britain's retreat from greatness. Its lack of a direct impact is revealed by the Sharpeville massacres which followed in South Africa and the formation of the right-wing Monday Club in the Conservative Party, to oppose the very policy he had proposed. Concerned that his speech was being interpreted too radically he subsequently stressed that he was not proposing 'a howling gale' (Sampson, 1967: 190).

The contradictions in Macmillan's speeches in accepting the Suez defeat while proclaiming Britain's greatness, and endorsing decolonisation while appearing to regret it, are clear. A similar contradiction was evident in the 'never had it so good' speech delivered in 1957. Many commentators assert that the speech was a serious warning about the threat of inflation yet while Macmillan wanted it on record that he recognised the inflationary dangers ensuing from an expansionist economic policy, he also wanted to convey a partisan propagandist message. His purpose was clear, and in stating that most British people had 'never had it so good' he added: 'Go around the country, go to the great industrial towns, go to the farms, and you will see a state of prosperity such as we have never had in my lifetime – nor indeed even in the history of the country.' It is striking that the warning about inflation was couched in terms of risking 'the old nightmare of unemployment' (Heffer, 2007: 202). To remove any ambiguity about his intention, a few days later in the Commons, he lauded full employment and a high standard of living and explicitly stressed 'what I said in Bedford, they have never had it so good' (House of Commons debs. Vol. 574, Col. 718). Later, he boasted that 'the luxuries of the rich have become the necessities of the poor' (Sampson, 1967: 159).

During Macmillan's political life television became the chief medium for public communication which fundamentally affected oratory and rhetoric. He never watched television as there was no television at his home, 'except in Nanny's house at the Lodge gates' (Catterall, 2003: 378). He understood that emotional appeals were not appropriate on this medium (Jamieson, 1988: 46). Instead he came across as 'urbane, witty, eloquent, moving' (Blake, 1980: 2). By 1959 he acted the authoritative statesman and the *Daily Mirror* described his final party political broadcast as 'a real corker' (Lord Egremont, 1968: 187). His advisors asked Norman Collins, an experienced television executive, to assist. Collins noted that at public meetings Macmillan stood 'bolt upright' with 'squared shoulders', a characteristic which Collins exploited by persuading him to broadcast standing up behind a reading desk, except when he strolled over to a globe and manoeuvred it as a visual aid to enhance his appeal as a world statesman. It was as if he had the world in his hands. To overcome nerves Collins filmed the rehearsal and only informed him afterwards that it was to be the actual telecast, with the result that Macmillan appeared very relaxed.

By the early 1960s the illusion that a British prime minister had the world in his hands was exploded and he was the first leader in modern history to have his public oratory mocked when the act of a faded Edwardian ceased to be 'an agreeable joke'

(Turner, 1994: 272). Macmillan can be credited with inventing *Private Eye*. Peter Cook's satirical act in the revue *Beyond the Fringe* in which he purported to deliver a Macmillan speech, demolished all the logos and pathos, and even undermined the ethos which Macmillan had acquired. In the speech, Cook described 'travelling round the world at your expense visiting some of the chaps with whom I hope to be shaping your future' (Aldous, 1996: 9) and continued, 'I then went to America, and I had talks with the young, vigorous President', and here Cook sounded old and weary, 'and danced with his very lovely lady wife. We talked of many things including Great Britain's position in the world as some kind of honest broker. I agreed with him, when he said that no nation could be more honest; and he agreed with me when I chafed him and said that no nation could be broker' (Becket, 2006: 98). Cook satirised the small circle which governed Britain when on Macmillan's claim to be Kennedy's trusted advisor, he added, 'at one time we even exchanged photographs of our respective families, and I was very touched, very touched indeed, to discover that here was another great world leader who regarded the business of government as being a family affair' (Aldous, 1996: 9). While attempts in the 1950s to mock him as 'Supermac' (Vicky the cartoonist) and 'Macwonder' (Harold Wilson) enhanced him, by 1961 the magic was tarnished. Macmillan had lost his ethos and so his logos and pathos were largely undermined.

Macmillan's oratory: evaluation and conclusion

An overall judgement about Macmillan's oratory is impossible. Political oratory is affected by the specific historical moment it occurs (Evans, 1981: 44) and politicians can also deliberately improve their communication skills over time. The quality of Macmillan's oratory changed during the course of his career which stretched from 1924 to 1986. In the inter-war years a journalist commented that 'he is an enthusiast who does not enthuse. There is no declamation in his speeches, no skilful manipulation of voice, and no display of structured gesture' (Horne, 1989: 780). His oratory improved, but despite achieving its apogee in his early years as prime minister it was beginning to pall by 1961, and his ethos and pathos no longer resonated in a changing social, political and economic context. Gaitskell could then condemn the Edwardian pose and the languid condescension of 'a fine actor ... a splendid showman, but when the showman is shown up, the play is over, illusion is shattered ... it is time for the players to depart' (Williams, 1979: 695). Macmillan had other critics. In the 1940s, a Churchill lieutenant, Brendan Bracken, described him as a 'pompous posturer' (Lee, 1996: 153) and Lord Boyd-Orr described a Macmillan broadcast as 'just blah-blah' (Hughes, 1962: 157). Henry Fairlie regarded him as an 'aged cynic', claiming he could

> calculate the hopes, fears, moods and attitudes of ordinary people with almost precise skill and by satisfying them he holds their support. He vulgarises his own opinions ... so that they will accord with them, and it is the essential vulgarity of his political

leadership which contrasts so notably with the privately civilised, educated and reflect-
ive being which he clearly was … The vulgarity is sometimes not even veneered.
(Hughes, 1962: 2120)

By contrast, Olmstead acquits Macmillan of demagoguery and fraudulent practice
while acknowledging that he stirred passions (Olmstead, 2006: 3). Her view that
oratory should connect with the times suggests that it was Fairlie who was out of
touch with electoral requirements, including Macmillan's instinct that affluence was
popular. Olmstead even regarded the contradictions or even duplicity in Macmillan's
rhetoric as serving a 'healing' function (Olmstead, 2006: 2).

Macmillan skilfully exploited ethos, pathos and logos. If his pathos was often con-
trived, his ethos was also linked to a consciously cultivated political personality. He
understood the importance of effective perorations, as the mood in which the audience is left is the most important characteristic of oratory. The main source for his
ethos was his political longevity, but his memories, whether of military greatness or
of inter-war unemployment, clouded his judgement in dealing with post-war problems (Dorey *et al.*, 2011: 128). His main achievement was to revive a depressed party
and nation in 1957 and then to retain power to enable him to manage change, most
spectacularly concealing from his party Britain's reduced world role. Macmillan's
oratory took his party in directions which it often resisted, particularly in his parliamentary performances. His policies did not signify an absence of ideological boundaries. Ideological change occurs when fundamental political principles collide with
political realities (Seliger, 1976). Parties can change without losing their identities
and they need to refresh and renew (Seawright, 2011: 40) and party and ideological
boundaries are always fluid (Freeden, 1996: chapter 2).

Macmillan was a chameleon who was learned and statesmanlike but also populist. He enjoyed expressing grand historical visions but was also adept in addressing short-term needs. He particularly relied on ethos. Even after the magic had
palled and his style was out of kilter with the times, his appeal was such that had
he not resigned in 1963, he would have proved a greater electoral asset than his
successor.

4

The oratory of Iain Macleod

Mark Garnett

Iain Macleod has been a hero to many Conservatives, particularly but not exclusively to those who identify with the party's 'One Nation' tradition. This is a fitting legacy for the man who co-founded (and named) the One Nation group of MPs. In part, he owes his continuing appeal to the fact that he died, at the age of just fifty-six, soon after reaching the pinnacle of his career by taking office as Chancellor of the Exchequer. The sense of promise unfulfilled is reinforced by the fact that, unlike so many moderate Conservatives of his generation, Macleod's reputation is unclouded by association with the misfortunes of the Heath government. Better than almost any British post-war politician, he seems to epitomise the qualifying clause of Enoch Powell's dictum that 'all political careers, unless they are cut off in midstream at a happy juncture, end in failure' (Powell, 1977: 151).

However, Macleod would not continue to attract admirers if his only claim on posterity was a premature death in Downing Street. His personal qualities inspired devotion from his closest friends, like the Conservative MP Nigel Fisher who wrote his first biography, and Ian Gilmour who made him editor of the *Spectator* magazine after his refusal to join Alec Douglas-Home's government in 1963. Above all, Macleod was physically and morally courageous. For most of his adult life he suffered lameness as a result of serious wounds received in France in 1940, and pain from a crippling spinal condition. This explained why Macleod, who was usually very entertaining in private, could be prickly and even taciturn on occasion. Far from trying to win sympathy by drawing attention to his physical disabilities, 'there was nothing he disliked more than to have a fuss made of him' (Watkins, 1982: 101).

Like most people whose friendship is worth having, Macleod was not afraid of making enemies. Few politicians of the 'consensus' era were so willing to exacerbate the partisan battle by berating opponents for their practical shortcomings, or by magnifying minor differences of principle. In such cases, Macleod was usually able to establish quite amicable relations with his victims. He was less fortunate in healing breaches on his own side of the House. While his rhetorical jousts with Labour politicians disguised a broad commonality of aim, his disagreements with Conservatives tended to be heartfelt; and opponents on his own side were less likely to be mollified because he met their objections with reasoned argument rather than the clever sound-bites he saved for encounters with Labour or Liberal MPs. Yet while Macleod's prospects of becoming Conservative leader were undoubtedly damaged by his beliefs – most notably, by his opposition to the Imperialist element within Conservative ranks – the attacks he encountered seemed to have had no impact on his views or his temper.

Macleod was a notable and generally successful minister under Churchill, Eden and Macmillan, before his brief period at the Treasury under Heath. His two-year stint as Colonial Secretary (1959–61) established his heroic status in the eyes of liberal Conservatives, and made him odious to the party's Imperial wing. However, his reputation has long outlasted the furious controversies of those years. Although Roy Jenkins was ungenerous in his claim that 'throughout nearly his whole career he scored more triumphs with words than with deeds', it is true that Macleod's glamorous posthumous image derives mainly from his oratory, rather than his considerable ministerial achievements. Indeed, even Jenkins was forced to admit in 1993 that many observers would give Macleod 'third place in the pantheon of British speakers of the past fifty years, after only Churchill and Bevan' (Jenkins, 1993: 36). His career spanned the brief period in which political reputations could be made or broken by performances in three very different settings, of roughly equal importance – the traditional parliamentary debate, the party conference, and the televised address. It was Macleod's ability to meet the challenges of this fleeting conjunction of circumstances which inspired Harold Macmillan to hail him as the *last* Tory orator (cited in Fisher, 1973: 25). Nowadays parliamentary speeches (as opposed to sound-bites at prime minister's question time) are barely noticed; and Macleod was one of the last politicians to rise almost from nowhere because of a brilliant display from the backbenches. He was the undoubted star of a succession of party conferences; and, while older orators like Churchill struggled to master the new medium of television, Macleod was judged a major asset for his party in election broadcasts. In the following assessment of Macleod's oratorical prowess, his performance is appraised in relation to Aristotle's categories of ethos, pathos and logos.

The attack on Bevan

After attending public school (Fettes) and graduating from Cambridge University with a modest second-class degree, Macleod supported himself largely through gambling. A world-class bridge player who wrote a book on the game, he could make the best of any hand he was dealt and was a penetrating analyst of his fellow competitors. On the evening of 27 March 1952 – less than two years after Macleod had won the Enfield, West constituency for the Conservatives, he rose to speak in a debate on the NHS, in circumstances which offered him the chance of landing a political jackpot.

On this subject Labour's Aneurin Bevan was sure to attract a considerable audience, adding his authority as founder-minister of the NHS to his well-deserved reputation as an orator. The prime minister, Winston Churchill, turned up in the chamber to hear Bevan speak. However, on this occasion Bevan was below his best form, and when he had finished Churchill prepared to leave the Commons. The order of speeches had been altered to accommodate a member's maiden effort; so instead of speaking *before* Bevan, Macleod was required to *answer* him. On hearing Macleod's first words, Churchill decided to stay and listen, asking the Chief Whip for the name of this MP and to judge his potential for ministerial office. The verdict on Macleod was obviously satisfactory. Less than six weeks later, he was appointed Minister of Health – not, at that time, a Cabinet position, but nevertheless a considerable first step on the ladder of preferment.

Even the bare report of Macleod's speech in *Hansard* explains why Churchill decided to linger in the Commons' chamber. During the Second World War Bevan had been one of the few orators with the ability and courage to confront Churchill, and the prime minister had referred to him as 'a squalid nuisance'. Macleod's opening remarks were just as rude, but not unjustified since in his own speech Bevan had accused the government of wanting to dismantle the welfare state and of taking the first step towards ending parliamentary democracy in Britain. Apart from promising to match Bevan's fire with a fusillade of his own, Macleod's introductory remarks suggested that he would develop a more constructive critique: 'I want to deal closely and with relish with the vulgar, crude and intemperate speech to which the House of Commons has just listened' (*Hansard*, Vol. 498, col. 886).

True to his promise, Macleod did produce a detailed analysis of Bevan's speech, sprinkled with dates, quotations, facts and figures, as well as more mischievous lines such as an accusation that Bevan had gone 'behind the back of his Cabinet and his leader to defraud the House of Commons' (*Hansard*, Vol. 498, col. 890). Unsurprisingly Bevan was goaded into an intervention, but Macleod was ready to use his pugilistic reputation against him. Refusing to withdraw his comments, Macleod remarked that 'The right hon. Gentleman has been a long time in this House and I do not think that he objects to this form of debating at all' (*Hansard*, Vol. 498, col. 891). If this was stretching the elastic of parliamentary decency, the gambler presumably calculated that he had already won the stakes. Apart from his arresting opening phrase, he had included in his speech one of the best of all parliamentary quips, when he congratulated Bevan on his recent recovery from illness. He was glad that Bevan could be present, he said, because 'a debate on the National Health Service without the right Hon. Gentleman would be like putting on Hamlet with no one in the part of the First Gravedigger' (*Hansard*, Vol. 498, col. 889). Originally Macleod had intended to say 'without the ghost', which would have been funny enough. The final form of words understandably 'brought a roar of appreciative laughter from the Conservative benches' (Fisher, 1973: 82). Sir Gerald Nabarro, who like Macleod belonged to the celebrated Conservative intake of 1950, later recalled that Bevan had been 'clobbered and reduced to frothy fulminations' (Nabarro, 1969: 3).

The speech is a remarkable example of ethos, pathos and logos at work. The central idea of ethos – that the speaker is someone worth listening to – was fulfilled by the opening passage which persuaded Churchill to stay and listen, even though he needed to be reminded of Macleod's name. While pathos suggests an appeal to the audience's softer sensibilities, the brutal 'Gravedigger' remark was sure to win the sympathy of Bevan's enemies (on both sides of the House), and even its victim would have been forced to admit that it was a brilliant debating stroke. However, the speech might still have been a failure had Macleod not demonstrated his mastery of logos – his ability to marshal relevant facts, thus adding ballast to the regular intrusions of invective.

Cementing a reputation: Macleod's oratory at party conferences

Apart from propelling him into high office, the Gravedigger speech guaranteed Macleod's ethos for the rest of his career – he was a speaker who could empty the bars and tea-rooms rather than filling up these places with Members who suddenly felt a need for refreshment. Yet brilliant parliamentary repartee, even when backed by solid evidence as well as a ready wit, cannot be the sole measure of oratorical eminence. The greatest orators also excelled at set-piece speeches, even in settings where they could not play off hostile hecklers. Addresses to party conferences are good tests of an orator's versatility. This is particularly true of Conservative conferences in the 1950s and 1960s, when the mood of the audience was generally deferential but had the potential to turn ugly on occasion.

In an interview with Macleod's most authoritative biographer, Robert Shepherd, Michael Foot expressed the view that Macleod was eminent as a debater rather than an orator, contrasting him in this respect with Churchill (Shepherd, 1994: 266–7). Yet Macleod's conference orations were invariably successful, and two contrasting examples explain his mastery of that forum. At Blackpool in 1958 he was speaking from a position of strength, having been praised for his handling of the London bus drivers' strike which had weakened the position of the militant union leader, Frank Cousins. In May, Labour had tabled a motion of censure against Macleod personally, and government policy in general, on this issue. Macleod had replied to the debate in cold fury, expressing his 'scorn and contempt' for the Opposition leader Hugh Gaitskell for introducing a motion which could only make it more difficult to settle the dispute on satisfactory terms. Clearly nettled, Gaitskell accused Macleod of being 'far, far below his best form' – a notable (if backhanded) compliment, since Conservative backbenchers were in raptures after Macleod's speech and even the *Manchester Guardian* acknowledged that it had 'not been matched in power for some years' (*Hansard*, Vol. 587, col. 1452, 8 May 1958; Shepherd, 1994: 139).

After the strike was settled, a lesser politician – or even an able one who did not share Macleod's vision of Britain as 'One Nation' – might have succumbed to the temptation to gloat at the expense of Gaitskell and Cousins. Macleod could not entirely disappoint his audience on this score, and he did make some slighting comments about the failure of Cousins to enlist the trade union movement as a whole in his cause. However, he utilised the strength of his own position to develop a more constructive argument, outlining what he considered to be 'the Tory approach to industrial relations'. These principles amounted to a voluntarist brand of 'corporatism', in which the government, the unions and the employers would engage in 'a partnership independent of politics'. However, in Macleod's version of corporatism the government would not seek agreement at the expense of its authority; rather, 'the final decision of government can only be taken by government itself'. In true 'One Nation' style, he claimed that the Conservatives were not beholden to any sectional interest, and were anxious only to promote 'the partnership on which in the end all sound human and industrial relations must rest' (Macleod, 1958: 58).

In short, Macleod delivered a speech which was calculated to appease any Tories who inclined towards triumphalism, while sneaking a more conciliatory course under their radar. At the Brighton conference of October 1961, Macleod faced a very different challenge. He was about to step down as Secretary of State for the Colonies, to take up the job of Conservative Party Chairman – indeed, at the conference he spoke in both capacities – along with the leadership of the House of Commons. As Colonial Secretary he had faced persistent criticism for his belief that Britain should promote the rights of the majority before granting independence to nations under colonial rule. In March 1961 the Marquess of Salisbury had encapsulated opposition to Macleod's policy in a pungent sound-bite, claiming that the Colonial Secretary was 'too clever by half'. It was an inappropriate accusation, in that Macleod had not pursued his policy by stealth; but when levelled against a brilliant bridge player it proved too effective by half.

In his 1960 conference speech, Macleod had tried to distract those who regard him as a traitor to kith and kin by reminding them of their duty to hate their partisan opponents more than people who sported Conservative colours. When someone as skilful as Macleod resorted to this unimaginative tactic it formed itself into a sentence which party activists remembered long after they forgot their self-defeating animosity towards Macleod himself: 'The Socialists can scheme their schemes and the Liberals can dream their dreams, but we, at least, have work to do' (quoted in Fisher, 1973: 165). Macleod habitually made a point of referring to the Labour Party as 'the socialists', and one suspects that this was his cunning method of putting the Labour Party as an institution at a distance from himself, even on those occasions when he felt closer to that party's policy than to the views of the Conservative rank-and-file.

Macleod chose to make his speech at the 1961 party conference into an open declaration of faith, which resolved itself into his faithful conference format of a list of principles. This time, however, Macleod was using his list to rout his internal critics, rather than to restrain the vengeful thoughts of those Conservatives who had supported his stance during the London transport dispute. He started with a point which would have irritated Salisbury and his supporters, arguing that it was not enough to buy off Britain's colonial subjects with material benefits; rather than slaking the appetite for political rights, such policies were sure to increase the clamour for democracy. Macleod's second principle was caged very differently. It began with a reference to Britain's continuing Imperial mission, and although this was qualified to mean a commitment to partnership with the countries of the Commonwealth – so that Britain's Imperial role ended up sounding very like the Conservative commitment to talk with trade unionists as well as employers – Macleod had managed to insinuate an acceptance of a continuing global destiny for Britain.

This might have seemed like appeasement to Macleod's admirers, but it was only designed to soften up the Imperialists for his last, and most provocative, principle. He prefaced his final remarks with a gesture of verbal surrender to the irreconcilable forces within his party: 'This is the last thing I shall say as Colonial Secretary.' But then came the punch to the Imperialist solar plexus, without further preamble: 'The third principle is that I believe quite simply in the brotherhood of man – men of all races, of all colours, of all creeds.' Reinforcing this message with the predictable quotation from Burns, Macleod followed up with a parting head-shot to Salisbury and his ilk, describing those who denied the commonality of all human beings as 'foolish men' who would be 'swept away' (Macleod, 1961: 25). There can have been few more sincere or inspiring attacks on racism from a British political platform – and, ironically, it was delivered at a Conservative conference by a long-standing friend of Enoch Powell. What is more, Macleod got away with it; although one Empire Loyalist shouted an accusation of betrayal, his speech earned a standing ovation. Robert Shepherd does not exaggerate when he describes the speech as 'one of the great political performances of modern times' (Shepherd, 1994: 253). Macleod's party had not been converted, however; after listening to the ensuing debate on immigration, Lady Antonia Fraser noted that 'It seemed so odd to be discussing a resolution to keep West Indians out an hour after Iain's moving speech for the brotherhood of man' (Fisher, 1973: 202–3).

Television performances

There is less plentiful evidence of Macleod's calibre as a television performer, but in a relatively brief period of exposure to that medium he showed that he would have been just as successful if he had lived longer into the era of televised politics. In 1966 Heath asked him to oversee the political strategy of Conservative election broadcasts. Although the party was soundly beaten in the 1966 election, Macleod showed a shrewd understanding of the task at hand. According to the relevant Nuffield Study, he regarded the invigoration of existing supporters, rather than the conversion of opponents, as the main purpose of such broadcasts, though he also tried to ensure that they were 'framed for undecided and intelligent floating voters'. As the party's key television strategist, he confined himself to an 'anchor man' role in the broadcasts themselves, so his prowess remained hidden from the general public (Butler and King, 1966: 137–8).

Macleod figured more prominently on the nation's screens in the 1970 campaign, with distinctly favourable results. Understandably he was showcased in the party's broadcast on the economy, the third in its series of five. Private polling showed such a favourable response that Central Office implored Macleod to front the following programme, which was intended to appeal to women voters (Butler and Pinto-Duschinsky, 1971: 197–8, 222). There is something particularly poignant in the fact that Macleod should perform with such skill in front of his biggest-ever audiences when he had only a few weeks to live. Although it is difficult to quantify the impact of these performances, the state of the economy contributed more to Labour's unexpected downfall in 1970 than any other political issue.

After 1966 Macleod also delivered televised addresses as Shadow Chancellor, in reply to Labour's budgets. Roy Jenkins, who served as Chancellor after the devaluation crisis of 1967, was unimpressed by Macleod's performance in the Commons on economic matters (Jenkins, 1993: 36). Even so, Macleod has got the better of Jenkins by adding to the vocabulary of political economy; even before taking the post of Shadow Chancellor he had coined the word 'stagflation' to describe the alarming new combination on high inflation and low growth (*Hansard*, Vol. 720, col. 1165, 17 November 1965). Although he was keenly interested in tax reform, he clearly regarded economics as subservient to politics. This probably explains why his broadcasts on the subject were successful. According to Nigel Fisher, as Shadow Chancellor he would prepare the text meticulously, but never needed to rehearse his speeches. If these qualities were not enough to endear him to camera crews, he also kept his temper when technical hitches arose. John Grist, the head of Current Affairs for the BBC at this time, told Fisher that Macleod was 'probably the first man in the Conservative hierarchy to appreciate and understand television'; after all, 'He was a communicator and he was interested in all forms of communication as a part of political life' (Fisher, 1973: 287–8). Macleod was also a reliable motivator of the grassroots members in constituency speaking engagements, although his spell as party chairman (1961–63) was blighted by the unpopularity he had generated as Colonial Secretary. Thus, wherever Macleod should be placed in the ranking of post-war orators of any party, none of his rivals for the crown surpassed his versatility.

Reasons for success

Iain Macleod, then, was a speaker of unusual gifts. It was no accident that, in the exhaustive list of entries under 'Macleod, Iain' in Nigel Fisher's 1973 biography, the first was 'his powers of oratory' (Fisher, 1973: 345). Reviewing Fisher's book, Macleod's former ministerial colleague William Deedes wrote that 'He was incomparably the best orator in his party' (Deedes, 1973). We have seen that he ticked all of Aristotle's rhetorical boxes. His ethos ensured that MPs left their leisure activities in order to hear him; like all masters of logos he was adept at developing an argument, though the overall structure could be somewhat mechanical; and although he won his greatest renown through his acidic wit, he could also make an instinctively hostile audience pause and consider whether politics should be about conciliation, rather than reinforcing and exploiting arbitrary divisions such as skin colour. John Major, who often cited Macleod as a source of political inspiration, recalled that 'whatever he said seemed to be said with total conviction, both moral and intellectual' (Major 1999: 204; Shepherd, 1994: 425). In other words, Macleod's use of logos and pathos gave him an ethos which ensured that his influence would last long after his death.

Why was Macleod such an effective orator? According to the late Alan Watkins, Macleod asked himself the same question, semi-rhetorically. '"I suppose it's mainly the voice. Some people can do it; others can't. I can. Just like Nye"', he added in a tribute to the protagonist who had provided the text and pretext for his most celebrated performance (Watkins, 1982: 103). This self-assessment, while superficially conceited, was actually unduly modest. Macleod's voice, though slightly high in pitch, was unusually resonant, regularly compared to a bell. This unearned advantage cannot have harmed Macleod's oratory, and helped to establish his ethos: people wanted to hear him in part because it was pleasant to listen. However, a resonant voice which spouts nonsense is unlikely to retain a parliamentary audience for very long. Indeed, the reaction to Disraeli's maiden speech shows that a brilliant speaker who strives for effect rather than conveying a message of substance can earn the derision of the Commons, which takes many years to efface. Despite the luck which attended the Gravedigger speech, Macleod could never have established his ethos without considerable assistance from logos – in that case, a knowledge of the Health Service which surpassed almost all of his contemporaries, Labour or Conservative. In turn, Macleod's oratory was underpinned by a superlative memory. According to the journalist Anthony Sampson, he could 'recite lists of thirty-year old Olympic results and Derby winners without strain' (Sampson, 1962: 83). Equally, in debate he could reel off the most relevant statistics without having to refer to notes.

To a lesser, but still significant, extent Macleod's fame as an orator relied on his ability to use pathos. Few frontbench performers could rival his wit; arguably his only rival in the Commons of his day was Harold Wilson, who reportedly feared Macleod more than any of his Conservative contemporaries. The fear was well-founded. Wilson was the target of one of Macleod's best Wildean *bon mots*, when he said that if J. F. Kennedy was an idealist without illusions, the Labour leader was an illusionist without ideals (*Hansard*, Vol. 725, col. 1225, 1 March 1966). Back in 1961, when Wilson was Shadow Chancellor, Macleod had made merry at his expense, congratulating Wilson for a speech which 'was, as always, witty, cogent, and polished – and polished – and polished' (*Hansard*, Vol. 648, col. 927, 7 November 1961). If anything, a joke which exploited Macleod's exquisite sense of timing was improved by the fact that it, no less than Wilson's speech on that occasion, must have been carefully prepared.

In terms of pathos, Macleod's attack on Wilson's 'polished' speech was the more remarkable because it was followed just a few seconds later by a passage which illustrated his profound commitment to racial equality. It was his first major speech as Leader of the House of Commons, and in his new capacity Macleod could not avoid comment on what became the 1962 Commonwealth Immigrants Act – the first legislative attempt to limit the right to migrate to Britain from the former Empire. Having so recently spoken of 'the Brotherhood of Man', Macleod had to defend himself against the imputation of hypocrisy. He did so with breathtaking candour, telling the Commons that he found the case for restrictions compelling while making clear his detestation of the necessity for action (*Hansard*, Vol. 648, col. 926, 7 November 1961). Later in the decade, Macleod risked provoking his old critics by voting against Labour's panic-stricken measures to limit migration from Kenya; and although he did not join other liberal Conservatives in supporting the government's subsequent Race Relations Bill, he made his views clear in a letter to *The Times*, referring to the 'ignorance and prejudice' which made it unlikely that legislation could succeed in changing attitudes (Fisher, 1973: 296–7).

Those few minutes in the Commons testify to a very unusual emotional range among politicians – Macleod could leap from humour to profundity while barely pausing for breath, with equal effect in both of those modes. If the extent of Macleod's physical disabilities had been more widely known, he could have played upon these to enhance the pathos of his performances – after all, the ability to make an audience laugh when one is in considerable pain is only granted to the very greatest speakers. In this respect, Macleod was helped by the relative reticence of press coverage during the course of his career; the severity of his condition was unknown to the public, but press insiders became aware of it through first-hand observation and their knowledge was bound to colour their commentary on his efforts. In fact, it is possible that Macleod's disabilities were of material assistance, adding an unusual physical ingredient to his oratory. After his death, the journalist David Watt recalled how Macleod would provoke his Labour opponents into ill-advised interjections, 'and slowly the whole of his body would swing round like some great gun being brought to bear' (quoted in Fisher, 1973: 321). In television broadcasts, Macleod's eyes remained fixed on the viewer because he was unable to move his head without considerable discomfort; this could easily add to the impression of sincerity, which was particularly important in the 1970 campaign when as Shadow Chancellor he was trying to convince the public that the economic outlook was not as comfortable as it seemed.

One could also speculate that Macleod's ability to hold an audience owed something to his gambling career. In card play, particularly, the ability to read an opponent and to anticipate future moves in the game are crucial. On this view, Macleod was ahead of his political competitors because, unlike them, he had learned the basics of human nature in two of the hardest schools – gambling, as well as war. But while the seasoned orator probably relied to some extent on this knowledge, we have seen that Macleod's temporary reliance on gambling for a livelihood could be held against him by rivals and opponents, even if the Marquess of Salisbury was the only one openly to target this Achilles heel.

In the case of an Oxbridge alumnus like Macleod, oratorical excellence is often attributed to the parliamentary dress rehearsals held in the Union Societies of Oxford and Cambridge. However, Macleod spoke only once in the Cambridge Union, and he was certainly not regarded as a potential political star at that time. He had featured more frequently in debates held at his public school, Fettes, and the report of his maiden effort (on the motion that 'No one should give up his seat to a lady') recorded that he had made 'a very good speech which had the merit of being short and to the point' (quoted in Fisher, 1973: 34). Almost by instinct, it seems, Macleod had known that the worst thing for an aspiring orator was to be regarded as a windbag; and the discovery was the more impressive since, far from thinking that he was serving an adolescent apprenticeship for a political career, he was not sure where his partisan loyalties lay at the time, let alone that he would one day adorn the parliamentary stage.

Whatever purpose he felt that he was serving in those schoolboy debates, Macleod was proving to his own satisfaction that he was an effective orator. Lacking any obvious careerist motive, he thus had no reason to take an active part in debates at Cambridge, or to throw himself into the rituals which led to high office within the Union Society. Instead, while going through the motions of reading for a History degree, Macleod indulged his real passions – an enjoyment of the company of other human beings, and a love for language. As Powell wrote after Macleod's death – and his words are no less sincere because he was probably thinking of himself as the time – 'no one can be a parliamentary and platform orator of Macleod's quality unless he vibrates to English words as a chord to music' (Powell, 1973). Even as a schoolboy at Fettes, Macleod had written poetry which could not be judged as distinguished even by a star-struck observer, but nevertheless showed that the author was desperate to find a more congenial format for self-expression. Card play satisfied Macleod's inherent desire to match his wits against others in a context which was collegiate as well as competitive. By the end of the war he had reason to feel that he could make a constructive contribution in a broader field, not least because the conflict introduced him to his future wife, Eve, for whose sake he was prepared to relinquish some (though by no means all) elements of his wayward bachelor life.

Overall, Macleod's career lends support to the view that the greatest orators are born, not made. Seeking to explain the romantic streak which underpinned his oratory, Harold Macmillan and even the seasoned journalist James Margach could only attribute it to the cultural heritage of the Highlands, disregarding the fact that Macleod was born in the Yorkshire market town of Skipton (Margach, 1970: 41). Even if one accepts this fanciful claim, it would not explain the strong element of rational calculation in Macleod's political armoury. Clearly this arose from contextual influences, few of which had anything to do with the Highlands. Despite his privileged upbringing – which had been secured by the intelligence of his father, rather than riches inherited from earlier generations – Macleod was not helped by contacts made at school or university. He left Cambridge as a graduate who depended almost entirely on his native resources, and when he joined the Conservative Research Department in 1945 he had added to his curriculum vitae a war record which, compared to his fellow Cambridge graduate Enoch Powell, was not particularly distinguished. Yet he had the uncanny ability to absorb the most useful lessons from his varied experiences, and to profit from these when suitable opportunities arose.

Macleod's eminence as an orator, debator and television performer could not carry him to the leadership of his party. Indeed, since his oratory made enemies in Conservative ranks he might have been more successful if he had been a *less* gifted communicator. If he had regarded the premiership as the only prize worth fighting for, Macleod's celebrated judgement failed him in 1963, when he refused to serve under Douglas-Home. This protest, reinforced by his celebrated attack on the 'magic circle' of influential Conservatives, had not been forgiven in 1965, preventing him from emerging as the perfect candidate for a party which was seeking someone who could spike Wilson's guns. At the time of the 'polished' jibe, Wilson had predicted that the Conservatives would 'never have the sense' to choose Macleod as Macmillan's successor; and the party was, if anything, even less sensible in 1965 (Shepherd, 1994: 267).

A remarkable blend of acumen and eloquence, Macleod was an irreplaceable asset to his party, and the significance of his sudden demise was only truly appreciated in distant hindsight. For example, in an interview conducted for a book published in 1994, Robert Carr said that 'We lost our trumpeter, which in Ted [Heath's] Government was our greatest need' (quoted in Shepherd, 1994: 538).

It could be argued that Heath's government was so consistently unlucky that not even the combined trumpeting force of Joshua and his priests could have kept it afloat through its various travails. Nevertheless, it is tempting to speculate about the likely course of events if Macleod's health had held up throughout the 1970–74 period. After all, the general election of February 1974 was inconclusive; and although the crucial factor which toppled the Heath government was the 'exogenous shock' of the 1973 oil crisis, avoidable policy errors were made along with the disastrous mistiming of the election itself. As Chancellor, as a former Party Chairman, and as someone who was respected by the prime minister, Macleod would have been well placed to prevent at least some of this self-inflicted damage. And if his interventions had proved insufficient to save the government, a healthy Macleod could have stepped out of the wreckage as the person most likely to lead the Conservatives back to office; he would certainly have been a more effective 'stop Thatcher' leadership candidate that Willie Whitelaw proved to be. The inescapable fact, however, is that Macleod was not really 'cut off in midstream at some happy juncture', in conformity with the remark of his old friend Powell. He had been seriously unwell for many years before his death, and his admirers should be glad that he was able to defy disability to achieve so much, rather than wondering what he might have achieved if he had not been forced to suffer for so long.

5

The oratory of Enoch Powell

Philip Norton

For two decades, Enoch Powell was one of the most controversial politicians in Britain. He was one of the few public figures to be known by his first name and the only one in modern British politics to have large protest marches take place in his support. His fame derived not so much from what posts he held, but from what he said. His public reputation derived from a particular speech he delivered in 1968 at the Midland Hotel, Birmingham. His parliamentary reputation derived from a capacity to express himself in such a way as to set him aside from fellow parliamentarians.

His years as a politician, though, were in contrast to his two careers prior to entering the House of Commons (Norton, 2012: 133–6). His first was as an academic. Born in modest circumstances in Stechford, Birmingham, in 1912 – his parents were schoolteachers – he was a highly intelligent child. His mother gave up working to learn Greek and teach it to her son. He won all the academic prizes available to him as he went through school and university. He began an academic career as a Fellow of his old college, Trinity College, Cambridge, before being appointed as Professor of Greek at the University of Sydney, making him – at twenty-five – the young professor in the British Empire.

His first publication was a translation and commentary of some of the Rendell Harris papyri, an exercise notable for its precision. As Margaret Mountford has noted, 'Emphasis on the precise written word is the distinguishing characteristic of most of the rest of Powell's scholarship' (Mountford, 2012: 239). He specialised in the works of the Greek historians Herodotus and Thucydides and had begun work on his *Lexicon to Herodotus* before he had even graduated. The book was published in 1938 and his *History of Herodotus* in 1939. His inaugural lecture, 'Greek in the University', delivered on 7 May 1938, was dedicated to showing not why Greek should be learned, but why it should be taught. Reproduced in Rex Collins' collection of Powell's speeches, *Reflections of a Statesman* (Collins, 1991: 87–96), the lecture was delivered in a style that would be recognisable to those who were to listen to him in his later career as a politician.

He was offered a chair at the University of Durham, but war intervened. This brought him to his second career, that of a soldier. He enlisted in the Royal Warwickshire Regiment as soon as war broke out. Throughout the war, he sought a combat role, but was always denied it – his understanding of logic and his linguistic skills made him a prime resource for military intelligence and planning. In North Africa, he played a crucial role in anticipating Field Marshall Rommel's moves. His work resulted in the award of a military MBE 'for gallant and distinguished services in the Middle East'. He was remarkable, though not unique, in rising through the ranks from Private to Brigadier. His rapid rise also meant that, at thirty-two, he became one of the youngest Brigadiers, though not quite the youngest, in the British army.

It was in these two careers that he shone in terms of what he did. His curriculum vitae for his early life set him apart.

After wartime service, he pursued a political career. After deciding that he was a Tory, he began working in the Conservative Research Department – alongside figures such as Iain Macleod and Reginald Maudling, both destined to be senior Cabinet ministers – before being elected as Conservative MP for Wolverhampton South-West in 1950. He transformed a marginal seat into a safe one, before controversially declining to seek re-election in 1974, ending his political career as Ulster Unionist MP for South Down, serving from 1974 until being defeated in the general election of 1987.

On the face of it, his political career was less distinguished than his academic and military careers. As a politician, he set no records. His rise through the political ranks was not rapid and he never scaled the heights achieved by his Research Department colleagues, Macleod and Maudling. The highest ministerial post that he held was that of Minister of Health. He served in that post for three years, but only one of those was in the Cabinet. He held no ministerial office after the age of fifty-one.

The reasons for the failure to scale the ministerial heights are twofold. One was his willingness to refuse office (which he did on three occasions) or to resign it (which he did once, in 1958, when he resigned as Financial Secretary to the Treasury, along with the Chancellor, Peter Thorneycroft, and Economic Secretary, Nigel Birch, over the government's refusal to rein in public spending). The other, and most significant, reason is to be found in what he said. He held and expressed views which set him apart and pursued his views with a single-mindedness that other politicians were generally unable to emulate. It was his single-mindedness that resulted in him declining or resigning office. It was also his willingness to express his views, in stark and uncompromising form, that led not to him declining or refusing office, but to being dismissed from it.

Powell's reputation derived, then, from what he said. To the public, the reputation was gained as a result of a particular speech. That speech both made and destroyed him as a major political figure: it established his national standing, but denied him the opportunity to hold high office. To parliamentarians, however, his reputation derived not from a single speech delivered on a public platform, but from his contributions delivered over his parliamentary career in the institution to which he was passionately attached: the House of Commons.

Parliamentary oratory

Enoch Powell is recognised, not least within Westminster, as a great parliamentarian. His reputation as such rests on the fact that he was an orator. Although a figure of great controversy, few if any would deny that he was a powerful and eloquent speaker. 'His speeches and writings', declared the *Daily Telegraph*

> will be read so long as there exists a political and parliamentary culture in which speaking and writing matter. And if there comes a time when such a culture is all but destroyed, those brave few who wish to restore it will find in the thoughts of Enoch Powell something approaching their Bible. (Cited in Heffer, 1999: 952)

He was a commanding presence in the House of Commons. Michael Foot wrote of Powell in 1986:

> in the House of Commons, he can compel attention, even from those who detest what he appears to say or stand for, as no one else has done since Aneurin Bevan, almost alone, faced the all-powerful Winston Churchill with the wartime parliament at his back. To elevate Enoch Powell into such company may at first seem a sacrilege, but most of those who have sat in the parliaments of the past two decades would not dissent. (Foot, 1986: 187)

His style and oratory were seen as superior to other leading politicians, including that of Margaret Thatcher. During the 1983 general election campaign, Terry Coleman wrote in the *Guardian*:

> I came to Mrs Thatcher's campaign after a short while with Mr Powell's. The fall was great. Gone was all attempt at reasoned argument. Gone was all sense of history. Gone was all gravitas. Mrs Thatcher shares with Mr Powell one thing – Will. But to Will, he adds intellect and passion. The descent from Powell to Thatcher is into bathos. (Cited in Foot, 1984: 123)

I utilise these last two quotes because they come from sources that may not be considered natural allies, certainly not ideological allies, of Enoch Powell. They demonstrate the recognition of Powell's impact as an orator.

By the 1960s, he already had a reputation as a noted parliamentary speaker. His greatest parliamentary speech was delivered in 1959, on the deaths of Mau Mau detainees in the Hola camp in Kenya (*Hansard*, Vol. 610, cols. 236–7, 27 July 1959). Delivered in the early hours of the morning, it was, declared Denis Healey, 'the greatest parliamentary speech I have ever heard' (Heffer, 1999: 252). Drawing on a thorough command of the papers that had been released, Powell dissected the reasons for 'this great administrative disaster' and, demonstrating the rigorous logic that was his hallmark, focused on who was to blame for the deaths. He rounded on a fellow Conservative who had suggested that those who died had been sub-human:

> It has been said – and it is a fact – that these eleven men were the lowest of the low; sub-human was the word which one of my hon. Friends used. So be it. But that cannot

be relevant to the acceptance of responsibility for their deaths ... In general, I would say that it is a fearful doctrine, which must recoil upon the heads of those who pronounce it, to stand in judgment on a fellow human being and to say, 'Because he was such-and-such, therefore the consequences which would otherwise flow from his death shall not flow'.

He reached a peroration:

Finally, it is argued that this is Africa, that things are different there. Of course they are. The question is whether the difference between things there and here is such that the taking of responsibility there and here should be upon different principles. We claim that it is our object – and this is something which unites both sides of the House – to leave representative institutions behind us wherever we give up our rule. I cannot imagine it is a way to plant representative institutions to be seen to shirk the assignment of responsibility, which is the very essence of responsible Government.

Nor can we ourselves pick and choose where and in what parts of the world we shall use this or that kind of standard. We cannot say, 'We will have African standards in Africa, Asian standards in Asia and perhaps British standards here at home'. We have not that choice to make. We must be consistent with ourselves everywhere. All Government, all influence of man upon man, rests upon opinion. What we can do in Africa, where we still govern and where we no longer govern, depends upon the opinion which is entertained of the way in which this country acts and the way in which Englishmen act. We cannot, we dare not, in Africa of all places, fall below our own highest standards in the acceptance of responsibility. (*Hansard*, Vol. 610, col. 237, 27 July 1959)

It was such powerful contributions that drew him to the attention of his parliamentary colleagues, but it was his speech, to a party meeting in 1968, that propelled him on to the national stage (the speech is reproduced in Collins, 1991: 373–9). When interviewed by a reporter for *The Times* during the 1964 general election campaign, he was asked what was the biggest issue on the doorstep and he had replied 'immigration'. The reporter, Norman Fowler, phoned in his piece, 'but it was never used. After all, who in 1964 had ever heard of a former Conservative Cabinet minister thinking that immigration was an important political issue?' (Fowler, 1991: 58). Four years later, Powell, by his use of language, was to ensure that it was. On 20 April 1968, he addressed the annual general meeting of the West Midlands Area Conservative Political Centre, of which he was president. The media had been alerted to an important speech and a television crew from ITV was present. Addressing the issue of immigration, he declared: 'We must be mad, literally mad, as a nation to be permitting the annual influx of some 50,000 dependents, who are for the most part the material of the future growth of the immigrant-descended population. It is like watching a nation busily engaged in heaping up its own funeral pyre.' He concluded, in what was to include the classical reference indelibly associated with him:

As I look ahead, I am filled with foreboding. Like the Roman, I seem to see 'the River Tiber foaming with much blood'. That tragic and intractable phenomenon which we

watch with horror on the other side of the Atlantic but which there is interwoven with
the history and the existence of the States itself, is coming upon us here by our own
volition and our own neglect.

It was a speech that appalled his party leader and other members of the Shadow
Cabinet, who had no idea of what he was going to say. Heath dismissed him the following day from the Shadow Cabinet. The reaction in the country was very different.
Powell received over 100,000 letters, overwhelmingly in support of what he had said.
London dockers went on strike and marched along the Embankment in support of
his stance. Opinion polls showed that most people endorsed his views (see Bower,
2012: 161). He became a popular speaker at meetings throughout the country. He
could fill halls in cities as well as towns, his controversial stance also resulting in him
being accompanied by personal protection officers, a protection not accorded most
senior ministers. During the 1970 election campaign, the Press Association assigned
one reporter each to Harold Wilson and Edward Heath, and two to Powell (Gale,
1970: 56). As Patrick Cosgrave observed, 'He had always been a most formidable
parliamentary orator; by June 1970 he had established himself as by far and away the
most powerful public speaker in politics' (Cosgrave, 1989: 282).

What, then, made Powell such a distinctive, indeed renowned, orator? I propose to
utilise the three modes that form the basis of this volume: ethos, pathos and logos. My
contention is that Powell's oratory was not characterised, as may popularly be believed
by pathos – of appealing to the emotions – but rather defined by ethos and logos.

Ethos

Ethos is central to the impact of Powell. He had an impact on his audience before
he uttered a word. He had a distinctive presence. He was always an intense and insu-
lar individual, his manner compounded by his appearance. He was, by choice or
inclination, rather than upbringing, a rather austere figure. He had a happy childhood and was devoted to his parents, but in his dealings with the wider world preferred to plough his own furrow. Michael Foot was later to characterise him as a
'loner', meaning someone who preferred to act alone in the last resort, who would
always follow their own star (Foot, 1986: 186). His capacity to be alone, as Cosgrave
noted, 'was evident from his schooldays' (Cosgrave, 1989: 13). During his time in
the Conservative Research Department, he was, recalled Iain Macleod, 'memorably
unapproachable' (Cosgrave, 1998). In the House of Commons, he was, according to
one Tory MP, 'unclubbable' (Roth, 1970: 63). He was not one to frequent the smok-
ing room or the tea room, preferring instead the library or the chamber. His distance
combined with an intensity of approach. There was, in John Campbell's phrase, 'the
hypnotic oddity of his personality' (Campbell, 1997: 73).

His appearance and demeanour did not help him in seeking to find a parliamentary seat – after fighting the safe Labour seat of Normanton in a by-election in 1947,
he made nineteen unsuccessful bids for a candidature. As Robert Shepherd records,

'Powell's prospects were not helped by his austere, intense and reserved manner that often gave a forbidding impression' (Shepherd, 1996: 73). Even when invited to appear before the executive council of the local party in Wolverhampton South-West, the chairman told the members 'Now I just want to say to you before the next candidate comes in, don't be put off by appearances' (Roth, 1970: 57).

Yet his manner was a notable strength as well as a weakness. As the chairman of the Young Conservatives in the seat recalled, although he seemed 'rather dour and serious', he was 'very commanding' and had a 'real presence' and was 'very sincere' (Shepherd, 1996: 74). His intense manner and demeanour were to remain with him for the rest of his life. When the Solicitor-General, Sir Peter Rawlinson, attended Cabinet during the Profumo crisis in 1963, he recalled that when he was called to speak, 'I looked down the long table. I remember looking straight into the intense eyes set in the white face of the Minister of Health as he leaned forward the better to hear. They never shifted while I spoke' (Rawlinson, 1989: 97). Labour MP Frank Field recalled that when he entered the House of Commons in 1979, Powell was one of the greatest political figures in the Commons. 'While admired he was also feared', he recalled, adding 'and herein lay his strength of his parliamentary presence and its weakness' (Field, 2012: 47). That fear was not confined to new MPs. Douglas Hurd recalled that, when he was a minister, there was only one politician that frightened him, and that was Enoch Powell (Norton, 2012: 12). Powell's staring eyes and intense manner caused panic before he had uttered his penetrating question or observation.

He also benefited from engaging directly with his audience, either relying on a few notes or no text at all. His sentences, though, came out perfectly formed. As John Biffen observed, they needed no correction: 'He was a Hansard reporter's dream' (BBC News Online, 1998). He was also fearless and willing to engage with whoever challenged him. He relished debate. In many respects, as I have previously argued, Powell was a latter-day Lord Randolph Churchill (Norton, 2012: 151). He could argue his case in flawless English and, indeed, in other languages. (He spoke at least eight.) When he took his campaign against UK membership of the European Communities to other countries, he made his case in Lyon in French, in Frankfurt in German, and in Turin in Italian (True, 2012: 20).

His fearlessness also added to his impact. Far from avoiding combat in the war, he actively sought it. Despite being an obvious terrorist target, he always published his home address and telephone number. He would pursue his arguments in the face of hostility. He did not shy away from conflict. This reinforced the impact of his presence.

Pathos

Pathos is perhaps especially associated with Powell as a consequence of his 1968 speech containing his classical reference. It made him a hero in the West Midlands and beyond, whilst simultaneously destroying his career as a front-line politician. It was a late decision to render the phrase in English. He had apparently intended initially to deliver it in Latin. Had he done so, the impact may have been so very different.

There are, though, dangers in generalising about Powell's oratory from that one speech. Though he maintained his stance on immigration, pathos was not his natural style. Roger Scruton contends that Enoch Powell delivered two kinds of speech: one offering rigorous analysis and the other suggestive invocation (Scruton, 2012: 114). He goes on to say what he was not:

> In neither case do Powell's words correspond to the popular image of the man, as a fiery rhetorician, summoning his countrymen with 'ancestral voices prophesying war'. On the contrary, his voice is characterised by a sober level-headed vision of the human condition, expressed with absolute clarity, and with the unambiguous syntax that his classical studies had implanted ... Most of all, the speeches are characterised by an economy of presentation, a way of going immediately and convincingly to the point, and leaving all argument to the contrary in shreds. (Scruton, 2012: 114)

Though his speeches may tap emotional sentiments on the part of his listeners, they were crafted for the purpose of winning the intellectual argument. There could thus be a notable chasm between how his listeners interpreted his words and what he meant by them. His critics, and indeed his most avid supporters in 1968, may have seen him as a British Le Pen, but in terms of the beliefs he sought to convey he was, as the *Economist* put it, more a British de Gaulle (*Economist*, 12 February 1998). For Powell his views on immigration were determined by politics and not race (see Norton, 2012: 154). He believed that the nation flourished through having a sense of self-identification and that would be diluted, indeed lost, if there was an influx into large conurbations of people without that sense of identity. His fellow Tory MP, Richard Body, argued that Britain was multiracial and always had been, but that the problem arose through seeking to render it multicultural (Body, 2001). Powell was punctilious in treating everyone the same once they were in the country, be it immigrants in his Wolverhampton constituency or constituents who were Nationalists in his South Down seat.

Logos

Powell was more prone to appeals based on logical argument. He was, as we have seen, a trained classicist. He pursued an argument to what he saw as its logical conclusion. The logic trumped over everything else. As Norman Shrapnel observed, 'Powell was not the first or last politician to be caught between the concept and the act, the purity of the idea and the twist and turns of real life, but in his case the gift for abstraction was so advanced that the gap yawned wider than for most' (Shrapnel, 1998). As I have argued elsewhere, Powell embraced the rationalist rather than the empirical approach to problem solving (Norton, 2012: 150). His concern was with what logically *should* be rather than with what *could* be.

His attachment to logic was such that he pursued his argument regardless of the audience. In many respects, it did not matter whether he was addressing the House of Commons, a party conference or a public audience. For him, the crucial fact was that it was a live audience. 'I need to be talking to somebody', he said, 'I need to be talking to heads in front of me' (cited in Shepherd, 1996: 78). He did not necessarily distinguish between the gatherings he addressed. The topic may not always be an obvious one for the audience he was addressing. On one occasion, for example, he spoke in the Lincolnshire market town of Louth and addressed the issue of trade union reform. He would address a particular premise – some would argue at times a false premise – and then dissect it with rigorous logic. He needed an audience, but his words were not designed to be popular with his listeners. His goal was to persuade them to his line of argument. As Patrick Cosgrave put it, 'Powell was never a populist in seeking to convince his listeners that he was one of them; and he never talked down to them either' (Cosgrave, 1989: 296).

He did not necessarily seek to empathise with his audience and on occasion in his parliamentary interventions could cause great offence to those he was addressing, whether it was Edward Heath over the issues of immigration, European integration and economic policy or Margaret Thatcher over the Anglo-Irish Agreement. One MP, Julian Critchley, recalled him crying 'imbecility, imbecility' at Tory Chancellor Tony Barber when the minister got into difficulty over the effects of a rise in oil prices (Critchley, 1994: 136). On occasion, there was some retaliation, Heath on one occasion accusing him of a lack of humanity (Hutchinson, 1970: 176).

His rigorous pursuit of logic was sometimes confused with ideology. Samuel Beer described him as not only an ideologue but also a demagogue (Beer, 1982: 176). He noted the un-Conservative nature of his pursuit of rigour and consistency and contrasted his intellectual style with that of Ian Gilmour, noting Gilmour's claim that Powell was 'the nearest thing the Tory party has, or rather had, to an ideologue' (Beer, 1982: 176).

This, though, is to misunderstand Powell and the reasons for the impact that he had. Powell had a set of beliefs: he was essentially a Tory neo-liberal (Norton, 2012: 146), with a strong attachment to the nation state, institutions, and the free market. He pursued his beliefs with intensity, beliefs that often, but not always, attracted other Tory MPs to his side. This was especially the case in his opposition to European integration and to the Heath government's U-turn on economic policy (Norton, 1978). He thus had supporters – Powellites, if you like – but there was no Powellism (Norton, 2012: 146). There was no overarching philosophy, and certainly not one to which others subscribed. Indeed, part of his appeal was that listeners were not always sure what line he would take. As Maurice Cowling observed, he was 'capable both of batting all around the political wicket and of moving the stumps in order to set up a wicket of his own' (Cowling, 1970: 13).

He was initially a great defender of empire, but once he realised it had gone he took the line that there was no point in seeking to preserve it. He was also an opponent of Britain retaining nuclear weapons, since he could not envision an occasion when a UK prime minister would deploy them. Such stances made him a rather unpredictable Shadow Defence Secretary, his party audiences holding him in awe while also being slightly petrified as to where he would go. His stance could appeal across parties and sometimes as much to his political opponents as to his allies. Michael Foot lauded the speech he delivered in the House of Commons in 1983 in opposition to Britain's retention of nuclear weapons. 'However, even in election times', declared Foot, 'good arguments can be overlaid by greater ones, and in the 1983 election the best contribution to the greatest argument of all was presented by Enoch Powell' (Foot, 1984: 106–7).

Indeed, the combination of the complexity, or unpredictability, of his views and the sincerity with which he advanced them often confused and impressed his political opponents. Though his speeches on immigration could still provoke condemnation, 'his magnetism and the protean character of his output was attracting more and more interest and attention (and even respect) in circles which had previously found him dangerous and abominable' (Cosgrave, 1989: 299).

His rigorous pursuit of logic also meant that he eschewed a device used by many politicians, that of wit. He had a sense of humour, especially in private, but on the public platform it was rarely a feature of his words. When he did deploy humour it was, as Cosgrave noted, grim humour (Cosgrave, 1989: 17). As the *Economist* observed, 'There were not many jokes in a Powell speech', adding 'but the audience was held by its taut language delivered with passion' ('Enoch Powell', *Economist*, 12 February 1998). He relied on the logic of his argument, reinforced by the intensity of his delivery and the telling phrase. In my Speaker's Centenary Lecture on Powell, I noted that he rated only one entry in *The Oxford Dictionary of Humorous Quotations*, but twenty-one in the *The Oxford Dictionary of Political Quotations* (Norton, 2012: 151).

The force of his oratory was also aided by the fact that he combined intellectual brilliance with an inordinate capacity for work. He researched his subjects intensely. Reginald Maudling recalled his experience of Powell when they worked together in the Conservative Research Department:

> At one stage when Enoch was detailed to become the expert on town and country planning, he acquired the standard textbook and read it from page to page, as an ordinary mortal would read a novel. Within a matter of weeks he had fully grasped both the principles of the problem and the details of the legal situation. Within a matter of a few months he was writing to the author of the textbook, pointing out the errors that he made. (Maudling, 1978: 42–3)

The combination of his intellect, his command of language, his austere and penetrating gaze, his intense manner, and his dedication to his work made him a powerful speaker, indeed an outstanding orator. In the House of Commons, his name on the annunciator was enough to bring MPs into the chamber. John Major referred to the 'spell which he could weave' (Major, 1999: 40). Yet the features which set him apart also constituted something of a liability. He pursued issues to their logical conclusion, regardless of their political saliency. Some of the issues he pursued bordered on the bizarre. When he was in the Conservative Research Department, he gave R. A. Butler a paper 'in which he argued that with ten divisions we could reconquer India' (Butler and Pinto-Duschinsky, 1971: 143). Churchill asked Butler if he thought Powell was 'all right'. An arch critic of the United States, Powell believed that the CIA was involved in the assassination of Lord Mountbatten in 1979. He was convinced that the works of Shakespeare were penned by the Earl of Oxford.

His powerful oratory may have impressed, but it did not necessarily carry his audience. Harold Macmillan, not surprisingly, was somewhat dismissive of Powell following his resignation as Financial Secretary in 1958. As he wrote of Powell and Nigel Birch, 'Although I had great personal admiration for their gifts, I distrusted their judgement, since they seemed to have introduced into the study of financial and economic problems a degree of fanaticism which appeared to me inappropriate. If they did not actually welcome martyrdom, they did nothing to avoid it and seemed rather to seek and enjoy the crown' (Macmillan, 1971: 372). Quintin Hogg, who, as we shall see, also had reason to distrust Powell, noted that 'I greatly admire his intellect and his scholarship, even when his conclusions are of the most bizarre' (Hailsham, 1990: 372).

Even those who might be considered more natural allies were not always persuaded by his arguments, however eloquently expressed. Tory MP John Boyd-Carpenter, commenting on Powell's resignation in 1958, observed that he 'had for years demonstrated an astonishing mixture of intellectual brilliance and appalling judgment' (Boyd-Carpenter, 1980: 140). Another Tory MP, Sir Gerald Nabarro, concluded that 'His views are often so quaint, so lustful for logic and so void of meaning to ordinary men and women, that I consider he could not command sufficient support in his Party to rise to the top or near it' (Nabarro, 1973: 98). And Derick Heathcoat-Amory's biographer, W. Gore Allen, observed that Powell 'had made a considerable impression both by his intellectual gifts and the fluency of his speech – an impression that was only tempered by the suspicion of a complete inflexibility of mind. A poet and a theorist, he had never learned that "politics is the art of the possible"' (Allen, 1958: 175).

Impact

Powell's failure to treat politics as the art of the possible serves to explain why his impact was limited. The thesis of my Speaker's Lecture was that he was a great parliamentarian, but not a great politician (Norton, 2012: 132–58). He could rouse an audience, he could carry some of his colleagues in the House of Commons with him in his attacks on the government, but he rarely mobilised supporters on a scale that affected the outcome of public policy. He had his supporters in Parliament, but they were in a minority. He had garnered only fifteen votes when he stood for the party leadership in 1965. Though designed as a marker for the future, his 'small vote may even have weakened his bargaining position' (Ramsden, 1996: 237; see also Heffer 1999: 385). During the period of the Heath government, forty-four Tory MPs could be classed as Powellites, but not a single MP followed him into the lobbies on all the issues on which he opposed the government (Norton, 1978: 250–1). He would rise to make a powerful case, holding the House in awe as he spoke, but he was not an organiser, be it by nature or design, and he was not willing to temporise.

Powell, as we have seen, followed the logic of his argument to wherever it went. Iain Macleod notably observed, 'I am a fellow-traveller but I prefer to get out one or two stops before the train crashes into the buffers at the terminus' (Fisher, 1973: 17). Powell himself recognised his limitations. He noted that one of Margaret Thatcher's remarkable characteristics:

> is her ability to put up with things and go along with them, even though she doesn't agree with them, until the time comes when they can be dealt with. Now not possessing that quality myself – having the loquacity which always impels me to say: 'I don't agree' – I admire this. (Norton, 2012: 155)

His refusal to temporise extended to an unwillingness to accept the boundaries imposed by membership of the Shadow Cabinet. Macleod at one point complained to Heath about Powell pre-empting Shadow Cabinet decisions (Heath, 1988: 291). His 1968 speech enraged the Shadow Home Secretary, Quintin Hogg, not only for its content but also for the fact that it encroached on his portfolio. 'I clearly understood', Hogg recalled, 'that if Enoch's speech was not publicly condemned by colleagues I would have to resign as Home Affairs spokesman and, barring accidents, my public life would be effectively at an end' (Hailsham, 1990: 370–1).

Powell stood by the logic of his beliefs wherever it took him. His views on immigration may have denied him a place on his party's frontbench, but it was his views on the party's economic policy that led to his refusal to seek re-election to the House of Commons in February 1974. For him, to do so would be fundamentally dishonest. As he told the South Kensington Young Conservatives in 1976, elections usually offered a choice between broad principles and programmes, but on occasion were called on a specific policy. 'The general election of February 1974', he declared,

> was a classic case in point. It was expressly called with the object of seeking support and authority for the Heath Government's prices and incomes policy. That being so, no Conservative Party candidate could declare himself opposed to that policy without rendering the electoral process meaningless.

He had fought the 1970 election, along with other Conservative candidates, on a policy of opposition to compulsory wage control, and when the government embraced such a policy 'I had attacked, denounced and ridiculed it, I had predicted its failure, and I had voted against it in the lobbies. How, short of humiliating and insincere recantation or open defiance of the very meaning of party and parliamentary democracy, could such a person stand as a Conservative candidate at any election fought primarily and explicitly on that very issue?' (Collins, 1991: 255–6).

Having thus set himself apart, in effect criticising all his former colleagues who stood for re-election, he went on, for good measure, to tell his Tory audience why he had advised electors to vote Labour in the general election of October 1974.

Powell's failure to accept or at least act on the recognition that politics is the art of the possible not only kept him on the backbenches but also limited his capacity to affect government policy. His one notable political success came in 1969 when he was instrumental in forcing the government to abandon its plans for reform of the House of Lords, but in doing so he was not alone.

The measure to reform the Lords, the Parliament (No. 2) Bill, achieved a large majority on Second Reading (Norton, 1975: 312–14), but the government feared there would not be a majority if it sought to impose a guillotine to limit debate. The Bill was thus at the mercy of opponents who were prepared to speak at length during its passage through the House. Powell joined forces with Michael Foot on the Labour benches to make the case against the Bill – for Powell it went too far and for Foot not far enough – and both spoke with feeling and on numerous occasions. However, it required more than this eloquent and dedicated duo to keep proceedings going into the early hours. They were supported by MPs on both sides of the House. One Labour MP, Robert Sheldon, spoke for two hours and twenty minutes on one amendment (Morgan, 1975: 214). Other MPs contributed in order to prolong debate. As government supporters lost heart and failed to stay up for late-night proceedings, the whips failing to mobilise the 100 MPs necessary to carry a closure motion, the government decided not to proceed with the measure. Powell has subsequently received praise for his role in opposing the Bill – Simon Heffer described it as 'perhaps the greatest triumph of Powell's political career' (Heffer, 1999: 521) – but it was very much a team effort.

Otherwise, Powell's impact was indirect, influencing the thinking of others, most notably Margaret Thatcher in her neo-liberal approach to economic policy and in demonstrating that there was an alternative to the social-democrat state (see Gamble, 1994: 81). However, insofar as Thatcher was influenced directly by anyone, Sir Keith Joseph was far more in her inner circle than Powell (Campbell, 2000: 263–5), and insofar as Powell's beliefs impacted on Thatcher's thinking they did so only in respect of one part of what was to become Thatcherism. Thatcherism embraced Powell's view on economics, but not his stance on social policy – he was, among other things, opposed to capital punishment – or, for that matter, defence.

Outside Westminster, he could rouse the crowds, enticing workers onto the streets in a way that no other politician could, and his message on immigration was one that resonated and was to endure, encapsulated in the popular phrase 'Enoch was right'. However, his impact on voting behaviour was not as dramatic as some supporters believed or liked to believe. One supporter, John Wood, published some essays on Powell and the 1970 election, the purport of which was expressed in the introduction: 'As is tentatively suggested by the contributors – and there can be no certainty about matters of this kind – it is at least possible that Mr Powell played a decisive part in the unexpected Tory victory' (Wood, 1970: 7). If there was a Powell factor in the election, there is little evidence of it having affected the outcome (Butler and Pinto-Duschinsky, 1971: 341, 405–8). If he brought voters to the polls to vote Conservative, he may also have been responsible, as some Tories believed, for an increase in the turnout of Irish, non-white and Liberal voters (Butler and Pinto-Duschinsky, 1971: 341).

Though Powell was to have a notable impact on the debate about immigration – bringing it to the fore – it was uncertain as to the effect of his words on the development of party policy. His speeches, which on immigration he tended to keep to public platforms rather than the House of Commons, may have forced Heath in 1970 to 'elaborate a policy on immigration' (Hurd, 2003: 183), but at the same time emboldened party leaders not to be seen to concede to what were seen as extreme views. Party leaders sought to ensure the issue had a low profile during the 1970 election campaign (Butler and Pinto-Duschinsky, 1971: 327–9) and Powell had no impact in 1972 when the government decided to admit Ugandan Asians expelled from Uganda.

Conclusion

Powell has variously been described as something of an enigma. John Major described him as a 'strange and brilliant man' (Major, 1999: 40). He conveyed the impression, as Douglas Hurd observed during the 1970 election campaign, 'of a solitary prophet' (Hurd, 2003: 188). A 'loner and intellectual maverick' (Davies, 1995: 389), he was more concerned with the purity of the logic than the effect of his words on colleagues. As Norman Lamont recalled, Powell doubted that 'such a thing as real friendship is possible in politics' (Lamont, 1999: 420). He went his own way.

The very thing that made him such a powerful figure in the chamber of the House of Commons or on the public platform also denied him the great offices of state. The point was well put by Roy Lewis. 'The principles and passion that made Powell a force in politics', he wrote, 'unmade his career as a man of office and power' (Lewis, 1979: 251). He gave voice to what many believed, but then veered in a direction that left them perplexed or hostile. His intense logic was perhaps less of a problem than his embrace of conspiracy theories. Even those who were his political or personal friends could be embarrassed by some of his utterances. His austere manner hid a shy and loyal individual, but probably few recognised those characteristics. What does tend to unite friends and foe alike is the recognition that he was an outstanding orator, one of the best of his generation.

6

The oratory of Keith Joseph

Mark Garnett

From Edmund Burke to Dr Gordon Brown, the fortunes of intellectuals in British politics have been mixed at best, in their oratory as in other respects.[1] If they refuse to make concessions to their audience, they run the risk of the sort of criticism levelled by Oliver Goldsmith at his friend Burke, who:

> … too deep for his hearers, still went on refining,
> And thought of convincing, while they thought of dining.

At the other extreme, a known intellectual who renounces the ivory tower and adopts a more down-to-earth speaking style is likely to be suspected of opportunism. This, at least in part, explains why the Fellow of All Souls Lord Hailsham failed to succeed Harold Macmillan as Conservative leader and prime minister, after announcing his intention to revert to plain(ish) Quintin Hogg in 1963 and striking populist poses at the party conference.

Hailsham/Hogg was not the only All Souls Fellow in Macmillan's last Cabinet line-up. Sir Keith Joseph, who became Minister for Housing and Local Government in 1962, had also secured that coveted academic accolade, supplementing his first-class degree in Jurisprudence. Yet if intellectual politicians can be divided into Burkeans and Hoggites, Joseph is usually bracketed among the former. While Hogg was a pragmatist who saw politics as an art which required continual adaptation, Joseph's approach was similar to that expressed by his friend Margaret Thatcher, using words attributed to St Francis of Assisi: 'Where there is error, may we bring truth.' In the later stages of his career he saw himself as a teacher more than a politician; and if he came relatively late to his real vocation, this was only because it took time for him to grasp what he took to be the essential truths of politics.

In Aristotle's terms, then, Joseph as an orator was primarily concerned with logos. Indeed, while Goldsmith was unfair to imply that Burke was incapable of using pathos to capture an audience – his performances at the trial of Warren Hastings would have been enough to refute that suggestion, even if he had never lived to write about the French Revolution – Joseph's fame as an orator rests almost entirely on the substance of the messages he conveyed, especially his speeches of 1974. It was in that year that he claimed to have become a true 'Conservative' for the first time; and for the remainder of his career he refused to let the short-term interests of his party prevent him from enlightening the British public.

Formative influences

The fact that Joseph took so long – until his mid-fifties – to adopt the faith which defined his career suggests a prolonged psychological journey, which must be explored before we can assess the nature of his oratory. In a scenario which is strongly reminiscent of Martin Wiener's thesis in *English Culture and the Decline of the Industrial Spirit* (1981), the fortune which Joseph's family had accumulated through hard work was invested in an education which was designed to make the young Keith conform to the model of an English gentleman. Descended from Jewish immigrants who arrived in Britain in the early years of the nineteenth century, Joseph's relatives included notable figures from the world of culture as well as politics and business. Numerous ties of marriage reinforced the semi-formalised bonds of mutual dependence arising from their various entrepreneurial ventures. It was a background which exemplified to the point of caricature Margaret Thatcher's dictum that individuals and families, rather than 'society', were the only realities; the principles adopted by Joseph's extended family meant that it acted like a welfare state in microcosm (Denham and Garnett, 2001: 1–24).

Keith's father, Sir Samuel Joseph, had crowned his business career by serving as London's Lord Mayor, gaining in the process a baronetcy which his son inherited in 1944. By that time the new Sir Keith Joseph had attended Harrow School and Magdalen College, Oxford, before seeing action in the Second World War, where he showed considerable courage without winning any notable honours. In 1946 he competed successfully for his All Souls Fellowship, and in the same year was elected unopposed to the Court of Alderman of the City of London Corporation, for the ward of Portsoken in East London. He was already playing a prominent role in the construction company, Bovis, which had been his father's main business interest. It seemed that Keith was well set to emulate, if not to improve upon, Sir Samuel's remarkable career. However, in 1948 he retired as an Alderman, apparently because of stress and over-work. It was not until 1953, after his marriage to a beautiful and earnest American, Hellen Guggenheimer, that Joseph decided to put his name forward as a Conservative parliamentary candidate. Narrowly defeated at Barons Court in the 1955 general election, Joseph was selected to fight the 'safe' seat of Leeds North East in a 1956 by-election. Although Joseph had few connections outside the south of England – and made it clear that he would be an irregular visitor to Leeds even if he won the seat – he was comfortably elected.

Backbencher and junior minister

A wealthy, good-looking and intelligent baronet was an excellent acquisition for the parliamentary Conservative Party of 1956. On paper, Joseph looked to be set for a

highly successful political career. His Judaism might be regarded by some as an insu-
perable obstacle to the highest office, but not to promotion within a party which
was looking to widen the social basis of its support. A more serious problem was
that Joseph's privileged background had left him with an over-developed sense of
guilt. However, in these years of broad agreement between the major parties over
key social policies, the fact that Joseph obviously cared about poverty seemed to
be an additional asset; and during the Leeds North-East campaign he had actually
focused on his concerns about the plight of the self-employed.

Joseph made similar business-friendly noises in his maiden speech, delivered
during the debate on Harold Macmillan's 1956 budget. However, more relevant for
the present purpose is the response of the speaker who followed him, the Labour
MP Arthur Blenkinsop. Obeying the rules of parliamentary courtesy, Blenkinsop
applauded Joseph's first effort; but his chosen compliments are highly instructive. 'I
do not know', he said, 'that I have ever listened to a clearer, more logical and more
interesting maiden speech' (Halcrow, 1989: 13). In other words, even at this early
stage Joseph's set-piece orations were notable for logos more than for pathos.

Ethos, though, was a very different matter. The arrival of a Jewish intellectual in
the House of Commons of 1956 would not be a cause for comment; but the fact
that this Jewish MP had established his credentials with an All Souls Fellowship was
bound to make Sir Keith Joseph a figure of considerable interest even before he had
opened his mouth. It was also noteworthy that Joseph sported Conservative colours; although he was not the first Jewish Tory MP, the overwhelming majority of
practising co-religionists to that date had been elected for the Liberals or Labour.

Thus the man who had nursed a sense of guilt because of his inherited wealth
found it impossible to escape another advantage of his upbringing: whatever his
inherent intellectual merits, it is very doubtful that Keith Joseph would have gained
an All Souls Fellowship (or even attended Oxford University as an undergraduate)
without his costly school career. However, he was far from being the only person at
Westminster who owed his position to good fortune rather than unaided personal
merit; and unlike many others in that situation, he took his duties very seriously.
From January 1957, when he became a Parliamentary Private Secretary, to the 1964
general election when he lost his office as Secretary of State for Housing, Local
Government (combined, rather awkwardly, with Welsh Affairs), Joseph seemed
untroubled by any qualms of conscience as he climbed the ladder of preferment.
Promoted to the Cabinet as a beneficiary of Harold Macmillan's 'Night of the Long
Knives' in July 1962, he was described by *The Times* as 'one of the party's progressive
intellectuals', even if he was 'not the most Bravura performer at the Dispatch Box'
(*The Times*, 14 July 1962). However, after speaking at his first Conservative conference as a Cabinet minister (October 1962) Joseph received rapturous press notices
which suggested that his new eminence had burnished his oratorical skills. *The
Economist*, for example, saluted his 'air of ruthless determination' (*The Economist*,
13 October 1962). After the following year's performance he was even compared
to J. F. Kennedy (Denham and Garnett, 2001: 119). The vacancy at the top created

by Macmillan's illness at the time of the 1963 conference came too soon for Joseph to be taken seriously as a contender, but some of his colleagues were sufficiently impressed to tip him as a future leader.

It might seem ironic that Joseph's reputation for public speaking should have grown at a time when, on his own later testimony, he was merely reciting the accepted wisdom of the time rather than uttering truths which he had discovered for himself. A profile of Joseph published in 1964 recalled his 1962 conference performance in words which merit lengthy quotation, not least because of the remarkable contrast with his later oratory:

> On came the new Minister of Housing, vibrant as a dynamo, visibly in command of his subject, properly contemptuous of Labour's claims, taut of visage and fiery-eyed. Instead of debate, the members got direction; instead of magisterially phrased sentences, carefully qualified by this and that, they got machine-gun bursts of facts justifying the Conservative housing record. And there was a prophecy, for no good conference speech lacks one: slums would be cleared in future at double and perhaps treble the previous rate. The roof shook with applause.

In part, the profile suggested, Joseph had struck the right note because he was acutely aware of 'the malaise that arises from too much wrangling about principles' (*The Times*, 22 September 1964).

This account, combined with the categories of Aristotle's *Rhetoric*, sheds crucial light on Joseph's approach at this time. He was well aware that he had been appointed by Macmillan (along with other new colleagues like Enoch Powell) to inject some energy into a flagging administration. The role expected of him at party conferences, therefore, was obvious – to sound businesslike and determined, throw out a few statistics, and if possible land some blows on the opposition. In other words, the success of his speech depended on pathos and ethos much more than logos; if he could make the audience believe that the government's record on housing was something to feel excited about, he would convince Macmillan that his confidence had not been misplaced. There was no need to discuss the philosophy which lay behind the government's record; indeed, the figures that he reeled off were less important than the impression that Joseph, his colleagues and the rank-and-file should all feel proud of them, and that they gave the Conservatives an advantage over Labour in a key policy area.

In short, Joseph's conference performances in his first ministerial spell were a moderated version of the 'showman' approach which his All Souls colleague Quintin Hogg had also adopted, at least in part to avoid difficulties which might accompany 'too much wrangling about principles'. The crucial difference was that while Hogg was an ebullient character to whom showmanship came naturally, those who had known Sir Keith Joseph before he became a minister would have been astonished that he could play this part so well. No one could accuse him of cynical crowd-pleasing; if he chose not to talk about principles, it could only be because this thoughtful man was convinced that he and the government were on the right track. It was not until the Conservative defeat of 1964 that serious doubts began to creep in, to the extent that logos re-emerged as the primary feature of Joseph's oratory.

A free market crusader (Mark I)

Shortly after the Conservative Party lost office in October 1964, Sir Keith Joseph visited the free market think-tank, the Institute of Economic Affairs (IEA), and took away some of its pamphlets. Other notable Conservatives – including Enoch Powell and Geoffrey Howe – had already made contact with the IEA, and Margaret Thatcher paid her first visit at about the same time as Joseph.

The IEA was important to all these politicians, but the impact on Joseph was particularly profound. Powell had made himself a hero to economic liberals in 1958, by resigning as a Treasury minister in protest against the Macmillan government's apparent irresolution in addressing inflationary pressures. The IEA, which had been founded just three years earlier, could provide Powell with an extra-parliamentary platform but little in the way of lessons. Geoffrey Howe was intellectually inquisitive and far more flexible in his thinking than the others; as such, he could admire the work of the IEA without becoming a devotee. For her part, Margaret Thatcher had been imbued with economic liberalism by her father; if anything, she found in the IEA a welcome feeling that her unreflective views could be supported by sophisti-cated intellectuals.

Like the others, Joseph had shown unmistakable sympathy with economic liber-alism long before 1964. However, there was no real urgency in his initial speeches after the election. In 1987 Joseph told Anthony Seldon that he had never considered any political allegiance except the Conservative Party, and one must presume that he regarded the party as the natural friend of entrepreneurs like his father (Seldon, 1987: 26). When he encountered the IEA, however, he heard a very different mes-sage. As befitted an educational charity, the Institute was determinedly non-partisan; indeed, it had been established precisely because it felt that no political party could be trusted to uphold the free market case in an era of post-war 'statism'. For someone of Joseph's character and background, the ideological certainties expressed by the IEA had life-changing potential. The beneficiary of entrepreneurial endeavour and academic training could now feel a revitalised sense of mission which reconnected him with both of these formative influences: he could become a teacher, reminding his party and the British public as a whole that success depends on the efforts of risk-taking individuals rather than the well-intentioned but invariably misguided initia-tives of the state. Furthermore, as a person with a well-developed sense of personal frailty, Joseph could convey this message without self-aggrandisement; if post-war British politics had proceeded on the wrong lines, he was perfectly willing to include himself in the indictment.

On paper, this new liaison between a rising politician and a hot-house of ideas should have been a perfect match. However, a serious difficulty became clear almost immediately. In a volume of essays compiled by the IEA in 1964, Enoch Powell had written that 'Those whose business it is to think, to study and to criticise have a positive duty to follow the Logos where it leads them; it is the business of others (or of the same people in another capacity) to speculate on what might be "politically practicable", and how, at any particular moment of time' (Powell, 1964: 262–3). This was pretty gnomic even by Powell's standards. At one extreme, it could imply that intellectuals who seek the truth are doomed to have their ideas rejected by people who accuse them of 'thinking the unthinkable' in political terms. Worse still, politicians who, *qua* intellectuals, uncover valuable truths, might on Powell's showing feel they have a positive duty to *suppress* their thinking if the moment is not propitious.

This dilemma affected Joseph particularly acutely, since as a minister before 1964 he had shown an unusual propensity to respect the boundaries of the 'politically possible'. As we have seen, his conference speeches followed the typical format of these years; instead of taking his stand on principle, Joseph recounted concrete achievements and set himself more exacting targets for the future. His new allies in the IEA quickly came to suspect that Joseph should have been a champion of the entrepreneur, but as a minister he had surrendered his critical faculties to those redoubtable guardians of the 'politically possible' – the civil service. Far from throwing off these bonds when his party returned to opposition, at least initially Joseph still seemed reluctant to 'follow the Logos'. No doubt his caution was affected by his Shadow responsibilities between 1964 and 1967, which lay in the acutely sensitive areas of Social Services and Labour (i.e. policy towards the trade unions). However, he seems to have interpreted his appointment in early 1967 as spokesman on Trade and Power as a licence to inject distinctive ideas into his public performances. In April, for example, he delivered a speech at Reading which was reported in *The Times* under the headline 'Tory errors confessed'. Joseph argued that successive Conservative governments had only 'half freed' private enterprise from the shackles imposed on it by the Attlee governments. His conclusion was that 'Private enterprise has not failed, it has not been properly tried'. *The Times* noted that this was just the first of 'a series of speeches' in which Joseph would seek to elaborate 'a Tory philosophy' in relation to key contemporary issues (*The Times*, 27 April 1967).

On a superficial reading, Joseph had done nothing out of the ordinary. The duties of government entail constant decision-making, leaving little opportunity for philosophy; as such, Joseph's speeches until some time after the 1964 election had been preoccupied with practical matters. Yet Opposition offers scope for reflection; and Joseph could be forgiven for feeling compelled to take a leading role in this task, since his status as an All Souls Fellow had clearly played a part in his promotion to frontbench duties. In other words, Joseph's original ethos was based on his reputation for intellectual distinction. In office, he could claim attention from his peers and the public by advertising the practical record of his department. Back in Opposition, the best way to justify his position was to fall back on the qualifications which had made him a politician to watch from the time of his first entry into Parliament. In short, he was entitled to feel that the maintenance of his ethos now depended on his mastery of logos.

Again the comparison with Hailsham/Hogg is informative here. The latter had first been elected in a celebrated 1938 by-election as a committed supporter of the Chamberlain government. Although he quickly repented of his mistake in support-ing appeasement and joined the Conservative rebellion which unseated Chamberlain in 1940, as a backbencher of intellectual distinction he felt the need to respond to his party's critics in speeches and in print. However, his prolific attempts to justify his party's record were controversial in nature; only in 1947, after the Conservatives had returned to Opposition, did he attempt a philosophical justification (Hailsham, 1947). He repeated this pattern later in his career, warning against the dangers of 'elective dictatorship' in his Dimbleby Lecture of 1976 but not allowing his worries about an overmighty executive to dissuade him from serving as Lord Chancellor under Margaret Thatcher from 1979 to 1987.

However, as we have seen Joseph's translation from government to Opposition in 1964 was far more momentous than the norm. His utterances were different from those of Hogg/Hailsham in at least two crucial respects. First, Hailsham's 1947 book, *The Case for Conservatism*, was unlikely to cause concern among his party's high command; rather, in elegant prose it sought to reassure Conservative support-ers at all levels that Labour's doctrinaire approach to politics was a temporary inter-ruption of the natural order. By contrast, Joseph's championship of the free market in 1967 was, in the relevant context, itself 'doctrinaire', threatening to make Labour, led by the pragmatic Harold Wilson, seem more 'conservative' than the Conservative opposition. Far from being delighted by Joseph's philosophical ruminations, the Conservative Party high command was likely to see his initiative as a thinly veiled attack on the current leader, Edward Heath. In January 1966 another Conservative frontbencher, Angus Maude, had openly called for a more clearly defined philosoph-ical approach – and been sacked by Heath for his pains.

The other difference was that while Hailsham was always careful to calibrate his fire – so that even when his own party had been less than foot-perfect, Labour was always presented as the chief culprit – Joseph went out of his way to equalise the blame. Taking the Reading speech at face value, the voters were being invited to pre-fer the Conservative Party in future because at least it, unlike Labour, was prepared to recognise its post-war failures. Joseph's colleagues could be forgiven for finding scant consolation in this message – not least because by April 1967 their party had been in office for more than thirteen out of less than twenty-two post-war years, and thus could be assumed to have more reason for apologies than Labour.

Since Joseph had criticised his party's performance in the whole post-war period – whereas Angus Maude only complained about the current lack of philo-sophical ballast – one might conclude that the former's offence was far worse, and that Joseph only survived because Heath could not afford another high-profile front-bench sacking. However, ethos clearly played a part; Maude had a reputation for independent thought and action which made him an accident waiting to happen, while Joseph had been impeccably loyal since becoming a minister and had openly campaigned on behalf of Heath before the 1965 leadership contest. There is no evidence that Joseph was even issued with a warning after his Reading speech. Instead, at Carshalton in July 1967 Heath expressed his own (pragmatic) economic ideas. Whether or not this was intended as a rebuke to Joseph, it seemed to work, at least in the short term; the promised (or threatened) follow-ups to the Reading speech did not materialise.

However, Joseph's reticence was enforced rather than voluntary, and in April 1968 his obedience to the official party line was sorely tested by the controversy over Enoch Powell's 'Rivers of Blood' speech on immigration. Although he was not an All Souls Fellow, Powell's intellectual credentials were at least equal to those of Joseph or even Hogg, as he testified by insisting that on a literal translation of Virgil's Latin, the River Tiber 'foamed' rather than 'flowed' with blood. Unlike Joseph's Reading speech, the reaction to Powell's oratory on this occasion went far beyond the readership of *The Times* newspaper, or indeed the Conservative Party faithful. However, Powell seemed to have combined ethos and logos to considerable effect without considering the impact of his pathos; the speech implied that recent immigration of all kinds was detrimental to the British way of life, and despite his education at Harrow and Oxford Joseph was acutely aware of his own descent from a family of recent immigrants. It was a sign that politicians who (on Powell's own terms) try to challenge the boundaries of the 'politically practical' could damage their own argument through overblown oratory. Whatever Joseph's feelings about immigration, he admired Powell and he certainly did not join the shadow ministers (including Hogg) who urged Heath to dismiss his turbulent critic.

Powell's departure seems to have increased Joseph's ever-active sense of personal responsibility; if he felt honour-bound to speak out in 1967, now that he was the senior economic liberal in the Shadow Cabinet it would be a dereliction of duty to stay silent. In November 1969 Joseph showed the text of a proposed speech to James Douglas of the Conservative Research Department. Rightly sensing a re-run of the Reading episode, Douglas advised him to consult a seasoned speech-writer (Denham and Garnett, 2001: 182). Inadvertently, the moderate Douglas had encouraged Joseph to form one of the most celebrated double acts of the Thatcher revolution – not exactly its Lennon and McCartney, but more appositely its Simon and Garfunkel. Joseph had already worked with Alfred Sherman, an abrasive co-religionist whose youthful Marxism had been replaced by an equally dogmatic faith in the free market. In the run-up to the 1970 general election, the collaborators produced several speeches which gave some credence to Harold Wilson's claim that Edward Heath and his party proposed a complete reversal of post-war policy, envisaging a limited economic role for the state. When Wilson tried to personify

Conservative intentions in the Neanderthal figure of 'Selsdon Man', it was Joseph rather than the party leader who provided his ammunition.

This time, at least, Joseph showed less inclination to convict his own party of offences against the market; despite (or perhaps because of) his born-again zeal, Sherman recognised the value of tact so close to polling day. On the basis of Joseph's speeches – for example, the one delivered on 7 March 1970 to an audience of Young Conservatives – one would have supposed that Britain's problems were entirely attributable to Wilson's mismanagement. It was, presumably, Sherman's tactical wisdom which dictated that the speech should include repeated assurances that the free-market revival would be accomplished within 'a context of humane laws and institutions' and that the ultimate aim was a 'social market' economy modelled on that of West Germany. However, the overall message of the speech contradicts those mollifying words; indeed, the word 'humanising' leaps from the page because it is the only humanising element in a text which (presumably to the dismay of Joseph's young listeners) extends over twenty-three pages of the Conservative Central Office handout (Joseph, 1970).

The collaboration with Sherman was crucial to Joseph's later reputation as a trailblazer for Thatcherism – and since Sherman later worked with Thatcher herself, it is instructive that phrases like 'rolling back the public sector' are encountered in Joseph's speeches at this time. However, the relationship is instructive in ways which do little to enhance Joseph's reputation as an orator. First, while Joseph disobeyed James Douglas to the extent that he plumped for Sherman instead of choosing a speech-writer who would temper his ideological fervour, his approach to Sherman was a tacit acceptance that he needed help with the composition of his speeches. Second, the partnership with Sherman was always an unequal one, with the unelected advisor clearly in command of the elected politician from the outset. Third, while Sherman could supply his compliant client with the kind of sound-bites which satisfied the modern media, at heart he was an intellectual like Joseph himself. The temperamental contrasts between the pair could not disguise their fundamental affinity, as intellectuals who in their different ways were trying to master the difficult task of conveying complex arguments to interested members of the electorate. From the outside, Sherman understood the game of politics much better than Joseph did; but he was intolerant of clever people as well as fools, and his impatience proved infectious. In this respect, as in others, Margaret Thatcher was far better advised to retain non-intellectuals (like the playwright Ronnie Millar) within her own speech-writing team.

A free market crusader (Mark II)

The fact that Joseph had conveyed a free-market message before 1970 was often forgotten as a result of his second stint as a government minister. As Secretary of State at the Department for Health and Social Security (1970–74) Joseph stuck rigidly to his brief. The job entailed regular requests for higher state expenditure; although in opposition Joseph had argued that increased spending would lead to higher inflation and other unpleasant consequences unless the market was liberated from 'statist' constraints, he was now in a 'spending' ministry and seems to have insulated himself from debates of more direct application to the economic sphere. Heath's failure to appoint him as Chancellor of the Exchequer in succession to Iain Macleod when the latter died within weeks of the 1970 election would have upset most politicians in Joseph's position, but he seems scarcely to have noticed the barely coded implication that he was regarded as untrustworthy on Treasury matters. Economic liberals in the IEA and elsewhere, who had pinned their faith on him as a worthy substitute for Enoch Powell, were now ignored; Joseph, it seemed, was only too willing to surrender his beliefs to the first 'statist' civil servant he encountered. Judged by his conference speeches, it seemed as if he had picked up the threads of his ministerial career without interruption; the message of economic liberalism had disappeared, without any sign that the minister had spent any time 'wrangling about principles'. Even if they had accepted Joseph's attempt to divert funding towards the most 'deserving' cases, his critics deplored his wasteful reorganisation of the NHS.

At the DHSS, Joseph coined one memorable phrase, identifying a 'cycle of deprivation' which prevented members of low-income families from realising their potential (Welshman, 2005). The fact that Joseph chose to signal his concern for the inter-generational transmission of social disadvantage at a conference of the Pre-School Playgroups Association, rather than a Conservative conference, is highly instructive. Joseph might have returned to relatively 'safe' ministerial mode, after his philosophical excursions of the late 1960s; but he was unwilling to let the chains of office restrain him entirely on a subject which mattered so much to him. His solution to the confinements of government responsibility was to make his attempts at broadening public debate outside the expected forums of partisan conflict. Presumably Joseph had also realised that, as an orator, he was most successful when he put his rational faculties to sleep. Now that he wanted to deliver a message close to his heart, his best chance of making an impact on public opinion was to speak in front of a specialist audience, which could judge him on logos rather than crowd-pleasing pathos. It was no accident that those who continued to see Joseph as a potential Conservative Party leader now tended to refer to his social conscience; the populist Joseph who had evoked comparisons with Kennedy had disappeared in 1964, when the IEA taught him that politics could be about teaching the truth, whether or not it was currently popular.

If Sir Keith Joseph had been a conventional politician, his behaviour after the downfall of the Heath government in February 1974 would have been easy to interpret. Since Heath's Chancellor of the Exchequer, Tony Barber, was retiring from politics, Joseph could have expected to be given the top economic portfolio now that the party was returning to opposition. Any other senior politician would have taken this double rebuff – following Heath's choice of Barber as Macleod's successor back in 1970 – as a licence to use any weapon at hand in his or her battle to dethrone the offending party leader.

Superficially, this is exactly what Joseph did. Denied the post of Shadow Chancellor, he refused any other conventional shadow brief and demanded a policy-making role unattached to the work of any specific department. To this end, he asked Heath for permission to establish a think-tank, eventually dubbed the Centre for Policy Studies (CPS). The CPS was Alfred Sherman's idea; unlike the non-partisan IEA, it would make no secret of its allegiance to the Conservative Party. In acceding to Joseph's request, Heath possibly thought that the new venture would keep Joseph quiet at least for a while; ostensibly, the CPS would absorb lessons from other European countries – notably West Germany – and the necessary research would take time. However, while Joseph continued to admire the West German social market economy, the CPS needed quick results if it was to keep its donors happy. Instead of giving Joseph a harmless occupation after the defeat of February 1974, the foundation of the CPS ensured that Alfred Sherman could draw a decent (if precarious) salary while working on some of the most important speeches of the 1970s.

With hindsight, Joseph's major orations from this time – at Upminster in June 1974, and Preston three months later – can be hailed as the first symptoms of an intellectual counter-revolution within the Conservative Party, leading to the down-fall of the post-war Keynesian 'consensus'. In reality, even after those speeches most senior Conservatives remained in the Keynesian camp. However, the Preston speech in particular attracted considerable attention from the broadsheet press – not just *The Times*, which was strongly sympathetic to Joseph's message and printed the text in full (*The Times*, 6 September 1974). Despite Sherman's input, the Preston speech contained few arresting phrases; the most memorable was the opening warning that 'Inflation is threatening to destroy our society', which most observers in 1974 could have worked out for themselves. What really excited Joseph's admirers – like Margaret Thatcher who received an advance copy along with other members of the Shadow Cabinet and regarded it as 'one of the most powerful and persuasive ana-lyses I have ever read' – was the statistical part of the speech, which implied that post-war unemployment had never been anything to worry about (Thatcher, 1995: 255). Since 1945, Joseph claimed, the number of unfilled vacancies had never been less than 600,000 and had sometimes come close to 1,000,000. Injecting demand into the economy in response to fears of mass unemployment – as the Heath gov-ernment had done after 1971 – was thus wholly unnecessary and indeed counter-productive, since it had only generated inflationary pressures which damaged British competitiveness. Although Joseph's argument purported to be economic – an attack on Keynes' legacy – it strongly implied that William Beveridge's welfare state had been too generous, encouraging 'the unenthusiastic, the unemployable, the fraudu-lent' to see a life on social security benefits as a more congenial alternative to low-paid work. Joseph's speech thus attacked both of the key pillars of post-war domestic

British policy in a way which, by accident or design, was sure to appeal to newly insecure members of the middle classes.

Typically, Joseph made no attempt to conceal his own sense of culpability – with justice, since as he freely admitted he had been a high-spending and heavily interventionist minister under Heath as well as Macmillan. However, while Joseph's self-deprecation made it difficult for senior colleagues to dislike the man, if anything it made his message more irksome. Since the February general election had left Britain with a minority Labour government, it was inevitable that Harold Wilson would call another poll when circumstances suited him; and by September 1974 he was ready to go again. Although by that time Joseph had clearly passed to a stage where general elections are happenings of limited consequence, more practical members of the Shadow Cabinet were unlikely to be impressed when he insisted on developing his critique just before the election (held on 10 October). Just a week before the poll, for example, he treated an audience in Luton to his musings on 'hooligans and vandals, bullies and child-batterers, criminals and inadequates' (Joseph, 1974a). Whether or not one accepted his portrait of 'permissive' Britain, since his own party had been in office for seventeen of the twenty-nine years since the war it was not a message which was calculated to inspire many floating voters to offer full-hearted endorsement to Conservative candidates.

In short, Joseph (with Sherman's assistance) had turned himself from a minister who was presiding in February 1974 over a key area of domestic social policy without showing undue symptoms of alarm, into an all-purpose prophet of doom just eight months later. Many Conservative activists were pleased with this unusual spectacle; but in the circumstances of 1974 a more pragmatic political operator would have been more impressed with the opinions of floating voters, and Joseph seems to have paid little heed to the reception of his speeches outside the limited circle of the party faithful. The Tories were in turmoil after the election of October 1974, but grassroots loyalty to the incumbent leader was still strong. Joseph could still be a significant contender if he chose to challenge Heath, but only if he gave the party good reasons to hope for a much better performance next time if he took over as leader.

Instead, on 19 October 1974 Joseph chose to deliver a speech at Edgbaston, in which he summarised his fears for Britain by warning that 'The balance of our population, our human stock is threatened' (Joseph, 1974b). The ensuing furore disabused him of any latent feeling that, for want of an alternative, he should challenge Heath for the Conservative leadership. His supporters within the party took the same view, and switched their allegiance to Margaret Thatcher. As Education Secretary under Heath, Thatcher's performance had been just as inglorious as that of Joseph; but at least she had been discreet enough to signal her sympathy with the economic liberal dissidents without perpetrating any noticeable verbal blunders.

Even if Joseph had confined himself to fairly technical matters, and not tried to inject some sparkle into his text by using a form of words which made him sound like a proponent of eugenics, his oratorical performances since February 1974 would have made him vulnerable as a leadership candidate. According to one account of the Edgbaston speech, Joseph spoke so rapidly that the audience were forced to follow his message with 'the air of Monday morning commuters blearily watching their train flash through the station when they had expected it to stop' (Denham and Garnett, 2001: 265). This was not a style of oratory which was likely to leave favourable impressions on less partisan audiences, as any Conservative leader would have to achieve if the party hoped to recover from its 1974 defeats. In a rare comment on political oratory which featured in an interview conducted after his retirement from office, Joseph recalled Harold Macmillan's speech to the 1922 Committee which helped the latter to succeed Anthony Eden as prime minister in 1957. Joseph remembered that Macmillan had 'peppered his brilliantly effective monologue, if you can apply peppering to silences, with long pregnant silences in which he could have heard a pin drop in that packed committee room' (Seldon, 1987: 27). There is no evidence that Joseph ever mastered such premeditated oratorical devices; although there were many instances after 1974 when he 'peppered' his utterances with silences, typically these would occur during media appearances when such interludes were wholly inappropriate and disconcerting to interviewers and audiences alike. It was as if Joseph had made it a personal mission to contradict the profile-writer of 1964 who credited him with avoiding 'the malaise that arises from too much wrangling about principles'.

In 1964, Sir Keith Joseph was recognised as a fairly accomplished orator by friends and foes alike. Ten years later, even those who acclaimed the content of his speeches had little to say about the style of delivery. In televised interviews, Joseph had also become hesitant, to the point where his nervous mannerisms became the subject of satirical content. After his ally Margaret Thatcher toppled Heath as Conservative leader in February 1975, exasperated colleagues gave him the nickname 'the Mad Monk' in testimony to his impractical approach to policy development. His subsequent conference speeches seemed designed to verify the sobriquet; in October 1975, for example, he tried to persuade his listeners that the party should abandon the quest for the 'middle ground' of politics and instead try to locate the 'common ground' which Conservatives already shared with the majority of voters. In the abstract it was an interesting argument, but it was far too complicated for a conference platform and left many in the audience – including seasoned journalists – feeling confused (Denham and Garnett, 2001: 297).

At party conferences, Joseph's ethos as the intellectual guru of what came to be known as Thatcherism ensured respectful applause, even (or even especially) from those 'hearers' who found him 'too deep'. However, the House of Commons was a different matter. In that unforgiving forum, long before the 1979 general election Labour MPs had begun to anticipate a Joseph speech with much greater pleasure than their Conservative counterparts. After the election, which brought the Conservatives back to office with Joseph as Secretary of State for Industry, the 'guru' was often treated as a figure of fun by Opposition speakers. For example, in

October 1980, as the government's monetarist approach seemed to have damaged British industry without providing any strategy for restoration, the Labour leader Michael Foot compared Joseph to a magician who smashes a watch and then has to confess that he has forgotten the rest of the trick. It was a brilliant sally in itself, but Foot made it all the more effective by comparing the look on the magician's face to Joseph's habitual 'puzzled and forlorn' expression (*Hansard*, Vol. 991, col. 607, 29 October 1980). As Industry Secretary Joseph was torn between his belief that British industry needed radical restructuring and the advice of civil servants in his high-spending ministry (reinforced by his own compassion for the victims of unemployment). The inevitable result was an incoherent strategy which was difficult to sell either to the Tory 'wets' or to Joseph's 'dry' allies within the party; for their part, senior figures within the IEA were dismayed without being unduly surprised. Whatever the merits of the message, Joseph was incapable of presenting it to best advantage. In April 1980 he announced the appointment of the businessman Ian MacGregor as Chairman of British Steel, for a fee which amounted to almost £2 million. It was not only Labour MPs who heard the announcement with incredulity; but the adverse reaction seemed to take Joseph by surprise, and he ran through the remainder of his statement as if reciting a shopping list.

Although Joseph's spell at Industry is often credited with having paved the way for the successful privatisations of Margaret Thatcher's second term (1983–87), the credit really lay with junior ministers (notably Norman Tebbit) rather than the Secretary of State himself. After the 1983 election Joseph was moved to Education, where he was accused of precipitating a teachers' strike and lambasted by his own side for a premature attempt to introduce a system of loans, in place of grants, to support students in higher education. When Joseph left the government in May 1986 – ostensibly at a time of his own choosing, but more realistically through an arrangement which football clubs describe as a departure 'by mutual consent' – the main cause of surprise was that such an apparently hapless minister had lasted so long.

Why *did* Joseph survive in office for seven years? While his ministerial career under Thatcher can be defended in hindsight, at the time it seemed that he had failed badly both at Industry and Education; and there is evidence that by 1986 Thatcher had identified his lack of success in getting his message across to voters as a specific reason to replace him (Denham and Garnett, 2001: 404). However, if Thatcher had been clear-eyed and unsentimental where Joseph was concerned she would have denied him a specific departmental role in her 1979 government; even at that time there was plenty of evidence to suggest that he would fail to convey a crisp and coherent message to the party faithful, let alone to Parliament or the electorate at large. Obviously Thatcher felt she owed Joseph a great deal because he had been the first senior figure to present a reasoned case against the economic approach of the Heath government; but between Heath's deposition in 1975 and the 1979 general election she had given Joseph plenty of scope to prove his effectiveness, and in terms of the Commons, the party and the electorate in general he had palpably failed.

Ultimately Thatcher's loyalty to Joseph arose not from his set-piece speeches between the two 1974 general elections, but rather to a spin-off from this second 'crusade' on behalf of the free market. After his failure to become Conservative Party leader, Joseph accepted a series of speaking engagements in British universities – according to Joseph himself, 150 in total over the three-and-a-half years between Thatcher's elevation to the party leadership and the 1979 general election. Since universities in general were regarded as hotbeds of leftist sentiment, few senior Tories would have participated in such events; but Joseph actively courted them. His intention was to reason with the cream of British youth, in the hope of convincing the opinion-formers of the future that the free market approach was right. This was proselytising on a truly heroic scale. Joseph was often denied a proper hearing due to physical or verbal intimidation; later he recalled that six of the 150 engagements had to be cancelled. When Joseph was allowed to speak, he delivered an oration of around half an hour, and was happy to answer questions afterwards. The speech contained little beyond Joseph's new stock of ideological certainties, and presumably he quarried the same source when he replied to questions from the audience. None of the accounts of Joseph's performances across Britain's campuses suggest that the speaker captivated his listeners either with the originality of his message or the brilliance of his repartee with hecklers. However, for many Conservatives of all ages this series of speeches was a source of inspiration merely because Joseph was brave enough to confront such hostile audiences. This was particularly important for Conservative students, who could easily feel intimidated by the mood in British universities at the time. The content and delivery of Joseph's standard speech might not be extraordinary; but the *context* fulfilled all the criteria of notable oratory. Joseph's ethos was clearly sufficient to recruit a passionate audience; he had earned his reputation through his logos, as befitted a Fellow of All Souls College; and to his undergraduate admirers, at least, merely agreeing to speak before unruly students bestowed an element of pathos on his endeavours.

Conclusion

Sir Keith Joseph is not readily comparable with other Conservative orators discussed in this volume. Even those (like Margaret Thatcher) who lacked natural talent took deliberate steps to rectify this defect because they understood that the fate of their message depended on rhetorical style as well as logos. Joseph, by contrast, became a *less* inspiring orator after his supposed 'conversion to Conservatism' in 1974: an apparent epiphany which would have injected new fire into the oratory of most politicians left Joseph groping for the right words, whether in speeches or television interviews. As a result, it would not be unfair to characterise him as, at best, a mediocre orator who delivered several highly noteworthy speeches.

Joseph could rely on widespread publicity for his major speeches of the 1970s due to a series of circumstances that owed little to his merits as an orator. From the start of his parliamentary career his All Souls Fellowship had been an indispensable asset, and one suspects that his elevation to frontbench status by Harold Macmillan owed more to a presumption of intellectual ability than the prime minister's recognition of his speaking skills. His retention of frontbench status for more than two decades is explained by luck (under Heath) and sentiment (until Thatcher was forced to accept that her cherished friend would be better served by retirement).

Although as an intellectual in politics Keith Joseph bore some resemblance to Edmund Burke, the parallel cannot be sustained. Unlike the latter, Joseph was never faced with the necessity of giving up 'to party ... what was meant for mankind'. Burke's livelihood depended on the favour of his party leaders; by contrast, despite fluctuations in the fortunes of the family business Joseph could be confident that he would survive in reasonable comfort whether or not he sat on the Conservative frontbench. This was true despite the fact that, by his own admission, he lacked the talents of the entrepreneurs whose cause he espoused with such sincerity. One is faced with the paradoxical verdict that if Joseph had known poverty at first hand he might have been inspired to combine ethos, logos and pathos more effectively; but by the same token, it is equally possible that, in a media-driven age, an impoverished background would have prevented an individual as thoughtful, conscience-stricken and lacking in charisma as Keith Joseph from gaining a public hearing in the first place.

Notes

1 According to one eyewitness, when a youthful Gordon Brown stood for Rector of Edinburgh University his main opponent was seconded by a PhD student. When this unfortunate individual started a speech Brown's supporters started shouting 'intellectual!'; clearly they took this as the best means of discrediting him, and the message was not lost on Brown himself, who concealed his doctorate (awarded in 1982) during his political career. See http://subrosa-blonde.blogspot.co.uk/2010/01/gordon-brown-phd_19.html.

7

The oratory of Margaret Thatcher

Peter Dorey

Margaret Thatcher was one of the most charismatic and controversial party leaders and prime ministers in British political history, providing a fascinating academic case study in the art of oratory. Three particular characteristics strongly impacted upon her oratorical style and rhetoric; her background (a grocer's daughter), her grasp of empirical detail which enriched her speeches, and her particular interpretation of Conservative philosophy, each imbuing her oratory with a strong sense of proselytising and didacticism.

Upon her election to the Conservative leadership, she was not yet a 'Thatcherite'. According to Peter Riddell (1985: 10), 'Mrs Thatcher became leader of the Conservative Party in February 1975 principally because she was not Edward Heath, not because of a widespread commitment to her views'. Nonetheless, to those who listened carefully to her views, it was already apparent that she believed too many post-1945 Conservatives had tacitly accepted that 'the task of Conservatives as one of retreating gracefully before the Left's inevitable advance' (Thatcher, 1993: 104). Consequently, in spite of not yet being a fully fledged Thatcherite, much of her support in the 1975 party's leadership contest derived from Conservative MPs who already viewed her as the candidate most likely to lead the party in a different political direction (see, for example, Cowley and Bailey, 2000: 628; Lawson, 1992: 13).

During her time as Conservative Party leader and prime minister, Thatcher's speech-writers included the journalist Patrick Cosgrove, the Conservative politician John Selwyn Gummer, the academic Shirley Robin Letwin, the playwright Ronald Millar, the journalist and author, Ferdinand Mount, the journalist Matthew Parris, the author and one-time Director of the Centre for Policy Studies Alfred Sherman, and the broadcaster and author George Urban.

However, some of these speech-writers – as well as some of her admirers and supporters more generally (see, for example, Dale, 2010: 15) – subsequently acknowledged that Thatcher was not a natural orator. True, she made some memorable and controversial speeches, but many of these were the product of intensive preparation, re-drafting and rehearsal. Certainly, Anthony King noted 'the attention to detail ... lavished on her public speeches and her appearances in Parliament'. Writing when Thatcher was half-way through her premiership, King explained that:

'Hours are devoted to briefing her for Prime Minister's Question time', and she would also spend time 'polishing each phrase and paragraph of a speech to be delivered three weeks hence'. (King, 1985: 128. See, also, Urban, 1996: chapter 2)

Similarly, the authors of a Thatcher biography observed that: 'Her speech-writing sessions may spread over weeks and will last at least several days, often spilling into the small hours of the morning', albeit adding that: 'She is not an exciting stylist and has long relied on others for expressive words; the appeal "give me a phrase" regularly punctuates meetings' (Wapshott and Brock, 1983: 160).

It was not merely the actual drafting of the speeches which proved onerous, but also ensuring that Thatcher articulated them in the manner intended. Given that she was not a natural orator, their final presentation was sometimes rather stilted, particularly when Thatcher was unenthusiastic about what she was saying. For example, at the 1983 party conference, Thatcher was persuaded by John Selwyn Gummer to allay public concerns about the future of the NHS by declaring: 'The National Health Service is safe with us.' However, Ferdinand Mount wryly noted that the phrase was delivered 'in the listless drone of a hostage reading a statement prepared by her captor – which is what it was' (Mount, 2009: 331).

'One of us': Thatcher's use of ethos

During the first few years of her leadership, ethos was particularly important in enabling Thatcher to persuade both the Conservative Party and sections of the British electorate that her relatively humble social background rendered her more 'in touch with' the aspirations and anxieties of 'Middle England'. Consequently, she often used conference speeches and media interviews to allude to her lower-middle-class family background, and to emphasise that her political philosophy was 'born of the conviction which I learned in a small town, from a father who had a conviction approach' (quoted in Ogden, 1990: 192).

For example, in a television interview (Granada TV, 1975) during the Conservative Party leadership contest, Thatcher emphasised that her political stance was:

borne out by the development in my own life going to an ordinary state school, having no privileges at all, except perhaps the ones which count most, a good home background with parents who are very interested in their children and interested in getting on, and that's what I see as the kind of Conservative approach.

Some of Thatcher's references to her relatively humble social background were intended to contrast her origins and experiences with those of more privileged Labour politicians, evident by her first (1975) annual conference speech as Conservative leader, when she defended grammar school education, asserting that: 'A child from an ordinary family, as I was, could use it as a ladder, as an advancement.' She reiterated this two years later, telling conference delegates that: 'People from my sort of background needed grammar schools to compete with children from privileged homes, like Shirley Williams and Anthony Wedgewood Benn', an assertion which skilfully invoked pathos too, by identifying two Labour ministers who were especially disliked by Conservatives and implying that it was they who were privileged.

On another occasion, when appearing as a guest on BBC Radio 4's *Desert Island Discs*, she explained that:

> I think the toughest thing of my childhood was that my father taught me *very firmly indeed*: you do not follow the crowd because you're afraid of being different. You decide what to do yourself. If necessary, you lead the crowd but you never just follow. Oh, it was very hard indeed but my goodness me, it stood me in good stead. (BBC Radio 4, 1978, emphasis in original)

Even after she had been prime minister for several years, Thatcher sporadically referred to her background if it was relevant to the particular audience she was addressing, and would consequently facilitate pathos. For example in her 1985 address to the Scottish Conservative conference concerning higher rates which had just been introduced in response to revaluation – prompting the subsequent development of the Poll Tax – Thatcher declared that 'I know how commercial ratepayers feel; I spent my early years living above the shop' (Thatcher, 1985a). Again, ethos was melded with pathos, as Thatcher sought to establish an emotional connection and shared identity with her audience, citing her own experience, thereby convincing her audience that she understood their concerns and was on their side.

In the same year, in a television interview with Dr Miriam Stoppard, Thatcher explicitly cited her family background by referring to: 'very ordinary people like us', adding 'you live according to your means', this last assertion clearly a manifestation of pathos as Thatcher sought to establish an empathy and strong sense of shared experience with those who also lived modestly, and who were aggrieved at the 'greed' of trade unions and the financial profligacy of Labour authorities (Thatcher, 1985b).

'I share your anxieties. I share your aspirations': Thatcher's use of pathos

Alongside the utilisation of ethos to emphasise her relatively humble social background, Thatcher was highly adept at invoking pathos to establish an emotional connection with various audiences, in order to assure them that she understood and shared their anxieties. Such pathos was established by invoking various rhetorical devices and discourses.

One such aspect of Thatcher's attempts at establishing a shared identity with her audience entailed conveying a belief in 'family values', such as hard work, individual liberty, personal responsibility, property ownership, self-reliance, sobriety and thrift, all of which were depicted as the timeless values shared by the majority of ordinary British people, but especially the (lower) middle class and socially mobile working class, but which were denigrated and undermined by left-wing intellectuals and liberal *bien-pensants*.

Certainly, during the 1970s, there was increasing resentment in Britain, especially among much of the *petit bourgeoisie*, against those deemed responsible for the country's economic, political and social problems – in times of crisis, many people are readily encouraged to look for scapegoats upon whom blame can be heaped, namely 'greedy' trade unions, the 'socialist' Labour government, employment (protection) legislation, punitive taxation, high inflation, 'exorbitant' wage increases, a burgeoning public sector, feminism/sexual liberation (undermining the family and marital fidelity), 'too much' immigration, the repercussions of the (1960s) 'permissiveness revolution', 'do-gooders' empathising with criminals and other law-breakers and the general undermining of the work ethic caused by an 'over-generous' social security system (see, for example, Hutber, 1977: chapter 2). While the ire of much of the population was directed at these targets, it was the entrepreneurial or thrifty middle class – viewing itself as the bedrock of British society – which often felt particularly aggrieved, believing they were under siege and that their own survival depended the survival of Britain itself.

Thatcher expressed enormous sympathy with these grievances, for in numerous speeches, she explicitly cited the plight of small businesses, an early example of which was a speech in Glasgow, just ten days after her election as Conservative leader, in which she argued that 'in no field has the vindictiveness of Socialist policies been more apparent than in their effect on small business ... the family business has been the backbone of commerce and industry'. Hence her rhetorical question at the Conservative Party's 1977 conference: 'What's the point of building up your savings or your own business if they're [Labour] going to take it all away from you?', in response to which she pledged that Conservatives 'want to hold out to the enterprising businessman a reward which matches the risks of building up a firm'. Thatcher reiterated this theme at the following year's conference, when she castigated 'Labour's bias against men and women who seek to better themselves and their families. Ordinary people – small businessmen, the self-employed – are not to be allowed to rise on their own'.

In various speeches during her premiership, she also drew comparisons between her government's economic policies and living within one's means or prudent financial management, characteristic of most small businesses. Hence Thatcher's insistence, in her 1980 speech to the Conservative Central Council, that 'all of us have cash limits. Every family, every independent company, every corner shop faces the same blunt truth: cash is limited'. In the same speech, she suggested that when her critics or sceptics complained about the government's 'draconian' cuts in public expenditure, they should realise that these were 'like the necessary economies which every family is called on to make in time of trouble'.

In delineating the sundry problems that Britain apparently faced, and identifying the apparent causes or 'enemies within', another aspect of Thatcher's pathos was to depict herself as on the side of ordinary British people, a strategy that was inextricably linked to ethos, whereby she had emphasised her humble origins. This provided the basis for much of her 'populist' appeal, whereby she explicitly aligned herself with those 'hard-working' or 'law-abiding' citizens, 'moderates' or the 'silent majority', and who were therefore contrasted favourably against 'extremists' and 'militants'. For example, she condemned the picketing by the National Union of Mineworkers as 'mob rule', and alleged many of the strikers were 'against democracy and the rule of law' (House of Commons Debates, 6th series, Vol. 72, col. 435). By contrast, the miners who refused to support the strike were feted as brave and courageous in defying the 'bullies' on the picket lines in exercising their 'right to work'.

Meanwhile, although all party leaders routinely use the pronouns 'our' and 'we' when addressing their colleagues and supporters (and *inter alia* aiming to appeal to the wider electorate), to establish or reinforce a sense of shared affinity, Thatcher's use of these pronouns was often prefixed to nouns and verbs which highlighted the bravery, courage or determination of like-minded Conservatives in adhering to the 'right' principles and pursuing the 'correct' policies: 'we will not be cowed'; 'our faith'; 'we are sticking to our policy'; 'our cause'; 'we have a duty to ...'; 'our new strength and resolve'; 'We are made of sterner stuff ...'; 'our great purpose'; 'we intend to fight'; 'our perseverance'; 'We do not shrink from it'.

Such rhetoric and phrases invited the audience to put their faith in Thatcher herself, for the clear signal was that, unlike her predecessors, she was leading a crusade from which she would not be deflected or defeated. This was precisely what many Conservatives had long wanted to hear, having hitherto abandoned any real expectation of being led by someone who genuinely understood and shared their frustrations and aspirations. These Conservatives were persuaded (or allowed themselves to be persuaded) by the rhetoric that she was 'one of us', and would rescue them, and thus Britain, from socialism.

One academic expert on linguistics notes that by deploying such 'conflict metaphors', and drawing a clear demarcation between the values and virtues of Britishness being defended by Conservative policies, Thatcher portrayed herself 'as the heroine who struggles against an imagined enemy' (Charteris-Black, 2011: 90).

'Common sense' conservatism

Part of Thatcher's pathos entailed persuading her audience that the Labour Party was dangerously dogmatic and doctrinaire, whilst her values were merely 'common sense'. Indeed, she used her first major parliamentary speech as prime minister to declare that 'the [Labour] Opposition have allowed Socialist ideology to blot out common sense' (House of Commons Debates, 5th series, Vol.967, col.75). This emphasis on 'common sense' conservatism was a recurring theme throughout Thatcher's premiership, exemplified in her speech to the party's 1981 conference, when she insisted that her government's controversial policies to curb inflation and restore sound money were simply 'sheer common sense', while a few weeks later, in the Debate on the Address (Queen's Speech), she insisted that: 'Sound common sense polices are as vital to a nation coming out of recession as they are to one that is still in its grip ... Common sense has prevailed' (House of Commons Debates, 6th series, Vol. 12, col. 23).

Meanwhile, during a BBC *Panorama* interview with Sir Robin Day in 1987, Thatcher outlined her political goals, but insisted that although 'People call those things Thatcherism; they are, in fact, fundamental common sense' (BBC, 1987), a perspective she reiterated a few months later at the 1987 Scottish Conservative Party conference, when she insisted that it 'doesn't strike them [ordinary British people] as a political dogma, but simple common sense'. This message was repeated in a 1989 speech in her Finchley constituency where she explained that 'Thatcherism didn't start with Thatcher. I pulled everything that was best out of the character of a people, everything that was commons sense and everything that was courage. And that is really how it works'.

Use of religious allegories and moral absolutes

Her rhetoric variously incorporated biblical references and religious imagery, as exemplified by a 1979 election campaign speech in Cardiff, when Thatcher (1979a) famously emphasised her rejection of 'consensus politics' by declaring that:

> The Old Testament prophets didn't go out into the highways saying, 'Brothers, I want consensus.' They said, 'This is my faith and my vision! This is what I passionately believe!' And they preached it. We have a message. Go out, preach it, practise it, fight for it.

Later the same year, in her first speech to the Lord Mayor's Banquet as prime minister, Thatcher (1979b) insisted that although her government faced 'a herculean task ... we are not faint-hearted pilgrims. We will not be deflected by a stony path'.

Many of her speeches also contained allusions to 'good' versus 'evil', such as the interview with Dr Stoppard, when Thatcher (1985a) asserted that 'we have a choice ... between good and evil'. She reiterated this perspective in a speech to the General Assembly of the Church of Scotland, declaring 'from the beginning man has been endowed by God with the fundamental right to choose between good and evil' (Thatcher, 1988).

Elsewhere, Thatcher criticised the socialist 'fallacy' that man's imperfectibility could be eradicated 'if we get our social institutions right; if we provide properly for education, health and all other branches of social welfare'. Regardless of such material progress she insisted: 'The Devil is still with us, recording his successes in the crime figures and in all the other maladies of this society', and added that 'As a Christian, I am bound to shun Utopias on this earth' (Thatcher, 1978a).

Of course, probably the most famous example of religious content or allusion in Thatcher's speeches was her peroration outside 10 Downing Street after the victory in 1979, when using *anaphora* she purportedly quoted St Francis of Assisi:

> Where there is discord, may we bring harmony.
> Where there is error, may we bring truth.
> Where there is doubt, may we bring faith.
> And where there is despair, may we bring hope.

However, doubts were subsequently raised about whether St Francis himself had ever uttered the words, leading a senior (One Nation) Conservative critic, Ian Gilmour (1992: 268), to ask acerbically: 'Was the sentiment she expressed as bogus as the source?' This disdain was evidently shared by another One Nation critic, James Prior (1986: 113), for he averred that 'quoting St Francis of Assisi could scarcely have been less apt, and from her lips were the most awful humbug: it was totally at odds with Margaret's belief in conviction politics'.

With regard to Thatcher's attempts to equate her mode of conservatism with Christianity and traditional morality, even one of her closest ministerial colleagues, Nicholas Ridley (1991: 18), felt that she was sometimes 'over-ambitious in trying to make this direct link between Christian morality and her political beliefs', and added that 'I would not seek to justify my views about economic or social or foreign policy on the back of Christ's teachings'.

Thatcher's use of humour

Thatcher's critics have viewed her as so ideologically driven and politically dour that she was bereft of a sense of humour. Yet such a characterisation overlooks the extent to which she often used mockery to deride her internal and external critics, while endearing those more closely to her, thereby strengthening their affinity. In other words, by injecting humour into speeches which were primarily manifestations of logos, she also further facilitated pathos by encouraging her supporters to laugh with her in mocking her opponents and critics. For example, in the parliamentary debate on the 1974–75 Finance Bill, the Labour Chancellor, Denis Healey, derided Thatcher for being 'La Pasionaria of privilege', to which she retorted: 'Some Chancellors are macro-economic. Other Chancellors are fiscal. This one is just plain cheap' (House of Commons Debates, 5th series, Vol. 884, cols. 1553, 1554).

Meanwhile, in her speech to the Conservatives' 1977 annual conference, Thatcher skilfully combined criticisms of 'excessive' government expenditure, high taxation and welfare provision by observing that: 'There's one hand-out that people really want today. That's the Government's hand out of their pocket.' In the same speech, she also attracted much mirth by ridiculing the recently established parliamentary pact between the Liberal Party and the Labour government, suggesting that 'instead of a government with steel in its backbone, we've got one with Steel in its pocket'.

Of course, one of Thatcher's most famous 'humorous' remarks was at the party's 1980 conference, when she was under pressure from some of her ministerial colleagues to change her government's economic policies and adopt a different approach. Her response was to advise her critics: 'You turn if you want to. The lady's not for turning.'

However, many of these were scripted for her, which meant, according to one of her biographers, that the humour was sometimes rather 'laboured', to the extent of being 'the least convincing part of her speeches, because she never sounded as if she understood them' (Campbell, 2000: 349). Indeed, the 1980 'You turn ...' line was inserted by her main speech-writer, Ronald Millar, but he was then exasperated by the fact that Thatcher had to rehearse it several times in order to get the intonation right, and thereby ensure that she heavily emphasised the 'You' at the start of the sentence; if it was all read in the same intonation, the aural impact would have been lost (Mount, 2009: 330).

On another occasion, after the newly formed Liberal Democrats had adopted a soaring bird as their logo, it was suggested that Thatcher mock this in her Conservative conference speech by citing Monty Python's famous 'dead parrot' sketch; 'This parrot has ceased to be. It has shuffled off its mortal coil ... This is an ex-parrot'. Not being familiar with the surreal comedy of Monty Python, Thatcher took a lot of persuading, and then considerable coaching to get the delivery and intonation correct. Just before going on to the conference platform from where the speech was to be delivered, Thatcher turned to her entourage and enquired: 'Monty Python – are you sure he's one of us?' (Whittingdale, 2012: 246).

Yet even if her articulation was somewhat stilted, and she herself did not always fully appreciate or understand the humour, her audience invariably found Thatcher's jokes and witticisms highly amusing, which thus further endeared her to them.

'There is no alternative': Thatcher's use of logos

Because of her logos, Thatcher appealed to a much wider audience while also enhancing her own credibility as a party leader and prime minister. She proved particularly skilful at marshalling an array of empirical evidence, philosophical premises and arguments to attack the policies of her opponents, and thereby elicit support for her particular version of conservatism. Many of her speeches, both to Conservative audiences and in the Commons, were broad-ranging and cited a plethora of statistics, yet they were rarely rambling.

On the contrary, Thatcher's oratory was remarkable for the manner in which she linked a variety of apparently disparate problems, and then deftly wove them together both to illustrate their inter-connections, identify the underlying causes or those she deemed responsible, and thence to argue that only a particular political response and set of policies would solve them. In this regard, the description by one of her main speech-writers, Ronald Millar of her 1975 conference speech, could be applied to many of her other speeches during the next fifteen years: 'The tour d'horizon went on, wide-ranging, but crisp and taut and cohesive. There was the ring of overwhelming conviction' (Millar, 1993: 239).

Logos aided Thatcher's election to the leadership in 1975 because many Conservative MPs had been greatly impressed by her parliamentary performance when attacking Labour's 1974–75 Finance Bill. In replying on behalf of the Conservative Opposition in the second reading debate, and then serving on the standing committee, Thatcher adroitly utilised logos to attack its sundry tax increases and the allegedly disastrous impact these would have on British entrepreneurs.

In these attacks, Thatcher did not rely simply on condemning Labour's penchant for higher taxes but displayed a more sophisticated awareness of different types of taxation, and the likely deleterious consequences of increasing them. In so doing, Thatcher displayed a clear grasp of statistical data and other factual material, while also placing many current and projected fiscal figures in historical context, illustrating how damaging the tax increases had been to the economy (House of Commons Debates, 5th series, Vol. 883, cols. 1383–98).

Indeed, the Labour MP who spoke immediately after Thatcher confessed to being 'much impressed by her fluency and by the logic of many of the arguments she put forward' (House of Commons Debates, 5th series, Vol. 883, col. 1398), while James Prior (1986: 99) averred that 'Margaret's stature in the Party has been enhanced by her performance at the despatch box'. Similarly, another Conservative colleague, Cecil Parkinson, observed that 'she made an outstanding speech ... She'd obviously mastered the subject and it was a big turning point for her' (quoted in Young and Sloman, 1986: 31). This grasp of empirical and statistical detail, and the concomitant adeptness with which she couched it in comparative or historical context, was to become a key aspect of her logos.

Logos was important to Thatcher because she was not merely seeking to persuade her audiences or the wider electorate that Conservative policies were better or more efficient than those of Labour, but because she fervently believed that she was engaged in nothing less than a battle of ideas. Indeed, Thatcher used this very phrase when, after being elected as Conservative leader, she informed the Conservative Central Council that: 'We also need to involve our friends in the universities, colleges, industry and the mass media. That is where our philosophy and our policies for a free society must be renewed and retold. That is where the Battle of Ideas must be fought – and won.' The reference to 'our friends' in universities, colleges and the mass media was highly significant because part of Thatcher's critique of post-war British politics was that much of academia and the media had been colonised by the left, which used these positions influence to promote socialism and egalitarianism.

During her subsequent premiership, she continued these attacks, saying in 1985 to the Conservative Central Council 'all of us ... who believe passionately in the individual freedom of man go over to the offensive in the supreme battle of ideas'. It was her determination to wage this 'battle' that had previously prompted Thatcher to tell the Conservative philosophy group, 'We must have an ideology. The other side have got an ideology ... we must have one too' (quoted in Young, 1989: 406).

Thatcher's logos was instrumental in promoting the image of a serious polit-ical leader who had intellectual *gravitas* and a remarkable grasp of detail, yet who could also articulate complex philosophical premises in a clear and persuasive manner. Indeed, on one occasion, Thatcher explicitly linked her skilful deploy-ment of facts and figures to her professional background, explaining that 'with a mixture of a scientific training and a certain period spent in the revenue bar [sic] and on dealing with Treasury matters, one has ... to adduce a mass of evidence to support the case which one is trying to put' (Thatcher, 1975a); her ethos thus underpinned her logos.

She later alluded to her pre-parliamentary background to explain how she sub-sequently developed ideas and arguments, emphasising that as a scientist, 'you look at the facts, and you deduce your conclusions', while as a lawyer, 'you learn your law ... You judge your evidence' (quoted in *The New Yorker*, 10 February 1986). This point was emphasised in one of the many biographies of Thatcher, with the authors noting that: 'She marshalled huge quantities of statistics with the strict logic of the lawyer and chemist', which were then articulated with 'vigour and certainty of deliv-ery' (Wapshott and Brock, 1983: 162).

Notwithstanding that 'facts' and 'evidence' are not irrefutable or value-free, but have to be interpreted, much of Thatcher's logos evinces this scientific and court-room methodology, particularly her speeches denouncing the character of post-1945 British politics, and the consequent problems. As noted in the chapter's introduc-tion, one of the features which had stood Thatcher in such good stead in the 1975 Conservative leadership contest had been her mastery of detail in her speeches. Thatcher's ability to support or oppose a policy by marshalling an eclectic range of comparative data and empirical 'facts' to advance an argument was a skill which she successfully deployed on innumerable occasions.

When making such speeches in Opposition, Thatcher was naturally aiming to persuade her audience that previous and current policies were ineffective, and even exacerbating the maladies they were intended to remedy. This in turn was supposed to lead logically to the conclusion that a wholly new set of Conservative policies was vitally necessary, thereby breaking with the politics and policies which had prevailed since 1945.

However, whereas many academics argued that Britain in the 1970s was experi-encing a crisis of capitalism, Thatcher insisted that 'what we face today is not a crisis of capitalism, but of socialism' (Thatcher, 1975b; see also Thatcher, 1976; Thatcher, 1978a). This is why it is important to emphasise that for Thatcher, the logos aspect of so many of her speeches was about persuading audiences that the intellectual basis or ideological premises which underpinned many previous and current pol-icies were erroneous. In this context, Thatcher recalls that when her first conference speech was being written, 'I told my speech-writers that I was not going to make just an economic speech. The economy had gone wrong because something else had gone wrong spiritually and philosophically' (Thatcher, 1995: 305).

Much of what 'had gone wrong', she argued, could be attributed to the intellectual influence of the left in post-1945 Britain, and the extent to which socialists had set the political agenda. She lamented the dominance of the left, arguing even Conservatives 'have been in danger of allowing our thinking to be dominated by socialism to a point where we even define our own position in terms of how, where and why we differ from socialism and socialists' (Thatcher, 1977).

However, following the victory in 1979, Thatcher began claiming that 'the Socialists had now lost the intellectual ascendancy they had claimed since the War' (speech to the 1922 Committee, quoted in *The Financial Times*, 19 July 1979), and by 1987, she was triumphantly informing the Scottish Conservative Party conference that whereas: 'For much of the 20th Century, it seemed that Socialism was advancing and Conservatism in retreat ... Today, it is Socialism which is in retreat and Conservatism which is advancing.'

Throughout the 1980s, Thatcher routinely displayed her mastery of empirical evidence and statistical data to 'prove' the success of her governments' policies, and how these had apparently led to the economic renaissance of Britain after the steady decline of the 1960s and 1970s. To give but one example, in her 1988 speech in the Debate on the Queen's Speech, Thatcher declared that:

> Ten years ago, 38 per cent of pensioners were in the bottom one fifth of national income. Today, only 24 per cent of pensioners are in the bottom fifth ... Domestic electricity costs 8.1 per cent, less in real terms today than it did five years ago ... We are now in the eighth successive year of economic growth, averaging over 3 per cent. In terms of output per ... after two whole decades – the 1960s and 1970s – when the United Kingdom was at the bottom of the growth league, in the 1980s we have climbed to the top of the table.
>
> Unemployment has now fallen for 27 months in succession. Over the last year, it has been falling in all regions, and the unemployment rate has fallen faster than in any other major industrial country ... manufacturing output is at its highest ever level ... total public spending, although it is at record levels, now accounts for less than 40 per cent. of national income – for the first time in over 20 years ... This year the number of small businesses is increasing at a rate of nearly 1,000 a week, and since 1980 manufacturing productivity has been growing at over 5 per cent. a year. Under the last Labour Government it averaged only just over 1 per cent a year ...
>
> For the public sector, the plans set out in the Autumn Statement provide an additional £2.25 billion of capital spending next year, taking the total to over £25 billion ... In the 12 months to June this year, the value of takeovers by overseas companies in this country was £2,900 million. In the same period, British businesses made over 550 overseas acquisitions, with a value of £13,700 million ... Investment by the private sector has been growing rapidly. Total private investment in 1987 – some £60 billion – was over 15 per cent; higher in real terms than in any year under the last Labour Government. Now, in the first three quarters of 1988, investment by the manufacturing, construction, distribution and financial industries is 13.5 per cent higher than it was in 1987. (House of Commons Debates, 6th series, Vol. 142, cols. 19–23)

Needless to say, such speeches were frequently embellished with mockery and ridicule of the criticisms and policies advanced by Neil Kinnock's Labour Opposition, and allegations about how dangerous and disastrous these would be if they were ever enacted. Labour's policies, Thatcher regularly claimed, would either bankrupt the country, or turn Britain into a Soviet-style totalitarian state, as every political problem and inevitable policy failure prompted yet more state intervention.

However, political arguments are rarely won solely on the basis of economic statistics or empirical evidence alone; they need also to persuade the audience, and thereby secure agreement and support. Consequently, there were other aspects of Thatcher's logos which were simultaneously intended to generate support for her particular mode of conservatism and its radical policies while also strengthening her pathos.

Binary opposites and antithesis

One of the most notable characteristics of Thatcher's oratory was her construction of 'binary opposites' and creation of *antithesis*. This, of course, was a variant on her distinction between 'good' and 'evil', and entailed such polarities as liberty versus equality, individualism versus collectivism, wealth creation versus national bankruptcy, etc., with the Conservatives always on the side of the former in each pair, and her political opponents on the side of the latter. Hence Thatcher's apparent conviction that 'There Is No Alternative', and her repeated insistence that her principles and policies were mere common sense. Indeed, in a 1978 speech to East Anglian Conservatives, Thatcher reportedly 'felt the majority of people in Britain were Conservative at heart. Yet they did not vote Conservative – yet' (*Eastern Daily Press*, 11 March 1978).

However, another manifestation of Thatcher's use of binary opposites was the occasional use of counter-intuition to secure support for particular policies, whereby she argued that instead of policies 'A' and 'B' being mutually exclusive or diametrically opposed, they were actually dependent on each other. For example, to those of her critics who claimed that the Conservatives' desire for curbs on immigration were racist, or at least would exacerbate racial tensions, she would insist that 'racial harmony is inseparable from control of the numbers coming in'; only if the public was persuaded that immigration was being strictly controlled would hostility or suspicion towards ethnic minorities be reduced. In other words, Thatcher promoted tough immigration controls as a measure which would actually reduce racism and benefit ethnic minorities already resident in Britain.

Meanwhile, Thatcher occasionally insisted that the government was not consciously choosing to prioritise the reduction of inflation over the reduction of unemployment, because the two were symbiotically linked. 'Inflation is the parent of unemployment', a point she elaborated on at the party's conference a year later, when she explained that 'it is not a question of choosing between the conquest of inflation and the conquest of unemployment. Indeed … we are fighting unemployment by fighting inflation'.

Similarly, to those who complained about her apparent authoritarianism, as evinced by her advocacy of strong law-and-order and apparent scepticism towards civil liberties, Thatcher repeatedly insisted that increasing the disciplinary powers of the state and the police was not inimical to a free society, but a necessary component of it, for as she also explained to delegates at the Conservatives' 1978 conference, 'We believe that to keep society free the law must be upheld'. In the same year, in a speech to the Bow Group, Thatcher approvingly quoted John Locke's observation that: 'Where Law disappears, tyranny begins.' The same argument was reiterated in her speech to the 1985 conference, when she insisted that 'without the law, there can be no freedom'.

Minorities versus the majority

Another aspect of Thatcher's logos, albeit one which was closely linked to the notion of 'binary opposites' or *antithesis*, was her tendency to identify minorities whose objectives or activities were a threat either to Britain's material interests, or to the views of the majority (either in society in general, or in particular organisations). The identification of such minorities was rendered relatively easy for Thatcher during the 1980s, partly because of various bitter industrial disputes involving trade unions, and because of the rise of the 'loony Left' and associated social movements whose values were markedly at variance with Thatcher's own traditional 'Victorian values'.

Certainly, Thatcher's stance towards trade unionism in general exemplified her populist device of distinguishing between the 'moderate majority' and the 'militant minority', so that when her governments passed six laws to curb union power, tilting the balance of power in industry back towards employers, these reforms were depicted as 'democratising' the unions, and 'handing them back to their members'. This classic Thatcherite distinction was clear in her response, in a television interview, to a question about opposition from the trade unions to these reforms:

> You said that my supporters liked the [1980 Employment] Bill … [but that] The Trade Unions don't. I think some of the Trade Union Leaders don't, but many, many, many members of Trade Unions are fully behind us in that Bill … you know, every opinion survey shows that the majority of Trade Unionists are behind us in what we're trying to do. (Thatcher, 1980)

Elsewhere, Thatcher articulated the apparent bewilderment and anger of the 'silent majority' against the 'loony Left' during the mid-1980s, as exemplified by her speech at the 1987 conference, when she fulminated that: 'Children who need to be able to count and multiply are learning anti-racist mathematics … Children who need to be taught to respect traditional moral values are being taught that they have an inalienable right to be gay'. More generally, with reference to high-spending Labour local authorities, Thatcher suggested to MPs that: 'It is a curious sort of freedom that argues that the profligacy of the few should be paid for by the sacrifices of the many' (House of Commons Debates, 6th series, Vol. 12, col. 24).

Meanwhile, in a 1984 speech which she presented to the Carlton Club, Thatcher even argued that 'consensus' was frequently lauded by those who simply wanted a quiet life, which meant a determined or vocal minority was able to impose its will on the majority, because the latter's desire for a quiet life meant it was less inclined to stand up for its own beliefs and interests. This, she insisted, was not a genuine consensus, but coercion of the majority. She insisted 'The concept of fair play – a British way of saying "respect for the rules" – must not be used to allow the minority to overbear the tolerant majority'. In such circumstances, she insisted: 'That is when we have to stand up and be counted, that is when we have to do what we believe to be right' (Thatcher, 1984).

Here, again, we see Thatcher melding logos with pathos, utilising (apparently incontrovertible) empirical evidence and logical argumentation to reflect and articulate the anxieties and grievance of 'ordinary' British people, and further persuade them that she and the Conservative government were 'out there' with them, and on their side. Moreover, such rhetoric was also intended to reinforce the image of Thatcher as the 'warrior' leader who would take up the cudgels on behalf of those majorities who were seemingly being bullied or manipulated by self-serving or politically motivated minorities.

Identifying enemies, domestic and foreign

Many of the minorities referred to above were portrayed, or even directly labelled, as 'the enemy within' because their activities and/or ideological objectives were deemed to constitute a serious threat to individual liberty, a market economy and parliamentary democracy. The main 'enemy within' she identified were left-wing trade unions and their leaders, the apparent Marxist infiltration of the Labour Party during the late 1970s and much of the early 1980s, and 'loony Left' local councils. The Campaign for Nuclear Disarmament (CND) was also denounced on various occasions, and its loyalty or patriotism impugned. Shortly after being elected as Conservative leader, and with specific reference to 'extremists' in the Labour Party and the trade unions, Thatcher warned that: 'These dangerous men … the extreme left … know exactly where they hope to go and what they want to achieve. It is nothing less than the destruction of private enterprise in this country and the enforcement of state control and direction in every aspect of our lives' (Thatcher, 1975b), while during the 1979 election campaign, she referred to the 'many similarities between the Labour and Communist manifestoes' (Thatcher, 1979a).

On other occasions, Thatcher insinuated links and similarities between the Labour left and the Soviet Union. For example, in a 1978 speech to the Bow Group, she claimed that: 'The Labour Left has also shown itself, astonishingly, more friendly to Russia even than some of the European communist parties' (Thatcher, 1978b). This yoked together an alleged domestic threat with a perceived foreign one. Indeed, Thatcher variously posited a link between domestic and foreign 'enemies' more generally, alleging that:

> At one end of the spectrum are the terrorist gangs within our borders, and the terrorist states which finance and arm them. At the other are the Hard Left operating inside our system, conspiring to use union power and the apparatus of local government to break, defy and subvert the law ... the Fascist Left. (Thatcher, 1984)

Thatcher spoke forcefully of the need to be 'strong enough to protect our people from wreckers at home and enemies abroad' (Thatcher, 1979c). As Robin Harris observes: 'Domestic and foreign policy appear as a seamless whole, in which the same truths are relevant, and usually the same enemies – in slightly different guises – are present' (Harris, 1997: xi–xii).

Thatcher's style of oratorical delivery

Having thus far examined Thatcher's oratory in terms of three categories, ethos, pathos and logos, we need briefly to consider the manner or style which she variously adopted for her speeches – *how* she delivered them.

The first point to emphasise, as noted by former director of the Conservative Research Department, Robin Harris, is the 'didactic quality' of many of her speeches. She was 'seeking to educate and persuade, not simply seduce or beguile' (Harris, 1997: xii). She perceived herself to be leading both the Conservative Party and Britain in general away from the philosophy and policies which had prevailed since 1945. Thatcher believed that only through pursuing a new path could national salvation and the renewal of Britain be achieved. This required that the Conservative Party itself was steered away from the consensual and paternalistic approach which it had misguidedly pursued for most of this period.

Following on from this was the extent to which Thatcher's speeches conveyed a sense of crisis and urgency, necessitating tough decisions and a willingness to stand firm in the face of criticism. Through 'binary opposites', Thatcher's speeches frequently painted an apocalyptic image of Britain, and a dystopian future if it did not immediately change political direction. In turn, this provided Thatcher with both the context and the justification for peppering her speeches with allusions to combat and biblical notions of good versus evil.

Another feature of some of Thatcher's keynote speeches was her use of *anaphora* to emphasise the *antithesis* between the stance of the Conservatives compared to

Labour on sundry policy issues. This rhetorical technique was particularly evident in her 1984 speech to the Conservative Central Council, when she declared:

> On high-spending councils, Labour supports the town hall bosses. We stand up for the ratepayers.
>   On de-nationalisation, Labour defends state monopoly. We stand up for the customers.
>   On trade union reform, Labour sides with the trade union bosses. We stand up for the members.
>   On council house sales, Labour loves to be the Landlord. We stand up for the tenants.
>   On taxes, Labour wants more of your money. We stand up for the taxpayers.

Another use of *anaphora* was evident in a 1987 speech, also to the Conservative Central Council, when Thatcher criticised the alleged brainwashing influence of the 'loony Left' in education, in defiance of the wishes of parents:

> Parents don't want their children banned from taking part in competitive games.
>   Parents don't want what is called 'positive images for gays' being forced on innocent children.
>   Parents don't want their children indoctrinated by Labour's so-called 'peace studies'.

Meanwhile, in her 1986 speech to the Conservatives' annual conference, Thatcher used *parison* in a speech which attacked the Labour Party's official policies, alleging that:

> What the Labour Party of today wants is:
>   Housing – municipalised;
>   Industry – nationalised;
>   The police service – politicised;
>   The judiciary – radicalised;
>   Union membership – tyrannised;
>   And above all – and most serious of all – our defences neutralised.

This also illustrates the earlier point made by Ronald Millar about Thatcher's ability to deliver speeches (or sections within them) in a manner which was 'crisp and taut and cohesive'. Certainly, many of Thatcher's speeches beyond Parliament were constructed of relatively short, emphatic assertions, facilitating rhythmic delivery.

Conclusion

In terms of ethos, Thatcher was readily able to invoke her lower-middle-class family background to establish an empathy with more *petit-bourgeois* Conservative Party members, particularly when addressing the party's annual conferences. 'She knew this audience, they were her people. She spoke their language as no one else, and year after year she gave them the reassurance they craved' (Millar, 1993: 284). Similarly, one of Thatcher's most eminent academic biographers noted that 'she was in her element among the small shopkeepers and disciplinarian matrons who typified the representatives, for she was unashamedly one of them. She spoke their language and shared their concerns' (Campbell, 2000: 347). Yet this ethos also enabled her to allude to her background and personal experiences in order to 'connect' with aspirational sections of British society, for she could portray herself as the personification of social mobility attained through hard work and deferred gratification.

This in turn underpinned much of her pathos. Thatcher's speeches had a sense of shared identity and common experience with her audience belief in 'family values', hard work, initiative, responsibility, sobriety and thrift. In depicting these qualities as 'common sense' Conservative values, Thatcher assiduously culti-vated her image of being 'out there' with ordinary British people against the lib-eral 'establishment' in academia, the media and the trade unions. In this respect, Thatcher's pathos was inextricably linked to her populism. Especially notable here was Thatcher's frequent use of the pronouns 'we' or 'our', rather than 'you' or 'your' to establish a direct connection with the audience, and persuade them that she was 'one of us'.[1]

Yet one notable aspect of Thatcher's populist pathos was that she imbibed the academic theories of New Right economists and philosophers like Friedman and Hayek, while depicting herself as anti-intellectual by implying intellectuals were usually left-wing and advocates of alien, non-British ideas – even though Hayek was Austrian. For example, she promoted the principles of monetarism to the electorate by comparing Britain's economy to a household budget, insisting both needed to be managed with care and restraint; spending should be frugal and borrowing mini-mised, and preferably avoided altogether.

In a polemical essay on Thatcher's (in)famous 1988 speech to the General Assembly of the Church of Scotland, Jonathan Raban argued that:

> Mrs Thatcher likes to get down to what she calls 'the nitty gritty' ... she lets them [her audience] know what's what in language more suited to the instruction of five year olds.
>   It is exactly this manner that makes her beloved to so many people. *She* is not afraid to go among the intellectuals ... the lah-di-dah classes with airy-fairy ideas, and get down to brass tacks with them in the sort of term you would use if your only regular reading was the [*Daily*] *Express*. She cuts fancy folk down to size. (Raban, 1989: 42–3, emphasis in original)

However, Thatcher also appealed to a much wider audience by virtue of her logos, given that she was adept at using both logic and philosophical premises to attack her political opponents to advance the case for a new mode of conservatism and style of political leadership. In so doing, Thatcher reduced the options facing the British people to a series of binary opposites: good/evil, liberty/totalitarianism, individualism/collectivism, etc., with the Conservatives always on the side of the former in each pair. Hence her conviction that 'There Is No Alternative', and that her philosophy, principles and policies were mere common sense; only those who were mischievous, misguided, malevolent or Marxists could possibly disagree!

Notes

1 'One of us' was a question apparently asked by Thatcher vis-à-vis her ministers and other close colleagues, by which she meant 'do they share my particular political values, objectives and vision of conservatism; do they support my radical policies and objectives?' So for example, Sir Keith Joseph, Nicholas Ridley and Norman Tebbit were undoubtedly 'one of us', whereas Ian Gilmour, Michael Heseltine and James Prior were certainly not.

8

The oratory of Michael Heseltine

Mark Bennister

Michael Heseltine may never have been Conservative party leader or prime minister, but he was always in demand as a speaker. Oratory was an essential part of his political persona and kept him firmly in the public eye. Heseltine was a flamboyant and exuberant performer. He was acutely aware of how performative qualities could generate support and woo audiences. However his rhetorical skill, confidence and flamboyance alienated many within the Conservative Party, and beyond the Parliamentary Party he never managed to transcend the caricature of Tarzan – the wild man of the political jungle – to be regarded as a credible leader. His oratory, rousing at party conferences, was individualistic and masked his policy positions which proved at odds with the Thatcherites in the party. Heseltine eschewed low-level political schmoozing in favour of high rhetoric, overly confident that his 'big beast' status would be enough to convince sceptics. Ultimately, though, his persuasive tools and grand oratory were not sufficient to sway the doubters, as he found himself on the wrong side of too many internal policy debates.

This chapter examines Michael Heseltine's performance in the three political arenas of the party conference, Parliament and the wider public arena. Although this chapter takes a broad view of Heseltine's oratory during his political career, there is a focus on three key speeches: the 1981 'Liverpool riots' conference speech; the 1985 'Ponting' parliamentary speech; and the 1986 'resignation' statement. Analysis of these speeches is augmented by an interview conducted with Lord Heseltine on 9 October 2012.

Michael Heseltine was a different type of Conservative politician. Although president of the Oxford Union, he did not walk straight into Conservative politics. Rather, on leaving Oxford he had to carve out a business career from a precarious financial position. Heseltine had managed to convert his ailing business interests into the highly successful Haymarket Publishing Group between 1962 and 1970. His wealth was based on his own business decisions and he was very much a self-made millionaire, prompting a degree of snobbery from many of his contemporaries – as one comment typical of the time demonstrates: 'The trouble with Michael is that he had to buy all his own furniture' (Crick, 1997: 1).

Heseltine entered Parliament as MP for Tavistock in 1966. He was then MP for Henley from 1974 until 1997. In government he served as Secretary of State for the Environment from 1979 to 1983 and Secretary of State for Defence from 1983 to 1986, until his abrupt and dramatic resignation in June 1986. On his return to Cabinet under John Major he took up his old post at Environment, before gathering the titles of First Secretary of State and then president of the Board of Trade from 1992 to 1995, and serving as deputy prime minister from 1995 to 1997. Heseltine was involved in most of the great political battles of the Thatcher and Major years: challenging CND, the sinking of the *Belgrano* during the Falklands War, pit closures, the Poll Tax and Europe. Heseltine's act of calm Cabinet rebellion did not, however, mark the ascent to the job Heseltine really coveted – that of prime minister. Although he never occupied the great offices of state or became prime minister, he managed to survive in front-line politics. He was always in the frame during the leadership crises of the Thatcher and Major years, but circumstance (and his 1995 heart attack) conspired against him. Heseltine's unusually long political career meant he was still at it at the age of seventy-nine, when he was tasked by George Osborne to review the government's growth strategy (Department of Business, Innovation and Skills, 2012). To survive, Heseltine had to deploy an array of persuasive skills and target them at audiences inside and outside the Conservative Party. He was not always successful; his oratory made him enemies as well as admirers and his approach often tipped from confidence into arrogance. He could be intimidating, imposing, and sometimes vain. Much of this reputation was based on his oratorical style and the techniques he deployed.

Whilst ethos, pathos and logos are asymmetrically interdependent, we can identify a stronger strand of pathos in Heseltine's party conference speeches, logos in his parliamentary performance and ethos in his engagement with the media and other external arenas. Political speeches in the classical sense divide between three genres: the motivational, deliberative and ceremonial or epideictic (Charteris-Black, 2012: 149). This chapter largely focuses on a motivational speech to party conference, a deliberative speech to Parliament and epideictic resignation statement to the media.

Heseltine was not a natural speaker; he had to work at it. He modelled his mannerisms on Lloyd George and drew on his own Welsh roots in Swansea. Heseltine had made slow academic progress; he was not a great reader and books were not a part of his everyday life growing up. He was later diagnosed with mild dyslexia. Speaking, however, fascinated him. He talked glowingly of seeing Aneurin Bevan speak in 1954: 'He was marvellously impressive and I can hear his beguiling Welsh lilt and his oddly compelling stutter to this day' (Heseltine, 2000: 36). At Oxford he was drawn into the cut and thrust of political debate. Heseltine recorded his own speeches and friends recalled him practising hand gestures and emphasis in the mirror (Crick, 1997: 43). He and his great friend Julian Critchley worked at tape recording each other to generate confidence in public speaking and familiarity in spoken word and delivery: 'And the game we played is one or the other would say to the other, "budgerigars," and you had to get your feet for one minute to talk about budgerigars.'[1] As with many future Cabinet ministers he was grounded in the debating societies at Oxford, rising to president of the Oxford Union in 1954. On generating positive reviews in his Oxford days, Heseltine noted that 'all that posturing in front of the mirror seemed worthwhile' (Heseltine, 2000: 31). But he was very much still learning on the way up. At a Cambridge Union debate with Harold Macmillan in 1953, Heseltine was underprepared and having not finished writing his speech in advance, bluffed his way through to the end. Macmillan noticed immediately: 'Take my advice. Always prepare the end first' (Crick, 1997: 45). Such an early lesson stuck with Heseltine, who saw the benefit of preparation as the key to successful speech-writing and the route to making an impact as an orator.

Party conference

In October 1975 the Conservative Party was in a state of disarray, having lost two elections and fought a divisive leadership contest earlier that year. The party needed reviving from the doldrums. Heseltine's first conference speech, telling his audience 'We are involved in a struggle for the very heart of society', hit the mark although Heseltine himself noted only that the speech was 'well received and earned me a standing ovation late in the afternoon from those delegates who had remained in the hall' (Heseltine, 2000: 175). Crick was much more effusive:

> Not since Iain MacLeod's great platform oratory in the 1960s, or the occasional turn by Lord Hailsham, had a speaker raised the spirits of party loyalists so effectively. They cheered loudly, clapped and stamped their feet in thunderous delight and gave Heseltine a standing ovation, which was an accolade bestowed much more sparingly by conference audiences. (Crick, 1997: 185)

This is a theme picked up by Critchley (1987: 47) who bemoaned the poor quality of Tory orators: 'by and large Conservatives do not bother to remove their silver spoons'. The response of the party was equally dull and uninspiring: 'applause was dutiful and restrained'. Conservative oratory was suffering a substantial dip, particularly in comparison with the Labour orators of the time such as Michael Foot, Barbara Castle and Tony Benn. Critchley insisted that in 1975 Heseltine 'took the stage by storm', wandering off his shadow environment brief and into the realms of passion and political confrontation. Keen to champion his friend's credentials, Critchley immediately saw the contrast with Heseltine's Conservative rivals from the competent (Peter Walker, Kenneth Baker) to the plain dull (Patrick Jenkin, Leon Brittan).

Heseltine did work with researchers on his speeches, but he liked to write drafts himself (particularly conference speeches), though both Dermot Gleeson and Michael Jones describe removing much of the incoherence evident in the early drafts written by Heseltine. Conscious that 'you could not waste a word' his speeches went through multiple drafts, reducing the content down to remove all 'redundant words'.[2] He also claimed to write all his own jokes (although as noted later in this chapter he was fed one in 1995). Gleeson later remarked that the standing ovation Heseltine received at the 1975 party conference was to do with the manner of the delivery rather than the content: 'If he'd read out the New York telephone directory with that vigour and style he'd have got a standing ovation' (Crick, 1997: 186).

Heseltine's performances were full of passion, fake and sometimes real rage. Once he had the taste for the party conference's adulation he responded each year, becoming a master of the claptrap.[3] Adept at deploying rhetorical tools, Heseltine was conscious that they had to be put into practice. Cicero called delivery 'a sort of language of the body', a political variation on acting (Glover, 2011: 236), and Heseltine's speeches in particular are remembered for the short, pithy but memorable line, often accompanied by visual emphasis. In October 1976, against the political backdrop of Chancellor Denis Healey scuttling off to the International Monetary Fund during the Labour Party conference and interest rates hitting 15 per cent, he told conference in Brighton:

> This government should go;
> and if it had a shred of pride it would go today.
> The reality lay in Blackpool last week:
> a one legged army limping away from the storm they have created.
> Left, left – left, left, left. (Quoted in Crick, 1997: 187)

He embellished the moment with a stiff-legged march to accompany the military command; a theatrical gesture which gained an instant response. Heseltine denied that this was a consciously theatrical approach, but was just 'what making speeches was about ... my speech-making style'.[4] However, performance generates a response, as Heritage and Greatbatch (1986: 150) concluded: 'The effectiveness of the rhetorical formats in generating applause was strongly, though differentially, influenced by performance factors.' Heseltine would also use musical references, such as the following from Gilbert and Sullivan:

> The idiot who praises with enthusiastic tones all centuries but this, and every country
> but his own. (Heseltine, 1982)

Later in 1991, having become adroit at turning a potential negative into a positive crowd-pleaser, he had to explain why the Council Tax was replacing the Poll Tax. Coming out fighting after the Poll Tax fiasco, he chose to attack Labour by drawing attention to the Lambeth councillors who had refused to pay the Poll Tax and, as a result, had been expelled from the Labour Party by Kinnock. Councillors who refused to pay local bills would be prevented from voting on matters affecting the level of local tax, Heseltine announced from the platform in an obvious deflection tactic. With a rhetorical flourish he used another musical reference to exclaim:

> Off with their heads
>   And into the political vocabulary of our times marched a whole new meaning to the words of the old song: Doing the Lambeth walk Oi! (Heseltine, 1991: 612)

In 1995 he even returned to his 1976 theme to poke fun at Labour's shift to the centre ground, drawing on physicality in delivery others would avoid:

> Twenty years ago I stood in this hall and warned you about the Labour party – a one legged army limping from the wreckage of their policies.
>   Left. Left. Left. Left. Left.
>   That didn't work. About turn.
>   Right. Right. Right. Right. (Heseltine, 1995)

Heseltine was acutely aware that party conference audiences have 'a general disposition to respond to negative rather than constructive assertions' (Heritage and Greatbatch, 1986). He structured his speeches to use attacks on the left to mask a difficult policy announcement or deflect criticism or simply to get the audience on board. Heseltine's speeches were peppered with such negative passages, but these were often precursors to passages less obviously in tune with the audience. Heseltine found that the success of his attacks on the Labour left in the 1970s created an expectation that each and every speech on whatever subject would contain a knockabout section on the Labour Party. Heseltine rarely disappointed. By 1995 he found it harder to deploy his usual mode of attack, presenting any shade of the Labour Party as unreconstructed left-wingers.

> New Labour hasn't forgotten Old Labour. Labour will always walk backwards into the future. Searching for yesterday's solutions to tomorrow's problems. (Heseltine, 1995)

Mastery of the use of the various rhetorical techniques is a key characteristic skill of the 'charismatic' speaker (Atkinson, 1984). The combination of carefully coordinated verbal and non-verbal signals (as invitations to applaud) mark out this charismatic skill. Heseltine deployed a freedom of expression, which lifted his performance beyond the script. He also had a quotability that suited the emerging sound-bite age. Closer examination of his speeches, however, shows long rambling passages that fade easily from the memory. Much as Heseltine protests, it was about the delivery, more deliberative and less forensic, more performative and less substantial.

Heseltine claims that the 1976 speech (Left, Left, Left) was a response to speculation that the Shadow Cabinet was about to be reshuffled. The ovation he received secured his position on the frontbench, although he was moved from the Trade and Industry portfolio to Environment. Heseltine points to another speech ten months earlier on industrial intervention which annoyed Margaret Thatcher enough to shift him. His popularity established, Thatcher preferred, and indeed saw the value of, keeping him in the tent. In fact she saw the value of deploying his rhetoric as Defence Secretary with a particular brief to counter the anti-nuclear protest movement.

Heseltine channelled his energy at conference into taking the attack to Labour and was still doing it to great party acclaim in 1995. Heseltine looks back with delight at his platform performance attacking Gordon Brown's neoclassical endogenous growth theory. The cringe-worthy pun which he said 'happened to be one of the best [jokes] I have ever used' was one of the few times he used a specific line presented to him by a colleague.[5] Chief Whip Richard Ryder had been given a joke which he passed on to Heseltine on the basis that 'only he could get away with it':

> Neoclassical endogenous growth theory and the symbiotic relationships between growth and investment, and people and infrastructure. Clear, unambiguous and to the point. Well last week the *Guardian* disclosed the speech had not been written by Gordon Brown at all but by a 27 year old choral-singing researcher named Ed Ball [*sic*]. So there you have it the final proof, Labour's brand new shining economic dream, but 'It wasn't Brown's. It was Ball's!' (Heseltine, 1995)

Apart from the obvious mispronunciation of Ed Balls' surname to make the joke work, it is of course true that only Heseltine could deliver such an awful pun and not only get away with it, but be able to use it as a means to ridicule Labour's economic policy. Generating laughter is accepted as a powerful spur to generating attentiveness (Atkinson, 2004: 33). Yet little beyond the joke remained memorable. Crick (1997: 187) suggests that Heseltine was adept at the political comedy, but was not a great phrase-maker.

It was not all knockabout stuff. Although speeches in the 1970s had established Heseltine as the conference favourite, it was his speech in 1981 that proved his most challenging. Coming after the Toxteth riots earlier in the summer, Heseltine had made a considerable personal commitment to intervening in Liverpool. He had expended much political capital: 'I do not remember any speech in my public life over which I anguished so long and so hard. I was as aware as anyone of the Powellite undercurrents that existed, not just in the Conservative party but throughout British society' (Heseltine, 2000: 230). He reflected in an interview that he was extremely nervous prior to delivering what can be regarded as the counterpoint to Powell's 1968 'Rivers of Blood' speech. Heseltine had defied the whip over the 1968 Race Relations Bill, when in opposition just after Powell's speech. Heseltine cites his experience in the hotel trade and his early years at Haymarket as convincing him of the necessity for race relations legislation. He took an interventionist and active role in Liverpool after the 1981 riots, and remained proud of his achievements (Hattenstone, 2001). But it was not just his actions, he was proud of this particular speech, one that 'had to be said' and 'had to be said by him'. He was nervous at the potential reaction, a speech that represented a 'different ball game'.[6]

Heseltine agonised long and hard over the words: 'No speech had gone through so many drafts', and reduced them to a simple message, in a crucial passage, containing *tricolon, anaphora* and *puzzle-solution*:

> We talk of equality of opportunity. What do those words actually mean in the inner cities today? What do they mean to the black communities? We now have large immigrant communities in British cities. Let this party's position be absolutely clear. They are British. They live here. They vote here. However tight the immigration legislation – and in everyone's interests they should be tight – there will be a large black community in this country tomorrow, just as there is today. There are no schemes of significant repatriation that have any moral, social or political credibility. (Heseltine, 1981)

This was far from the usual Heseltine performance. It was serious and challenged the Conservative Party to think in a different way. He reflected that it would only take one person to shout out to ruin the moment.

Heseltine had committed much personal political capital to understanding what went wrong in Liverpool and how the government could have a more positive impact. His extensive engagement and listening exercise heading up the Merseyside Taskforce culminated in a paper, the title of which he said embodied the phrase that was most frequently heard during his time in Liverpool: 'It took a riot' 'to bring you here and to make government listen'. The report was never officially published, though a copy was leaked and published in *The Times*. Margaret Thatcher in particular would not countenance Heseltine's interventionist six-point plan for Liverpool, and disliked the determinist overtones of the title. The legacy of his intervention can be seen though in the partnership projects taken up by Labour and the localism Heseltine himself continued to preach (Department for Business, Innovation and Skills, 2012).

The rhetoric deployed in 1981 at the party conference showed that while Heseltine may not have won the battle for additional funds in Cabinet he was prepared to use his oratorical skills to make his point. This speech had a considerable impact on the party. David Dimbleby remarked that Heseltine had 'picked up the Conservative Party, shaken it and put it down where he wanted it to be'. This was a media response that Heseltine approved of, commenting that 'this phrase made it all worthwhile after 30 years'.[7] The legacy of the speech was substantial; it created greater distance from the Powellite undercurrents still prevalent in sections of the Conservative Party. Yet Heseltine did not have it all his own way as the sentiment was not universally accepted. Norman Tebbit delivered his oft-quoted call for the unemployed to 'get on their bikes' later on the same platform, just as his father had done in the 1930s: 'he didn't riot', pointed out Tebbit.

Parliamentary performance

Although Heseltine will be best remembered for his oratory at party conferences and the personal relationship he had with party members once a year, he was a formidable (if generally reluctant) parliamentary performer. Heseltine claimed to enjoy the exhilaration of the battle in Parliament. He was energised and excited by the cut and thrust of parliamentary debate: 'it is the frontier of the political game and there's no quarter given. Winner takes all.'[8] When he was centre stage the adversarial arena suited his combative approach to politics.

Pathos (persuasion through the arousal of emotion) is perhaps the tool most regularly associated with Heseltine. The media delighted in the Tarzan epithet, given to him in the early 1970s by a Labour opponent (Stanley Clinton-Davis) in reference to his Johnny Weissmuller looks. Heseltine seemed not to mind and began to revel in the attention. The emotional aspect of Heseltine's politics was critical to his political career. It went beyond his charismatic appearance, hair flowing, gesticulating wildly. It has origins in the infamous 'mace incident' of May 1976, which is perhaps better for the lack of televised footage, allowing conflicting stories to emerge. During a procedural debate on Labour's Aircraft and Shipbuilding Industries Bill, Labour reneged on a 'pair' and won the motion by a single vote. The Labour benches erupted into a chorus of the Red Flag, an incensed Heseltine responded by picking up the mace as a symbol of the authority of the House and offering it to the government – an act he admitted was 'provocative and theatrical' (Heseltine, 2000: 173). Heseltine's action became embellished somewhat and gave great ammunition to those that already saw him as unreliable and volatile in character.

On several occasions Heseltine was required to use his skills in the Commons to defend a government position under particularly difficult circumstances. In February 1985, as Defence Secretary, he had to move the government motion in the Commons that the sinking of the *Belgrano* had been a 'necessary and legitimate action in the Falklands campaign'. More challenging, in light of the acquittal of the official Clive Ponting over leaking a week earlier, he also had to defend the position that 'the protection of our armed forces must be the prime consideration in deciding how far matters of national security and the conduct of military operations can be disclosed'. Heseltine described his speech as the most difficult he ever had to make in the House. It was also Heseltine's longest parliamentary speech (almost an hour and a half in length) and proved to be a rare Commons occasion, with packed benches and the government's reputation on the line. Heseltine relished the challenge and expressed his delight at the sight of the SDP leader, David Owen, entering the chamber with piles of books and notes ready to deconstruct his argument only to scuttle away well before Heseltine had finished. The Ponting case had infuriated Heseltine, who felt betrayed by his official, taking the parliamentary stage to defend not only the government but his own reputation. Whilst he looked back with admiration on his Commons performance, others described it as a 'second prosecution' (Crick, 1997: 261). The speech contained several stinging attacks on Ponting:

> I was entitled to expect that a man in such a position of trust would give me his full and dispassionate advice, but he did not. Parliament is expected to believe that, before Ministers make statements to the House or its Committees, civil servants in senior

positions will advise on the text of such submissions. Mr Ponting did not. (*Hansard*, 18 February 1985)

The performance made it into the 100 greatest speeches in *Hansard*'s 2009 Centenary volume as nominated by Michael Portillo (Portillo, 2009). The speech created a lasting impression on Portillo (2005): 'Over the course of seventy minutes Michael Heseltine forensically destroyed Clive Ponting'; 'When Heseltine had finished, I seriously expected Labour's spokesman to put up his hands and surrender'. The speech was not only a spirited defence of the government's position, but highly political, raising the spirits of a beleaguered government, reeling from Ponting's acquittal. Yet the speech was not classic Heseltine fare. He was precise, detailed and measured in his argument. Logos was deployed heavily throughout the speech. As Portillo, surprised at the 'relentless factual and logical' content, pointed out: 'It was all the more remarkable because Heseltine did not have a reputation for being a man for detail' (2009: 427). Heseltine described such concentration on the factual persuasion in this case as a 'bombshell of an argument'.[9] The qualities inherent in the speech itself are as important as the character of the speaker and the delivery; purpose, substance, structure and evidence matter (Glover, 2011). The logos aspect is to state the purpose of the speech, prove it and destroy the opposition case.

Heseltine found a form of words that turned the tables on the Labour Opposition, and in particular Tam Dalyell who had received Ponting's leaked documents:

> The constitutional novelty that the House is expected to support, if the Opposition have their way, is that the most trusted civil servants, in the most secure parts of our defence establishments, should be free anonymously to draft questions for Opposition Backbenchers to submit to Ministers on which the self-same leaking civil servants may then brief the Ministers on the answers which they consider appropriate. The Opposition may perhaps be beginning to wonder whether they have been any better served by Mr Ponting than I was.

And again, emphasising the phrase that was to resonate from the speech:

> So we have another *constitutional novelty*. A senior and trusted civil servant upon whom Ministers were entitled to rely for loyal and conscientious service claims it proper to sit in silence believing that Ministers are deceiving Parliament so that at the moment that it happens he may leak anonymously the advice of his own Civil Service colleagues which he has done nothing to counter. (*Hansard*, 18 February 1985)

Heseltine took few interventions, so presenting an almost uninterrupted chronological defence of the government's position. He insisted on putting the events on record in a precise timescale and refused to deviate from this precise and preplanned approach. 'I shall give way, but not in the middle of a sequence of events which it is important for the House to hear in one piece' and 'For the House to judge the credibility of this explanation, I shall set out the actual time scale of Mr Ponting's involvement'. The sequencing was critical to his argument. The strength of

Heseltine's speech lay in the context; the government was in a hole and he crafted a way out, turning defence into attack. In addition, he used the parliamentary platform to attack Ponting and dismantle the opposition's case. Heseltine took great pleasure in setting a trap and drawing the opposition in: 'you would be less than human if you didn't feel a certain exhilaration as you pull the trap string'.[10]

Heseltine, however, was no great parliamentarian. Even Tories like Portillo accepted the Commons was not his natural habitat. His defence of the 'constitutional principle' in the Ponting case and assertion of the national interest were less about the rights of Parliament and more about his own ministerial (and the government's) position. The irony of his rhetoric, using the 'constitutional principle' to defend his position and then resigning from Cabinet complaining of a similar breach was not lost on many observers. Heseltine had felt personally betrayed by Ponting and was furious that he had been acquitted. The parliamentary performance enabled him to get his own back. The speech was universally recognised to have pushed the Opposition onto the back foot and lifted the government out of a hole. It also had a considerable impression on up-and-coming Conservative MPs, like Portillo. Yet Heseltine's parliamentary performances did not reach such heights again, often deployed to manage crises and frustrated in his ambition. The closest Heseltine got to the prize of prime minister at the dispatch box was as deputy prime minister, infrequently standing in for John Major at Prime Minister's Question Time.

Public and media

Ethos, though, goes beyond the explicit expression of character based on personality and background. It relates to the identification of strongly held values and beliefs. Drawing on this appreciation of the role of ideology in public speaking, Heseltine reflected: 'conviction matters. The more I believed, the more I was able to transmit.'[11] Yet Simon Hoggart wrote that Heseltine's style of performance was in part due to the nature of his rather ambiguous ideological position within the Conservative Party:

> Like many people whose political opinions are fairly middle of the road, he needs to work himself into a lather of rage when he makes a big speech, which is why his conference set-pieces were always more successful than Mrs Thatcher's: she was so confident in her beliefs that she didn't need to shout them out. (Hoggart, 1997)

What Heseltine believed in was hard to define. He was certainly pro-European; he was a rather traditional and paternalistic Tory; and he was willing to intervene in the economy where necessary. This theme and his commitment to localised solutions to boost economic development were still championed in 2012 (Department of Business, Innovation and Skills, 2012). But Heseltine also strongly advocated privatisation, and competitive tendering. Originally a Heathite, he was regarded as an 'outer wet' (Young, 1989: 199). His ideological positions were rather contradictory at times, a pro-European, pro-industrial intervention, 'One Nation' Tory much in the traditional mould of patrician conservatives. Yet he was a *bête noir* for the left, taking up the attack on CND in the 1980s, closing the mines, driving forward the privatisation agenda under John Major. Even so Andrew Adonis (2011) praised Heseltine as one of the left's favourite Tories, not for being Thatcher's enemy, but for his institution building, claiming his hand in council house sales, Docklands, the Thames Gateway, High Speed 1, the Jubilee Line and the Docklands Light Railway. His failures were also heroically on the right side of the argument, according to Adonis: Poll Tax, Westland and latterly elected mayors. He was also prepared to share a platform (together with Kenneth Clarke) with senior Labour figures in 1999 to make Britain's case for entry into the single European currency. As his political agenda appeared more in tune with New Labour (or as he would say New Labour shifted towards his brand of centrist politics), he felt the need to increase his rhetorical attacks on the Blair/Brown centrist project.

As Heseltine was often at odds with large swathes of opinion within his party, he saw the benefit of utilising the arena beyond the party conference and Parliament. Heseltine enjoyed his jousts with the media, becoming a regular feature in the mainstream television studios. Although in his later years he admitted a respect for the Paxmans and Humphreys (perhaps due to his brief and unsuccessful foray into interviewing at Granada TV in 1960), he could in his pomp be an intimidating and difficult interviewee. This extended to walking out of a live Channel 4 news interview in 1986 when he learnt that a recording of an interview with Clive Ponting was to be broadcast on air.

It was during Heseltine's five years out of government that he did most to engage beyond the formal political arenas. He toured constituencies, rarely turning down invitations to speak (largely from those that would support him). He preferred the public circuit to remaining in the Commons – 'I did what I was good at'. His diary was full to bursting; he was rarely disloyal and always in his element on the so-called 'rubber chicken' circuit. In his wilderness years the media ensured his survival, they gave him support and built him up as the heir apparent to Thatcher. Heseltine was only too happy to go along with this. He was always good copy for journalists. He would craft words that presented himself as a loyal party member, at the same time as sending signals that the leadership should head off in a different direction. In interviews he gave as good as he got and he had acquired the experience to sound loyal and supportive whilst carefully presenting an alternative approach to the prevailing policy narrative.

Generally Heseltine prepared his answers in advance of interviews and made sure these were the ones he delivered. His approach was largely to make sure that interviews were conducted on his terms and not those of the interviewer. This approach is commonplace now as politicians are trained to stick to the prepared line. Heseltine was always reluctant to be trained or schooled in the emerging dark arts of media relations. However, he succumbed to the prevailing party political centralisation. In the late 1990s he was required to go to Central Office media training, which alarmed him at first, then as an old hand he agreed, only to find himself being upbraided by the trainer for being too relaxed in front of the camera.[12] Ever the smooth operator, Heseltine was still at it in October 2012, as he toured the media outlets to promote his alternative growth strategy, presenting a loyal front praising the current coalition leadership and 'nimbly dodging political booby traps' (White, 2012).

Heseltine may have roused successive conference audiences and gained a reputation as a grand orator, but he was less successful at the heresthetic approach – the art of manipulation. Heseltine was less interested in the lower level activities associated with heresthetics, the 'deliberate attempt to structure political situations so that opponents will either have to submit or be trapped' (Hargrove, 1998: 32; Heppell, 2013). He was a singular figure who expected his set-piece oratory to be enough to persuade the doubters. Although a political survivor, Heseltine was less able to structure situations to his advantage. In particular after his resignation from Cabinet in 1986 until his return in 1990 he was unable or indeed unwilling to spend time in the Commons cultivating his supporters and indulging in the type of heresthetical approach that would enhance his leadership credentials and support. He later admitted that he would have been wiser to spend more time with the 'doubters' in the House of Commons rather than take the easy public invitations. The rhetorical devices of gentle persuasion behind closed doors, in the bars and tea rooms were not for him. Probed about this aspect Heseltine's response is revealing:

> 'I'm not good at small talk [...] I have close good friends, but not many. I'm not the life and soul of the party.' He insists he was always good at keeping in touch with those he worked closely with. But not very good at keeping on side with those he had to? 'Yes, yes, yes, I think that's probably right.' There's a long pause, as he struggles with his words. 'Difficult ... the party became very divided in the 80s. They had a view about who was "One of us" as the phrase was, and I never was' (Hattenstone, 2001).

Such conscious isolationism was best demonstrated by the most dramatic political event of his career, when he chose to walk away from Cabinet over an inability to structure the Westland crisis in his favour. This may have been a structural problem of prime ministerial dominance that Heseltine could not face down (particularly when Margaret Thatcher pulled a pre-prepared note from her handbag to sum up the Cabinet discussion). Yet it is telling that the formal Cabinet minutes do not record any other Cabinet ministers offering support to Heseltine (in contrast to accounts in some memoirs). The Cabinet minutes from 9 January 1986 released under a Freedom of Information request in 2010 (BBC, 2010) simply record:

> The Secretary of State for Defence said that there had been no collective responsibility in the discussion of this matter. There had been a breakdown in the propriety of Cabinet discussions. He could not accept the decision recorded in the Prime Minister's summing up. He must therefore leave this Cabinet.

Heseltine walked straight out of the Cabinet room and out of Number 10. He crossed the road and approached the single cameraman waiting in Downing Street to declare to the startled journalist that he had resigned and would make a full statement later. The initial confusion as to whether he had really resigned gave way once it was relayed that he had announced it to the media. Heseltine, ever keen to engage with the media first and put his personal stamp on matters, chose to eschew the normal constitutional convention whereby resigning ministers make a statement to the House as early as possible. With the Commons not televised until 1989, Heseltine, keen no doubt for his resignation performance to gain the largest possible audience, summoned a press conference for four o'clock that afternoon. Even more unusually he delivered his resignation statement from the Ministry of Defence, with the agreement of the permanent secretary. The speed with which Heseltine drafted and then delivered his statement was viewed with much suspicion by those who believed the act was pre-planned (Crick, 1997: 289; Young, 1989: 447). Of course Heseltine himself (2000: 311) denied this, insisting he began with a blank sheet of paper and, using all the resources of the Ministry of Defence (which he admitted was 'a constitutional curiosity'), ended five hours later with his permanent secretary still making corrections as the press conference started. As with the Ponting speech his resignation statement was detailed, intricate and thorough (again fuelling speculation of a calculated act). The statement is a chronological exposition of the Westland affair detailing, from Heseltine's own vantage point, the duplicitous behaviour of officials and ministers and the sense that his preferred European helicopter option was not even being properly considered.

> The ad hoc [ministerial] meetings [chaired by the Prime Minister] were both ill-tempered attempts to overcome the refusal of some colleagues to close off the European [Westland] option. (Heseltine, 2000: 537)

It highlighted the fissure between Heseltine's Ministry and Leon Brittan's Department of Trade and Industry. More damaging still, it referred to Heseltine's thwarted attempts to get the issues addressed collectively: 'I sought on a number of occasions to have the issues properly addressed.' The statement ran to 3,000 words and took twenty-two minutes to deliver. Despite the strong emphasis on logos to stress fact and sequencing of events, the passage that is oft quoted and remains in the public consciousness is the final passage, drawing on Heseltine's more familiar pathos (with a touch of ethos to start):

> To be Secretary of State for Defence in a Tory government is one of the highest distinctions one can achieve. To serve as a member of a Tory Cabinet within the constitutional understandings and practices of a system under which the Prime Minister is primus inter pares is a memory I will always treasure. But if the basis of trust between the Prime Minister and her Defence Secretary no longer exists, there is no place for me with honour in such a Cabinet. (Heseltine, 2000: 542)

This was Heseltine playing to the external audience. The statement was reprinted in full in the next day's broadsheet newspapers. Heseltine was particularly impressed with the headline in *The Times*: 'A Very Good Resignation', claiming later that the lead editorial would have been difficult to improve on from his point of view (Heseltine, 2000: 311).

The resignation statement, crafted to establish his side of the Westland saga and position himself in advance of any potential leadership challenge, showed Heseltine as a singular, often isolated, politician. His use of rhetoric to justify his actions well beyond the Parliamentary Party is striking. Heseltine's unwillingness or inability to indulge in the necessary political manoeuvring to bolster his support ultimately cost him the prize of becoming prime minister. The image from his early years of a volatile extrovert stuck and, added to the high drama of his resignation from Cabinet in 1986, a perception of an emotional, irrational politician developed. Heseltine accepts that he was portrayed in this manner. 'If that adds up over 50 years of public life to emotion, so be it. The rest of the time on balance, I'm totally unprovokable. I've never sworn. I don't use bad language. I don't storm out of meetings. In fact I always act reasonably.'[13] But he remained wedded to the notion that his response (in 1986) was justified on the basis that his opponents (both inside and outside the party) had cheated. He had a strong belief that the rules of the political game needed to be adhered to, whether over the mace incident, Ponting or Westland. His rhetoric often came back to this theme that he could not abide people who 'cheat' the system: 'I'm always prepared to discuss at length the issues, but I will not be cheated.'[14]

Conclusion

Heseltine was a considerable orator and party conference darling, his early performances marking him out as a star attraction. A conference revue in the late 1970s captures the sentiment perfectly: as two drunken peers leave the stage after a Heseltine performance, one says to the other 'You can shay what you like about that fella Hesheltine, he cant half find the party's clitoris [*sic*]' (in Crick, 1997: 187). Heseltine was a different type of orator, one who could, rather unusually, get a slumbering party to its feet. He used his performative qualities, making a conference speech a great visual event, wonderfully captured by Simon Hoggart (in Crick, 1997: 186):

> The fascination lay in the terrible things that were happening to his hair. Something had gone terribly wrong with the engineering system holding it up. Great chunks of it crashed down, like cliffs falling into the sea, covering his forehead and sometimes blotting out his eyes. Now and again he tried to shore it up in mid-speech, but then a bit would sheer off and crash around his ears. By the end the whole noble edifice was in ruins, a sad reminder of man-made things.

Conversely his oratory and success in rousing the party proved his weakness. His popularity gained him enemies; the traditional Tory grandees found his 'annual demagoguery' vulgar and undignified. Margaret Thatcher avoided being present on the platform.

Heseltine worked hard at his oratory to develop his career and survive at the top of Conservative Party politics, even when at odds with the leadership. He drew strongly on ethos, drawing on his personal charisma and occasionally evoking his colourful entrepreneurial background. His use of pathos to emotionally connect with the audience was evident. He roused the party with his virulent anti-Labour rhetoric, though often the bulk of the content chimed only with a particular section of the party. The logos he deployed set clear dividing lines with Labour, always passionate and combative, but setting out 'home truths' to his own party.

Heseltine argued that his political style had a long-term impact. Private–public partnerships, European engagement, and urban regeneration became part of mainstream politics due to his policy insistence and rhetorical doggedness. Often against the grain, he drove a pro-European strand and favoured an activist state industrial policy. In 1992, he promoted the 'interwoven nature of the public and private sectors' and promised to 'intervene [to help British companies] before breakfast, before lunch, before tea and before dinner' (Heseltine, 1992). Yet the rhetorical narrative is one that sees him as an individual unwilling to engage in the low-level political activity necessary to build alliances and coalitions using a different type of rhetoric.

Heseltine, at his strongest at party conferences, was a less committed parliamentary speaker. The Ponting speech was the highlight in a career that saw him appear at the dispatch box in a wide range of ministerial portfolios. In the public arena he always gave as good as he got in interviews and generated a reputation as an impressive performer beyond the narrow confines of the conference and Parliament. Ultimately his persuasive, heresthetical tools and grand oratory were not sufficient to convince the doubters in his own party of his readiness for the highest office.

Notes

1 Interview, 9 October 2012.
2 Interview, 9 October 2012.
3 Claptrap: 'a trick, device or language designed to catch applause' (Atkinson 1984: 48).
4 Interview, 9 October 2012.
5 Interview, 9 October 2012.
6 Interview, 9 October 2012
7 Interview, 9 October 2012.
8 Interview, 9 October 2012.
9 Interview, 9 October 2012.

10 Interview, 9 October 2012.
11 Interview, 9 October 2012
12 Interview, 9 October 2012.
13 Interview, 9 October 2012.
14 Interview, 9 October 2012.

9

The oratory of John Major

Timothy Heppell and Thomas McMeeking

John Major served as prime minister between November 1990 and May 1997. For a Conservative his journey to Downing Street was unconventional. After leaving school with limited qualifications he experienced unemployment in his youth, before working for the Standard Chartered Bank, joining the Young Conservatives and being elected as a member of Lambeth London Borough Council (1968–71). He would enter Parliament at the age of thirty-six in 1979. Of his fellow entrants from that year he was the first to reach Cabinet in 1987, having worked in the Whips' Office (1983–85) and within the junior ministerial ranks of the Department of Health and Social Security (1985–87). After two years as Chief Secretary to the Treasury (1987–89), he was briefly (and surprisingly) Foreign Secretary in 1989 (May to October) before being appointed Chancellor of the Exchequer in October 1989. He was then dramatically elected as leader of the Conservative Party in November after the removal of Margaret Thatcher.

However, despite the human interest of his humble beginnings and the length of his prime ministerial tenure, he has been overshadowed by his predecessor, Thatcher, and his successor, Tony Blair. Both of them were able to win three successive general elections and govern for over a decade. Both of them challenged traditional assumptions about their parties through Thatcherism and New Labour. Without their electoral records, or a narrative or governing approach to associate with his name, Major has seemed inconsequential by comparison.

Although Major did win the general election of April 1992, a perception developed thereafter that he was an ineffective prime minister. It stemmed from the following factors. First, his reputation for competence was fatally undermined by the humiliating ejection from the Exchange Rate Mechanism (ERM) in September 1992. Second, a series of sexual and financial scandals engulfed the Conservatives, reinforcing doubts about their integrity and commitment to public service. Finally, the Parliamentary Conservative Party (PCP) lost its reputation for internal discipline and unity. Major seemed powerless as the party went into convulsions tactically over the ratification of the Maastricht Treaty and strategically over the single European currency. The cumulative effect of these factors was that the Conservatives under Major no longer possessed the characteristics of a party of government (Norton, 1998: 77–8).

As a consequence he was an easy target for criticisms from his political opponents. He was regularly subjected to parliamentary attacks by John Smith and Tony Blair. Smith captured the electoral mood after the ERM disaster with the line: 'he is the devalued Prime Minister of a devalued Government' (HC Debates, Vol. 212, Col. 22, 24 September 1992). Later, Blair captured the inability of Major to provide effective political leadership within his divided party by arguing 'I lead my party, he follows his' (HC Debates, Vol. 258, Col. 655, 25 April 1995).

However, it is important to acknowledge that Major faced immensely difficult circumstances, i.e. the 'ghost of the past' in the shape of Thatcher, and the 'grim reaper' of being forced to operate with a small and dwindling parliamentary majority (McAnulla, 1999: 193–4). For example, Thatcher celebrated Major's victory at the general election of April 1992 by arguing that 'I don't accept the idea that all of a sudden Major is his own man'. She then concluded that 'Thatcherism will live' and that 'there is no such thing as Majorism' (Thatcher, 1992). The combination of dealing with the legacy of Thatcherism, and operating with a small parliamentary majority, clearly shaped Major's outburst in his accidently recorded comments to ITN's Michael Brunson (in his infamous 'bastards' outburst) in July 1993:

> The real problem is one of a tiny majority. Don't overlook that. I could have done all these clever decisive things which people wanted me to do – but I would have split the Conservative Party into smithereens. And you would have said that I acted like a ham-fisted leader. (Brunson, 2000: 199)

However, rather than dismiss Major, this chapter regards his oratory as of importance as he was communicating to the electorate on the ongoing appeal of conservatism during a period of crisis. Therefore, the focus when analysing his oratory will be on his tenure as prime minister alone, which is justifiable given his incredibly low profile as a junior minister between 1985 and 1987 and when in the Cabinet between 1987 and 1990. Overall, although not particularly skilled at the performance aspect of oratory, the chapter will demonstrate that Major had an *awareness* of a significant range of oratorical approaches but that his impact was blunted by circumstances which limited his persuasive abilities. In assessing his oratorical skills the chapter will consider Major in three political environments: first, in Parliament; second, at party conferences; and, third, in wider public performances which can be cobbled together under the theme of electioneering. The chapter will showcase the following with regard to Major. In Parliament, he became increasingly combative and partisan, where his reliance on logos and factual evidence to justify his position was reinforced by pathos to establish an emotional connection with his own supporters, and here humour was his primary method. At conference, he relied more on his credibility and his own political reputation (ethos) as his weapon of persuasion, but this was often reinforced by *antithesis* and contrasting his positions with those of his principal opponents. When engaging in wider electioneering, Major would replicate some of the methods that would inform his conference oratory and rely on *utilitas* or shared objectives, often buttressing this through his reliance upon *dignitas* or *bonum* (what is worthy or good). Having outlined illustrations from within each forum the conclusion will offer explanations as to why (despite displaying an awareness of the many of the techniques that make for an effective orator), Major became regarded as a poor political communicator.

Major and Parliament

Assessing Major in Parliament is dominated by his performances at Prime Minister's Questions (PMQs). Major had initially wanted to rely on logos and evidence to justify policy choices. In doing so he hoped to change PMQs by offering 'honest answers' to 'sincere questions', creating a forum for discussion and debate that was 'good mannered' (Burnham *et al.*, 1995: 553). The timing of his acquisition of the premiership coincided with the Iraqi invasion of Kuwait, and thus defence matters would dominate the first ten PMQs (Bates *et al.*, 2014). This aided Major in his objective as Opposition leaders (Neil Kinnock and Paddy Ashdown) took 'care to show their backing for the government, usually prefacing their questions with some supportive comment' (Burnham *et al.*, 1995: 553).

However, the immediacy of the general election, and then governing with a small majority, would force Major in a combative and partisan direction. Instead of 'defending his government's record' he increasingly 'used questions from MPs as a vehicle for attacking the opposition's policies'. Major also became more evasive. He took refuge in 'non-contentious' issues where he would become 'long winded' and would devote more time here as he was 'more likely to increase his authority' (Burnham *et al.*, 1995: 553).

In terms of how Major dealt with each Leader of the Opposition that he faced, it is clear that he developed a more confrontational and emotive style after 1992. Logos and evidence was to be meshed with pathos and emotional appeals. Outward signs of aggression emerged towards Smith and Blair. In the case of Smith this was most notable in March 1994 surrounding the deadlock over EU enlargement and the use of qualified majority voting. He commented that 'we aren't going to do what the Labour Party do, which is to say "yes" to everything that comes out of Europe without any actual examination', before turning on Smith. Using *tricolon* (the three-part list), Major claimed Smith would 'sign away our votes, sign away our competiveness, and sign away our money' before dismissing him as 'Monsieur Oui, the poodle of Brussels' (HC Deb, Vol. 240, Col. 134, 22 March 1994). Major would later show his disdain for Blair. When Blair repeatedly asked him whether his government would agree to join the European single currency, Major provided an adequate partial reply by stating that 'I will not make a judgement that is crucial to the constitutional and economic future of this country until I see the economic circumstances of the day', before adding to the end of the sentence that 'only a dimwit would ask me to' (HC Deb, Vol. 254, Col. 138, 8 February 1995).

Much of his rhetoric on the central policy tension of his premiership, Europe, could be seen as Eurosceptic in the sense that limits towards further European integration were clearly outlined. For example, prior to entering the Maastricht negotiations, Major specified in detail how and why he could not and would not 'accept a treaty which described the Community as having a federal vocation' (HC Debates, Vol. 199, Col. 275, 20 November 1991). Major returned post-Maastricht to emphasise to Parliament the merits of his negotiated opt-outs on the single currency and the social chapter. Over the course of its tortuous passage through Parliament, Major would try to persuade rebels with more emotive language. To dampen down expected rebellions Major tried to reassure Eurosceptic doubters by arguing that 'for the first time we have begun to reverse the centralising trend' (HC Debates, Vol. 208, Col. 496, 21 May 1992). However, the most challenging speech that Major delivered to Parliament was in the aftermath of the expulsion from the ERM. What makes this such an interesting speech to assess is how he challenged conventional thinking. To justify his policy position he emphasised how broad the support for entry to the ERM had been. Using the technique of *testimonia* (see Atkins and Finlayson, 2010), he sought to limit the validity of criticism of membership by noting that the City and the CBI had also been advocates of membership. He even more provocatively sought to justify his position by noting that his political opponents – the Labour Party, the trade unions and the Liberal Democrats – had also been supportive of membership (Seldon, 1997: 321). Ignoring his own support for membership, Smith made his memorable 'devalued Prime Minister' put-down, which resonated more than Major's claim that the whole political class (except the Conservative Eurosceptic right) had been in unanimity about membership.

One of his most challenging speeches to Parliament was after the death of Smith. Here his oratory was designed not persuade people to endorse him or his party, but to empathise with the loss suffered by his political opponents. Seldon notes that it was one of his 'best judged and most moving parliamentary performances' (Seldon, 1997: 461). Major stated that:

> When I think of his premature death, I shall think of the waste it has brought to our public life; the waste of a remarkable political talent; the waste of a high and honourable ambition to lead our country; and the waste of a man who in all his actions retained the human touch. (HC Debates, Vol. 243, Col. 430, 12 May 1994)

Here Major used both *anaphora* by repeating the same word at the beginning of each clause, and *parison*, as each clause had the same construction. Seldon noted that 'his language may not have been Churchillian, but he spoke from the heart, and often extempore, and he judged the mood perfectly', before noting that 'their relationship was never as friendly as Major understandably painted it that afternoon' (Seldon, 1997: 461). The reality was that in Parliament Major was overtly partisan. In this context, Major relied on pathos, and within this he became particularly adept in his use of humour. The best illustration of this was how he exploited the decision of the

Shadow Cabinet minister, Harriet Harman, to send her child to a grammar school, a decision which Blair had supported despite the hostility it provoked within Labour ranks. Major offered his sympathy to Blair on his 'current predicament', after which Blair thanked Major for his 'kind words of concern over pressure', before emphasising that 'the difference between us is that I will not buckle under it'. Major then exploited Blair's infamous 'tough on crime and tough on the causes of crime' quote, and mocked Blair by saying 'I just want to be tough on hypocrisy and tough on the causes of hypocrisy' (HC Debates, Vol. 270, Col. 141, 23 January 1996). Major left the chamber with Conservative backbenchers cheering 'more, more, more' (Seldon, 1997: 629).

Major had also used humour to great effect during the course of his campaign to be re-elected as Conservative Party leader in June and July 1995. As he remained as prime minister he faced the difficult task of facing Blair over the dispatch box after his own Welsh Secretary, John Redwood, had resigned to contest the leadership with Major. Blair asked Major whether Redwood should have resigned earlier if he was in disagreement with the policy objectives of the government. Major expertly used the contents of Redwood's resignation letter days earlier which had included a reference to him being 'devastated' when hearing of Major's resignation. Avoiding the substance of Blair's question he noted that, 'I understand that he resigned from the Cabinet because he was devastated that I had resigned as leader of the Conservative Party' (Major, 1999: 638). During the course of the same PMQs Major delivered another humorous put-down when his weak position should have made him vulnerable to Labour attacks. Earlier in the day there had been media reports that supporters of Michael Portillo had ordered that extra telephone lines at a proposed campaign HQ should be installed in anticipation of his entry into a possible second ballot. When asked about this Major responded by denying knowledge but noting that 'the speed at which these matters can be done is a tribute to privatisation' (Major, 1999: 638). Seldon concluded that the 'whole performance was masterly: not only had he paraded oratorical skills under duress, but also belittled his principal antagonists' (Seldon, 1997: 581–2). That Seldon referred to antagonists, i.e. Blair *and* Redwood and his Eurosceptic critics, rather than simply Blair as Labour Party leader, was significant. Finding ways to placate (or appeal to) his own party was to be a dominant theme of Major's oratory at conference.

Major at conference

Assessing the oratory of Major within the conference arena involves consideration of the following themes. First, the way in which Major used his own social background to underpin his political positions and his own leadership. Second, the way in which Major used his oratory at conference to critique the policy choices or the shifting ideological position of Labour. Finally, Major attempted to use conference speeches to map out his interpretation of conservatism, and within this the most controversial example was to be Back to Basics.

It is clear that Major felt his own social background was suitable for use within his conference speeches. Foley notes that Major constantly reminded the party and the electorate of his humble beginnings, elevating it to the 'defining characteristic' of his political persona (Foley, 2000: 81). As he became more embattled he would use them to emphasise his strength of character and his resilience. For example, he informed the 1994 conference that 'I didn't fight my way from a small terraced flat to this platform for the hell of it' (Major, 1994). He emphasised the difficulty in the journey that had culminated in him being prime minister by arguing that 'you don't just drift into Downing Street' (Major, 1994). Similar sentiments were expressed in his last conference speech in 1996, when he attempted to rally Conservative activists by stating that 'I didn't come from two rooms in Brixton to 10 Downing Street not to go out and fight with every fibre of my being' (Major, 1996). As his position as party leader became increasingly questioned, and the threat of a challenge intensified, so Major used speeches to the party faithful to emphasise his determination to continue. When addressing the Conservative Party Women's Conference in June 1993, he addressed the constant rumours of an imminent challenge with the following warning: 'I will tell you what I am tired and weary of. I am weary of gossip dressed up as views, malice dressed up as comment and fiction reported as fact. But I have news for some people. I am fit, I am here and I am staying' (Major, 1993a). That emphasis on character was tied to Conservative values within his 1995 conference speech, when he sought to promote the importance of individual responsibility and the value of small businesses. He informed conference that:

> When I was a small boy, my bread and butter was paid for by my father's small business. He made garden ornaments forty years ago and some people have always found that very funny. I don't. I see a proud, stubborn, independent old man who ran that firm and taught me to love my country, fight for my own and spit in the eye of malign fate. I know the knockers and sneerers who may never have taken a risk in their comfortable lives aren't fit to wipe the boots of the risk-takers of Britain. (Major, 1995)

Thus, Major relied heavily on ethos as his primary oratorical technique at conference. This was his attempt to utilise the representative claim, by arguing that he stood for, and could speak for, a particular constituency (Saward, 2006). This exploitation of his own past became central to his identity and his means of relating to an audience and persuading people to endorse his view. His emphasis on ethos served two purposes. First, he was saying to the wider electorate outside the conference hall that they could put their trust in him because of who he was, and what he had been through. His claim to empathy flowed from having experienced social deprivation in his own childhood. Watching the experience of his father's own bankruptcy, and his own period of unemployment, was to be exploited within his oratory as it helped to make him seem genuine in his concerns. Second, Major had overcome these disadvantages; thus his rise to the apex of a supposedly hierarchical and traditional political party could be used as a living embodiment of his vision of a classless society.

Major was thus using ethos for partisan advantage, as exploitation of his ordinary background placed him personally on the political ground that Labour claimed belonged to them (Foley, 2000: 81–4).

Major would increasingly use conference speeches as a vehicle to belittle the policy choices and political positions of Labour. Major would deliver a message about the unsuitability of Labour for government, and notably after 1994 of Blair as an alternative to him as prime minister. He informed the 1994 conference that the 'time is ripe for grown up politics', which was clearly a rebuke not only for Blair, but also for Michael Portillo, who was seen at the time as a possible Thatcherite and Eurosceptic alternative to him (Major, 1994). Rejecting the shallowness that he saw in Blair, and wanted the electorate to share, Major concluded that:

> No windy rhetoric, no facile phrases, no pious cliché, no shallow simplification, no mock-honest, mock-familiar, adman's speak can conceal the infinite complexity of Government ... My trade had never been in adjectives. I shall be patient. I shall be realistic. I shall ask for patience and realism in others. And I shall put my trust in results. (Major, 1994)

Here Major meshes together ethos (the assumed, but perhaps misplaced, belief in his own credibility) with *antithesis* (the comparison to Blair), which is then supported by repeating the same word to commence each clause (*anaphora*) and with *parison*, in that each clause at the beginning and end points being made has the same construction. *Antithesis* and ethos (and Major's personal experiences and values) highlighted the 'shallowness' and 'inexperience' of Blair. Major reinforced this in his 1996 conference speech, in which he observed:

> It simply won't do for Mr Blair to say, 'Look, I'm not a socialist anymore. Now can I be Prime Minister please?' Sorry, Tony. Job's taken. And, anyway, it's too big a task for your first real job. (Major, 1996)

Major was less successful at outlining his political vision. Some of his interventions in this regard seemed less driven by Thatcherism than One Nation conservatism. For example, he informed the Central Council Conference during the 1992 general election campaign that he wanted to 'bring into being a different kind of country, to bury forever old divisions in Britain between North and South, blue-collar and white-collar, polytechnic and university' (Major, 1992a). He was more overt in his commitment to One-Nation values when he informed the Central Council Conference during the 1997 general election campaign that 'I dream of a people's Britain', where 'the have-nots become the haves', creating a Britain 'for everyone, for those for whom life is a struggle, for those who don't have the best education, don't have a decent house, don't have a safe neighbourhood, don't have a job'. He claimed that was 'what I have always wanted to do' (Major, 1997a). He ended by stating that 'I came from them. I care for them all. I long to see them have their fair share of the good things in life' (Major, 1997a).

However, by the far the most controversial speech that Major delivered to conference was the 1993 speech. Major spoke of the 'old values of neighbourliness, decency, courtesy' which he claimed are 'still alive' even if 'somehow we feel embarrassed by them' (Major, 1993b). He would claim that 'fashionable theories' had caused greater damage to society, be that the building of tower blocks, the rejection of teaching spelling or times tables, or preaching that criminals needed treatment, not punishment; these theories, he informed conference, were 'wrong, wrong, wrong' (Major, 1993b). Major then concluded with the phrase that was to be the emblem for the speech: 'we must go back to basics; we want our children to be taught the best; our public services to give the best; our industry to beat the best' (Major, 1993b).

Major had inserted into the speech a line that Seldon claims was added 'deliberately' to 'defuse the danger of moral posturing', which stated that government could not make people good, and that 'this is for parents, churches, for schools' (Seldon, 1997: 403–4). However, the emphasis that he placed on traditional values left his theme open to use by social conservatives. It became a vehicle through which to attack single mothers and preach sexual fidelity. The theme would implode upon Major as numerous Conservative parliamentarians were exposed in sexual scandals which seemed duplicitous when judged against the now distorted premise of Back to Basics (Heppell, 2007: 384). It was not the first speech that Major was to deliver that would subsequently undermine him.

Major and electioneering

Assessing the oratory of Major in terms of wider electioneering and projection of conservatism and the Conservative Party involves consideration of the following themes. First, there are clear illustrations of how Major sought to project his vision of the meaning of conservatism. Second, through his wider electioneering Major used critiques of Labour to identify its limitations as a way of justifying Conservative choices. Finally, it is clear that much of Major's wider communication to the electorate was geared towards attempting to explain away the ideological disagreements that existed within the party, most notably over Europe.

Major would claim to reject the labels that had defined Thatcherism – wet versus dry, or Europhile versus Eurosceptic – which he regarded as damaging to party unity (Foley, 2002: 27–30). While he was more a technocrat than a philosopher, an appraisal of his wider media comments showcases his adherence to a traditional and pragmatic One Nation strand of conservatism. For example, when he famously entered Downing Street by uttering the words that he wanted to see a 'country at ease with itself', it suggested the influence was Macmillan, not Thatcher (Major, 1990). Such sentiments influenced his campaigning oratory during the 1992 general election campaign, when he argued that:

> I want a Britain that offers dignity and security to older people. I want a Britain where there is a helping hand for those who need it. Where people can get a hand up, not just a hand out. A country that is fair and free from prejudice, a classless society at ease with itself. (Major, 1992a)

This type of One-Nation-inspired rhetoric was not as present during the 1992–97 term, but was to resurface during the 1997 general election campaign. As he headed for inevitable defeat, Major decided to 'make a heartfelt statement of his beliefs' (Seldon, 1997: 728). Major informed the electorate that his kind of conservatism was 'not just for the privileged but for the underprivileged as well, not just for the confident but for those who have doubts'. Later, Major spoke of his determination to bring economic prosperity to 'the circle of people who are still locked outside it' (Seldon, 1997: 728).

However, Major did not often receive positive reporting of such electioneering speeches. He was to suffer as the press bias that had previously aided Thatcher was lost during his tenure. Thus the trials and tribulations that his government did suffer were not covered in an understanding manner (Bale and Sanders, 2001: 97–9). One example of when Major was widely ridiculed was when he delivered a speech expressing his admiration for his country. Major spoke of a 'country of long shadows on county grounds, warm beer, invisible green suburbs, dog lovers and pool fillers' but also of 'old maids bicycling to communion through the morning mist'. Seldon comments that the 'lyrical vision was deliberately nostalgic' and that the 'sentimentality of his words reflected a yearning within him for simpler, more decent times' (Seldon, 1997: 370).

Major was to become comfortable when attacking Labour during his electioneering. For example, to emphasise how the Conservatives were the party to harness opportunity and Labour was the party that would restrict it, he parodied the famous 'I warn you' speech that Kinnock had made during the 1983 general election:

> I warn you not to be qualified.
> I warn you not to be successful.
> I warn you not to buy shares.
> I warn you not to be self-employed.
> I warn you not to accept promotion.
> I warn you not to save.
> I warn you not to buy a pension.
> I warn you not to own a home. (Major, 1999: 297)

Here, although the structural origins of the idea stem from Kinnock, this is an illustration of Major not only using *antithesis* and *utilitas*, but more specifically this is an oratorical style based around *parison* (each clause has a similar construction) and *anaphora* (repeating the same word at the beginning of each sentence). Underpinning it was his hostility towards his opponents. Later on in his tenure he became particularly aggressive when discussing Blair. He was to cover a wide range of negatives designed to bind the Conservatives together. Underpinning this antithesis strategy was the 'jeopardy thesis' (Hirschman, 1991). Whether it was on the damaging potential impact of the devolution plans that Labour were proposing that would ultimately lead to Scottish independence, or on the issue of the single European currency, Major relied heavily on this oratorical approach in the 1997 general election campaign. Days before his premiership would end Major replicated the oratorical methods identified earlier, notably *antithesis* and *utilitas*, as he informed the electorate of the 'sharp dividing line' on the issue, before offering them a choice:

> I say no to handing more powers to Brussels in a new employment chapter, Mr Blair says yes.
> I say no to the extensions of qualified majority voting, Mr Blair says yes.
> I say no to new powers to the European Parliament, Mr Blair says yes.
> On European control of foreign policy, Mr Blair says maybe, which means yes. (Major, 1997b)

However, his oratory on Europe was unable to persuade the electorate in part because he could not even persuade his own party of the merits of his pragmatic 'negotiate and decide' approach on the single European currency. Thus his attempts to highlight the limitations of opponents failed to gain traction. Moreover, on matters European Major was to suffer from a similar problem to that which we identified from his Back to Basics speech. This is best described as the boomerang effect, as Major delivered a speech on the importance of continuing membership within which his rhetoric was to be used against him as circumstances changed. In his speech to the Scottish CBI in early September 1992, Major staked his reputation on staying inside the ERM (Major, 1999: 326). He dismissed those who questioned ERM membership as 'quack doctors peddling their wares', before warning his audience that 'miracle cures simply don't work – never have, never will'. Major then concluded with words that would humiliate him within days:

> All my adult life I have seen British governments driven off their virtuous pursuit of low inflation by market problems or political pressures. I was under no illusion when I took Britain into the ERM. I said at the time that membership was no soft option. The soft option, the devaluers' option, the inflationary option, would be a betrayal of our future. (Major, 1999: 326)

Throughout his premiership Major would deliver speeches on European policy that when assessed over time might appear contradictory, but more accurately reflect the difficult balancing act that he was trying to maintain between the Eurosceptic and Europhile factions. He had begun his premiership (July 1991) with a commitment to place Britain at the 'very heart of Europe' (Seldon, 1997: 166), but the threat to him from the Thatcherite Eurosceptic right would lead him to inform the 1922 Committee (October 1992) that he was the Cabinet's 'greatest Eurosceptic' (Seldon, 1997: 340). However, the desire of the Eurosceptic right to see Major reassess his position on ratifying Maastricht, or committing to a referendum or ruling out entry to the single European currency, meant that some of Major's public comments provoked them. This was clearly evident when Major (April 1993) stated that the Maastricht Treaty was the 'scapegoat for many and nameless fears' that were being peddled by the Eurosceptic right (Seldon, 1997: 370).

When seeking to manage the ideological schism over Europe Major produced a bizarre performance during the 1997 general election campaign. Major said that he would negotiate on Economic Monetary Union in the interests of the UK as a whole, not on the 'convenient party political interests of the Conservative Party'. Then, in a dramatic gesture of clasping both hands in an appeal to his backbenchers, 'like me or loathe me, do not bind my hands when I am negotiating on behalf of the British nation' (Foley, 2000: 168). Seldon notes that he proceeded to give a 'lucid exposition of the case for and against Britain joining the single currency', but that it looked more 'akin to a video made of a jaded hostage filmed by their captors' (Seldon, 1997: 722). Blair retorted that 'there are two Conservative parties fighting this election [and] John Major is in charge of neither of them' (Seldon, 1997: 723).

Analysis and conclusion

Major made a deliberate attempt at portraying himself as the antithesis of the personality driven leader. This reflected his circumstances, but also his temperament, as his approach to politics was embedded in 'realism' rather than 'oratory' (Foley, 2002: 153). Nonetheless, Major was to deliver some notable oratorical moments in his prime ministerial tenure, whether in the heat of parliamentary combat, at party conferences or through the wider media. On the basis of the analysis above, four concluding observations about the oratory of Major can be identified.

First, his most notable oratorical flourishes were tied up with addressing the internal disputes within the Conservative Party. Nothing encapsulates this more than his choice of words when justifying his decision to resign the leadership of the Conservative Party and stand for the vacancy that he himself had created. As Major argued that 'I am not prepared to see the party I care for laid out on the rack like this any longer ... In short, it is time to put up or shut up' (Major, 1999: 626), he was clearly hoping (mistakenly) that his Eurosceptic critics would be cowards. However, that Major was driven to this shows the limited impact of his oratorical use of *utilitas*, his attempts to persuade his own party of what was in their advantage – unity. Ultimately, indeed tragically, his most memorable oratory reflected and then reinforced the central problem of his premiership – the ideological schism surrounding European policy – which served to embed the central reason why the Conservative Party did not warrant re-election. Through his oratory he constantly reminded his party that they needed to display discipline, loyalty and unity. These impotent pleas occurred with hideous frequency. This was the case in his 'don't bind my hands' speech during the 1997 general election campaign. Here Major identified the following central issues. Joining (or not joining) the single European currency was the most important issue facing Britain for a generation. The electorate should vote for the party that he led despite its divisions on this seminal dilemma. And despite the importance of the decision, he was not going to tell what he would do if the electorate did endorse his party in the forthcoming election, as his position was 'negotiate and decide' or 'wait and see'. With the convoluted logic of a trapped man, Major believed that he would enhance his chances of re-election by publicly demonstrating how deep the divisions were within his party, and his inability to deal with them. A Conservative prime minister seeking re-election by creating the imagery of himself as a powerless victim was an unedifying spectacle, yet his oratorical approach was shaped by the ideological schism that he inherited and struggled manfully to manage.

Second, just as his attempt to use *utilitas* would boomerang on him, so his reliance on other oratorical approaches would have the same impact. His attempt to promote a shared interest and identity (*utilitas*) and contrast with Labour (*antithesis*) through the Back to Basics speech would use *dignitas* or *bonum* (what is worthy or good), but due to a combination of media distortions and the personal behaviour of some of his own parliamentarians, this oratorical strategy famously rebounded on him. A similar attempt using pathos, in the shape of the classless society narrative, opened him to criticism from the socially conservative right. Equally, his speech immediately prior to the UK's forced ejection from the ERM involved emotional (pathos) and personal rhetoric (ethos) that made continued membership central to his political credibility. When that was not feasible the extent of the policy failure was magnified by reference to the comments made in his speech.

Third, although Major undermined himself with boomerang style oratory, he also suffered from the emergence of New Labour. A central component of Thatcherism was demonising oratory based around *antithesis*. Thatcher was adept at using rhetoric about the dangers of socialism and trade union power domestically. In foreign policy her oratory could mobilise bias by emphasising the threat of communism and the Soviet Union within the context of the Cold War. All three threats had been removed by the time Major became prime minister. Critically, the oratorical value of referring to the 'Winter of Discontent' (a key component of Thatcherite oratory) was nullified by the passage of time, but was also predicated on the compliance of the Labour Party by its continued adherence to socialism. The diminishing importance of the trade unions ran alongside the cultural, ideological and organisational metamorphosis of the Labour Party into New Labour. The strategic positioning of New Labour as a non-socialist party of the centre-left was problematic for Major. Injecting fear into his rhetoric about socialism, or a return to excessive trade union power, seemed less credible given their repackaging as New Labour. Major was left with few political enemies around which he could create fear and an 'other' to unite both the PCP and the middle classes. The alternatives to socialism and trade union power domestically that Major attempted to use, such as, for example, left-wing educational establishments, failed to gain traction. Meanwhile, while the Eurosceptic right would have liked Major to use the European Union and Brussels as the new rhetorical enemies abroad, this would provoke the Europhile left, and thus Major could never fully commit to this approach.

The final observation about Major's oratory relates to the extent to which he relied on ethos as a means of persuasion within his speeches. As mentioned above, his ability to use *antithesis* and *utilitas* was undermined by the modernisation and moderation of New Labour. It is this factor, alongside the difficulties that he experienced in constructing a clear narrative of the meaning of post-Thatcherite conservatism, that may explain the increasing emphasis on ethos. This created the oddity of a modest man, who eschewed visionary oratory, evolving a method of political persuasion within which conservatism became modelled around him (Foley, 2000: 81, 181–3). This was noted early on in his premiership by Hugo Young, who suggests that 'this was the unexpected coda to the Thatcher era', for while 'Thatcher was often charged with hubristic domination', she was 'never so shameless in representing her own life as the proof of all she had to say' (Young, 1991). However, the analysis of Major's leadership by Jones and Hudson suggests that building the image of the party around the personality of Major, partly shaped through his oratory and the narrative of his life story, had electoral limitations. This is because whilst the electorate might respond positively to the personality of the leader, what matters more will be perceptions of a party's governing competence. Major's narration of his life story may have contributed to him being seen as likeable, and indeed more popular than the party he was leading, but it could not override the stain of incompetence created by the ERM disaster (Jones and Hudson, 1996: 239–44; see also Broughton, 1999).

The oratory of Major was shaped by his political environment – the legacy of leading a long-term administration that was fundamentally divided and opposed by a resurgent and charismatic opposition leader. But his oratorical style was also shaped by his own temperament, where his lack of charisma contributed to weaknesses in terms of performance. He was not a stirring orator who could fire up the emotions, and he receives no mention from Glover in his seminar work on the art of great speeches (Glover, 2011). But he did not claim to be a great orator. Indeed he admitted to being 'uneasy with [the] flowery froth' that he associated with 'idle' oratory (Major, 1999: 32). His central political appeal, which had propelled him to the party leadership after the leadership cult that was Thatcher, was his status as a team player and a unifying figure for his party. Major, however, would spend an inordinate amount of time talking to the British electorate about the ideological fissures that defined the immediate post-Thatcher period. It defined his oratory and reflected and reinforced the erosion of his political reputation.

10

The oratory of William Hague

Judi Atkins

William Hague first came to prominence in 1977, when he addressed the Conservative Party conference at the age of sixteen. This speech was well received by delegates, with Margaret Thatcher describing it as 'thrilling' (BBC, 2007a). On 23 February 1989, Hague entered Parliament as MP for Richmond (Yorkshire), and eighteen months later he was appointed Parliamentary Private Secretary to the then Chief Secretary to the Treasury, Norman Lamont. Hague performed well in this role and was subsequently promoted first to the position of Parliamentary Under-Secretary in the Department of Social Security (DSS) in 1993, and then to Minister of State for Social Security and Disabled People in 1994 (Nadler, 2000: 137–47). As a junior minister, Hague soon became known for his debating skills and quick wit, and few were surprised when he was elevated to John Major's Cabinet as Secretary of State for Wales in 1995. Aged just thirty-four, he was the youngest Cabinet minister since Harold Wilson (Nadler, 2000: 157).

Following the Conservatives' crushing defeat in the May 1997 general election, Hague was chosen as Major's successor for the party leadership. Although he sought to renew the party institutionally, Hague made few attempts either to move it onto the centre ground or to broaden its appeal beyond its core supporters. He instead focused on the traditional Conservative priorities of crime, Europe and immigration, a position that was congruent with both his Thatcherite beliefs and the instincts of many grassroots party members (Bale, 2011: 372–4, 81). This strategy failed to win over the wider public, however, and the Conservatives suffered a second landslide defeat in 2001. Hague then resigned the leadership and withdrew from front-line politics until December 2005, when David Cameron appointed him to the post of Shadow Foreign Secretary. He finally returned to government in May 2010 as Secretary of State for Foreign and Commonwealth Affairs in the Conservative–Liberal Democrat Coalition.

This chapter evaluates Hague's rhetoric through the lens of the 'representative claim' (Saward, 2006, 2010). Such claims were present in Hague's 1977 conference speech, where he positioned himself as a spokesman for his generation, and they were accepted by his audience because they accorded with his Young Conservative ethos. During his tenure as party leader, Hague presented himself as the 'voice of middle England' (Wood, quoted in Bale, 2011: 155) and attempted to speak on behalf of this 'forgotten majority'. However, these representative claims were unsuccessful because Hague failed to convince the public that he was 'one of them'; his claims were not tied to a credible ethos of ordinariness. Likewise, Hague's representation of his audience as small-c conservatives was rejected by large sections of the electorate, which suggests that he had fundamentally misunderstood their values and attitudes. Indeed, this core vote strategy only served to reinforce the caricature of the Conservatives as a 'harsh, intolerant party', and consequently failed to bring them net gains in 2001 (Lynch and Garnett, 2003: 253).

Although unable to cement his authority as party leader, Hague is an accomplished parliamentary orator. This is clear from his ability to combine factual evidence (logos) with humour (pathos), which in turn contributes to an ethos of competence. These qualities not only facilitated Hague's rise through the junior ministerial ranks, but also his return to the frontbenches four years after he resigned the leadership. It is worth noting that, as (Shadow) Foreign Secretary, Hague toned down his populist rhetoric and avoided making representative claims. This approach proved highly effective, enabling him to cultivate an ethos of statesmanship.

The representative claim

In recent years, the issue of representation has received renewed attention from scholars. One such theorist is Michael Saward, who explores it through the notion of the representative claim. Saward proceeds from the assumption that 'in representation an individual or collective stands for, speaks for, or acts for, another', in the sense that a subject (e.g. an elected MP) stands for an object (e.g. a constituency). He then proposes that an individual or a collective agent (the 'maker') constructs a claim in which he, she or it puts forward a subject, which represents the idea of an object that is related to a referent, and presents it to an audience (Saward, 2010: 36–7). So, for instance, Mrs Thatcher (maker) regularly offered herself (subject) as standing for the interests of 'ordinary people' (object) to the electorate (audience). A representative claim is therefore 'a double claim: about an attitude or capacity of a would-be representative, and also about relevant characteristics of a would-be audience' (Saward, 2006: 303).

On Saward's view, 'representation is performing, is action by actors, and the performance contains or adds up to a claim that someone is or can be representative'. As such, representation requires the careful projection of characteristics that are possessed by, or ascribed to, the subject of the claim (Saward, 2010: 66). The performative aspect of representation is captured in the Aristotelian concept of ethos, whereby the (real or imagined) character of the speaker forms the basis of a persuasive appeal. Such appeals have become increasingly important, as contemporary politicians are required to prove their credibility to an ever more sceptical electorate. This chapter will demonstrate that they are also central to the success of representative claims, on the ground that an audience is unlikely to accept attempts to speak on its behalf if a politician has not first established their fitness to do so.

By portraying a constituency or the nation in a particular way, a speaker offers a new construction of the 'object' they claim to represent. Saward explains that a maker of representative claims will suggest to their potential audience: '(1) you are/ are part of this audience, (2) you should accept this view, this construction – this representation – of yourself, and (3) you should accept me as speaking and acting for you' (2006: 303). Thus, a politician may seek to portray his or her audience as, for instance, the 'squeezed middle' or 'hardworking families', and position him- or herself as their representative. These constructions are then accepted or rejected by their target audiences. For Saward, it is through these processes of claim-making and consequent reception by audiences that representation is produced (Saward, 2006: 303).

We find a typical example of a representative claim in the opening sentence of Hague's 1977 conference speech, where he asserted that: 'As a 16-year-old, I represent what may well seem to be the last generation for the Conservative Party'. In Saward's terms, Hague (maker) offered himself (subject) as standing for the interests of young people (object) to party members (audience). Hague then called attention to the lack of support for the Conservatives among first-time voters, which he attributed to the perception that the party stood for the 'maintenance of the existing political and economic order'. Using *antithesis*, Hague contrasted this stance with Labour's bold promises of a shift to the left, and argued that the Conservatives needed to 'reverse the progress of socialism' by positioning themselves as 'the party of radicalism and change'. This in turn would enable them to 'capture the imagination and support of the younger people' (Hague, 1977).

Hague returned to the theme of age with the question: 'What sort of world do young people want?' Using the technique of *anthypophora*, he answered it immediately by listing their aspirations for the future. In particular, Hague claimed, young people wanted to live in 'a society where effort and initiative are rewarded instead of stamped upon, where those who work the hardest receive the greatest reward, where those who take the greatest risk receive the largest profit'. However, he continued, their main priority was 'to be free, free from the government, the government that they think should get out of the way, not intervene, not interfere in their lives'. Hague then added playfully: 'And I trust Mrs Thatcher's government will indeed get out of the way.' After all, 'half of you may not be here in 30 or 40 years' time, but I will be and I want to be free' (Hague, 1977). Hague's cheekiness and his repeated references to his youth enhanced his Young Conservative ethos, and as such were vital to the acceptance of his representative claim by party members. We will see below that humour is central to Hague's rhetoric, along with his commitment to Thatcherite principles.

In government, 1993–97

In 1993, Hague was appointed Parliamentary Under-Secretary in the DSS, where he was charged with the preparation of the Major government's Pensions Bill. Although this was a challenging brief, Hague showed 'exceptional mastery of detail' in steering the legislation through Parliament (*Financial Times*, quoted in Nadler, 2000: 147). This is evident from the following extract, in which he responded to a question about the government's intentions regarding pensions and benefits:

> That raises the debate which often arises … about pensioners' living standards which, as one of my hon. Friends observed, have improved by 42 per cent on average over the past 15 years. The percentage of pensioners in the bottom quintile of income distribution has fallen from 38 per cent in 1979 to 24 per cent on the latest figures. Therefore, some of the points that the hon. Member for Newport, West (Mr Flynn) made earlier are not valid. His comments about pensioners' incomes are not true. (HC Deb., 16 February 1994, col. 1025)

Here, Hague appealed to logos to legitimate the Conservatives' position and disprove his opponent's argument. Such demonstrations of competence also augmented his ethos, and indeed convinced his colleagues that 'all the predictions about his golden future were well founded' (Nadler, 2000: 144).

Also vital to the effectiveness of Hague's parliamentary rhetoric was his use of pathos, in the form of humour. We find an example in the pensions debate where Hague, after quoting figures to support his claim that benefit claimants were better off under the Conservatives, employed *antithesis* to contrast his party's record with that of the Labour governments of the 1970s, when 'spending on families fell by seven per cent in total'. The Liberal Democrat MP Archy Kirkwood hit back with the question: 'Where were you in the 1970s?' to which Hague replied, 'I was at school, but I was watching closely the activities of the Labour Government. I recall writing down these figures at the time' (HC Deb., 16 February 1994, col. 1027). This exchange displayed Hague's knowledge of welfare policy, while playing up to his image as a political 'anorak' for the amusement of his audience.

On 20 July 1994, Hague was promoted to the post of Minister of State for Social Security and Disabled People. In a debate on Incapacity Benefit, he again appealed to logos by drawing on statistical data (HC Deb., 2 February 1995, cols 1233–4) and government reports (HC Deb., 2 February 1995, col. 1238) to support his case for reforming the benefits system. Hague also made repeated references to the involvement of outside experts, telling MPs that 'I am trying to show that the development of the new [all work] test has been an open process. We have consulted widely … We have consulted leading disability organisations' (HC Deb., 2 February 1995, col. 1236).[1] By emphasising the contribution of practitioners to the development of this policy, Hague sought to confer additional legitimacy on the government's approach, which in turn was intended to facilitate the passage of the legislation through Parliament.

Hague's skilled use of deliberative rhetoric in championing the Disability Discrimination Act further boosted his profile, and in July 1995 he was elevated to the Cabinet as Secretary of State for Wales. He identified as his priorities 'the economy, education and the environment', a combination of a three-part list and alliteration that was designed to ensure that 'the three [were] linked in people's minds and actions'. Taken together, Hague continued, these themes represented: 'Opportunity – the opportunity of learning, of gaining qualifications, of mastering a skill, of gaining a job, of continuity for communities, of a future for young people, and the opportunity to live in a healthy environment and to enjoy the variety of spectacular scenery that Wales has to offer' (HC Deb., 27 February 1997, col. 457). In this statement, Hague employed *anaphora* – the 'repetition of the same word at the beginning of successive clauses' (Lanham, 1991: 211) – to create a logical connection between education and its economic benefits. Although the sequence is broken by the word 'and', this conjunction establishes a direct link between Hague's first two priorities and his commitment to the environment.

A vital part of Hague's role was to advance the Conservative argument against Labour's plans for Welsh devolution (Nadler, 2000: 158). To this end, he attacked the proposed Assembly as an 'expensive roomful of hot air' (HC Deb., 29 February 1996, col. 1039, see also HC Deb., 27 February 1997, col. 467), using metaphor to represent this tier of government as a talking shop that would cost a great deal but achieve nothing. Furthermore, Hague argued, 'Labour's proposals are a recipe for constitutional chaos. They would put at risk all the benefits that Wales derives from the Union: higher public spending per head, representation at Westminster and a voice at the Cabinet table' (HC Deb., 29 February 1996, col. 1039, see also HC Deb., 27 February 1997, col. 468). This extract contains alliteration and a three-part list, which together heightened the rhetorical impact of Hague's argument. Hague also appealed to pathos by listing the negative consequences of devolution, a move designed to induce fear in his audience and thus convince them to reject Labour's proposed reforms.

Leader of the Conservative Party, 1997–2001

Major's resignation on 2 May 1997 triggered a contest for the party leadership. The challengers were Kenneth Clarke and Stephen Dorrell, who were associated with the Europhile left; Michael Howard, Peter Lilley and John Redwood from the Thatcherite Eurosceptic right; and Hague, 'who had softer associations with the right, although committed Thatcherites doubted the depth of his commitment to their cause' (Heppell, 2008b: 23). Dorrell's campaign collapsed at an early stage, while Howard, Lilley and Redwood were eliminated in the initial rounds. This left the pro-European Clarke and Hague, who was the most moderate of the four Eurosceptic candidates, in the contest. However, many on the Thatcherite right regarded the prospect of a Clarke victory as insupportable, to the extent that Thatcher herself abandoned her neutral stance and endorsed Hague: 'I am supporting William Hague. Now, have you got the name? William Hague for the same kind of principled government which I led, vote for William Hague on Thursday. Have you got the message?' (quoted in Heppell, 2008b: 26). This last-minute endorsement boosted Hague's campaign, enabling him to defeat Clarke by ninety-two to seventy votes and to assume the party leadership on 19 June 1997 (Collings and Seldon, 2001: 625).

According to Peter Snowdon, Hague presented himself as 'the candidate who could make "a fresh start", as the youngest candidate and the one least associated with the old regime' (Snowdon, 2010: 43). To this end, he adopted the campaign slogan 'Fresh Future', which encapsulated his desire to 'make the Conservative Party fresh, clear, open and united' (BBC, 1997). These aims not only signalled a break from the divisions of the past, but also a commitment to give the party a 'philosophical overhaul akin to the one it had had under Margaret Thatcher after 1975' (Kelly, 2001: 197). However, Hague acknowledged that this would be a difficult process and, in an interview with the BBC, he warned MPs: 'don't vote for me unless you want to work hard and don't vote for me unless you want to take some tough decisions. We've got to take tough decisions about the organisation of the Conservative Party, tough decisions about our policies in the next few years, tough decisions about making sure we've got discipline in our Party' (BBC, 1997). Here, Hague employed *anaphora* to establish a logical connection between the components of his modernisation programme, while repetition and a three-part list provided emphasis. His warning to MPs contributed to an ethos of strong leadership, which was designed to show the public that he possessed the character and vision required to modernise his party, and thus make it electable once again.

A key component of Hague's 'Fresh Future' strategy was the reform of the party's organisation. In particular, he pledged to give party members the final say in leadership elections and to introduce 'membership ballots to endorse or reject major policy proposals' (Collings and Seldon, 2001: 627). As Hague explained, these changes would form the basis of a 'new contract' between party members and the leadership:

> The members understandably say they want a greater control, a greater role to play in the Party, and a greater role over their leadership – their control over the leadership of the Party. The quid pro quo of that is that the leadership must have greater authority to intervene in particularly difficult or embarrassing situations for the Party. And again, I found in my tour of the country – that I've just completed, and I've spoken to nearly 2500 Conservative activists, and heard their views and questions – I think there is a great deal of support for that kind of concept in the Conservative Party. (BBC, 1997)

In this extract, Hague used a three-part list, *anaphora* and repetition to link together the demands of party members and emphasise their magnitude. He also sought to legitimate his approach by invoking the testimony of the activists he had met and their support for 'Fresh Future'. However, it is significant that Hague said relatively little about the leadership's side of the bargain. This may be attributable to the fact that, at root, 'Hague's plans involved centralisation [while] the demands from the party in the country were really about democratisation' (Bale, 2011: 74). Nonetheless, his reforms were passed, an early success that ensured Hague's continued popularity with party members even though he led them to a second defeat in 2001.

Hague suffered from two major difficulties that blighted his leadership from the start. The first was his own legitimacy, which was weakened by 'the perception that his was a default victory because the best candidates [such as Michael Heseltine and Michael Portillo] were not available'. Moreover, as the sole candidate of the Eurosceptic centre-right in the final ballot, Hague won support simply because he was 'anyone but Clarke' (Heppell, 2008b: 26). His youth and relative inexperience also counted against him, and undoubtedly diminished his authority among party members. From a public relations perspective, however, Hague's image as the youthful, modernising candidate was seen as an advantage in terms of appealing to the electorate (Fletcher, 2012: 186). Additionally, he was the most centrist of the six challengers for the leadership, and like Major he had come from an ordinary background (Snowdon, 2010: 43). On paper at least, it appeared that Hague would be able to broaden the Conservatives' appeal beyond their core supporters, and that his attempts to speak for this wider audience would be accepted. In practice, and as we will see below, Hague's second major problem was his failure to establish a rapport with the public.

As Leader of the Opposition, Hague's ability to use logos served him well and he drew on a range of sources to attack Labour's record.[2] In the 1998 Debate on the Address, for example, Hague expressed his support for the bipartisan approach to the Northern Ireland peace process but argued that the government had made a serious error:

> Seven months after the agreement was signed, more than 200 terrorists have been released from prison early, but not one gun or one ounce of Semtex has been decommissioned. We believe sincerely and strongly that continuing to release terrorist prisoners without any decommissioning by paramilitary organisations in return should stop. Such lack of reciprocation breaks the promise that was given to the people of Northern Ireland.

To give his argument additional force, Hague quoted the then Secretary of State for Northern Ireland, Mo Mowlam, who had previously told Parliament that 'several things must happen in parallel in order to build confidence. That has always been the situation, whether it be decommissioning, the release of prisoners'.[3] He then urged the government to 'stand firm and say to the terrorists … "You cannot have both the bullet and the ballot. You have to choose." We must get the terrorists to choose' (HC Deb., 24 November 1998, col. 17). This statement contains alliteration, which supplies emphasis while helping to fix the Conservatives' position in the mind of the audience. Meanwhile, Hague's tough stance on decommissioning was perhaps intended to contribute to an ethos of strong leadership, and so bolster his standing with his Parliamentary Party and the electorate.

In this period, Hague frequently made jokes at the expense of his political opponents. Of Charles Kennedy, he lamented: 'What a shame that the Liberal Democrat leader has gone in a few short months from *Have I Got News for You* to *I'm Sorry I Haven't a Clue*' (HC Deb., 17 November 1999, col. 16). Hague's pun on the title of a popular television programme was intended to mock Kennedy, and thus to undermine his authority. However, these attacks sometimes left Hague vulnerable to ridicule, with Tony Blair observing in 2000 that: 'The jokes were good – they are always good. There is probably a little debate in his office: "Do we go for jokes or for policy?" Let me congratulate him on at least one sound judgment. Frankly, I think it is better to stick with the jokes' (HC Deb., 6 December 2000, col. 29). On such occasions, writes Alastair Campbell, Blair 'turned the Tory leader's strength – wit and great one-liners – into a weakness, masking lack of strategy and judgement'. The charge of '"jokes, not judgement" spoke to a real concern about Hague', Campbell continues, 'but also put him off his stride on the joke front too' (Campbell, 2007). This accusation gained credence from Hague's failure to mention the economy in his comments on the Queen's Speech (Blair, HC Deb., 6 December 2000, col. 23), an area of policy that, together with health and education, was neglected by the party leadership in favour of typical Conservative concerns such as Europe, tax and immigration (Bale, 2011: 373–4).

Hague's parliamentary rhetoric also featured populist appeals, which were targeted at MPs and the electorate alike. In the words of Daniele Albertazzi and Duncan McDonnell, populism 'pits a virtuous and homogeneous people against a set of elites and dangerous "others" who are together depicted as depriving (or attempting to deprive) the sovereign people of their rights, values, prosperity, identity and voice' (2008, quoted in Bale, 2011: 102). We find an example in Hague's assertion that: 'The Labour Government pursue their own political priorities ... They should [instead] turn the common sense of the British people into common sense policies for the country. That is what the Opposition have to deliver – the common sense revolution.' Here, Hague utilised *antithesis* to contrast an allegedly arrogant government that neglected the needs of the country with the Conservatives, who he claimed were in touch with the 'common sense instincts of the British people' and thus could deliver the policies Britain needed (HC Deb., 17 November 1999, col. 23). However, this populist argument had little impact, with Blair dismissing the Conservatives' economic strategy as 'Haguenomics – revolutionary it may be, but common sense it certainly is not' (HC Deb., 17 November 1999, col. 30). Blair's retort tapped into the concerns about economic competence that had haunted the party since Black Wednesday. It also challenged Hague's assertion that the Conservatives were offering the right policies for Britain and, by implication, his claim to be in tune with the instincts of the 'British people'.

Populism notwithstanding, Hague was 'widely admired for his performance at Prime Minister's Question Time' (Garnett and Lynch, 2003: 2). His skills in debate regularly left Blair rattled, giving backbench morale a much-needed boost and thus strengthening Hague's position within his party (Fletcher, 2012: 190). Indeed, this debating prowess may have allowed Hague to remain as Leader of the Opposition for a full parliamentary term despite his consistently low opinion poll ratings (for figures, see Broughton, 2003: 205). It is important to note, however, that 'the formal debating style [demanded by Parliament] is a world away from the informal, conversational manner that the public has come to expect in the television age' (Fletcher, 2012: 190). Hague's inability to adapt his communication style to suit the electoral arena only reinforced his aloof, 'nerdy' image, and so failed to endear him to this wider audience.

The theme of Hague's 1998 conference speech was the 'British way' which, he explained, 'is about smaller Government and bigger citizens'. This idea was consistent with the views expressed in his 1977 address and lends weight to Jo-Anne Nadler's claim that 'Hague remained at heart an unreconstructed Thatcherite' (Hague, 2004, quoted in Bale, 2011: 80). Like Thatcher before him, Hague aligned the Conservative Party with 'the people', telling his audience: 'Our character is the character of the people. Our beliefs: the beliefs of the people. Our purpose: the defence, the advancement, the elevation of the people. Our history is that of a Party that trusts the people' (Hague, 1998).[4] In this statement, Hague employed *parison*, where each clause has a similar construction (Lanham, 1991: 104), to make his words more memorable. Emphasis was supplied through *symploce*, the use of repetition at the start and end of successive clauses (Glover, 2011: 93).[5] However, while Thatcher's claims to stand for 'ordinary people with ordinary hopes and beliefs' (Thatcher, 1976) were widely accepted, due to the centrality of such ordinariness to her leadership ethos (Scammell, 1996), Hague's representative claims failed to gain traction with the public, as we will see next.

In his 2000 conference address, Hague spoke of his reasons for entering politics, and he invited his audience to:

> Come with me to the Rother Valley, to the heart of South Yorkshire ... Come and meet the people I grew up with. Children of proud mothers who struggled with small budgets ... who hoped for a better life for their sons and their daughters. Children of fathers who worked hard in mines and on farms and in steel works ... who had no choice but to live from one week's pay packet to the next. (Hague, 2000b)

He proceeded to explain that many of his peers now had their own families and, though they were better off than their parents, nonetheless shared their desire for security and their aspiration for a better life. For Hague, these people, 'and millions like them, are the mainstream of our country. They are the people who motivate me'. However, he continued, they frequently feel let down by politicians who are out of touch on issues such as crime, taxation and keeping the pound, and he appealed directly to this neglected majority by pledging that the Conservatives 'will govern for hard-working families. We will govern for people of every community and background. We will govern for the mainstream that New Labour has ignored. We will govern for all the people' (Hague, 2000b).

On one level, this anecdote formed the basis of a representative claim, whereby Hague (maker) offered the Conservatives (subject) as standing for the interests of the 'forgotten majority' (object) to party members and/or to the electorate (audience). On another, it can be read as an attempt to incite identification with Hague as an 'ordinary person' (Atkins and Finlayson, 2013: 167–8), and thus to persuade the public to accept him as their representative. However, the story felt forced, and indeed did nothing to dispel Hague's image as a 'Hansard-reading teenage conformist and tweed-jacketed Young Conservative', who was 'aloof, out of touch, remote from ordinary people' (Nadler, 2000: 211–12). Likewise, the efforts of Hague's advisers to overturn this perception by setting up photo opportunities of him participating in 'normal' activities, such as visiting a theme park and drinking cocktails at the Notting Hill Carnival, were widely ridiculed and only diminished his authority further (Bale, 2011: 83). This lack of a convincing ethos of ordinariness ensured that Hague's representative claims were rejected by large sections of the public; he had failed to persuade them of his fitness to speak and act on their behalf.

The early rejection of Hague's 'Fresh Future' approach, with its calls for 'a more "pluralistic" and "inclusive" Conservatism' (Kelly, 2001: 197), can also be attributed to problems of ethos. As Nigel Fletcher explains, 'a modernising leader first has to embody change; Hague did not, and probably could not do so ... Hague was the authentic voice of his party as it stood, and that was his – and their – biggest problem' (2012: 195). Hague subsequently retreated to a core vote strategy with 'common sense Conservatism', which was based on the belief that 'there was a "silent majority" of voters simply waiting for and wanting to be mobilised by right-wing populism'. However, the party never provided any evidence in support of this assumption (Broughton, 2003: 202–3), which suggests that Hague had gravely misjudged his audience. Indeed, it soon became apparent that the Conservatives were 'damagingly out of tune with the attitudes and values of parts of British society' (Lynch and Garnett, 2003: 256), who not only rejected Hague's construction of them, but also his attempts to position himself as their representative.

Hague made an appearance on the BBC's *Newsnight* programme a week before the 2001 general election. Jeremy Paxman opened the interview by listing a series of discarded party slogans, among which were '"Fresh Start", "The British Way", "The Right Way" ... [and] "the common sense revolution"'. He then attacked Hague's credibility by observing that 'all these different slogans that you've adopted during the time you've been leader, people say are symptomatic of flip-flops of yours on policy'. One such initiative was the tax guarantee which, though central to the Common Sense agenda, was dropped within months (Bale, 2011: 109), leading Paxman to ask: 'When did you realise you'd made a mistake?' Hague attempted to deflect the question by saying, 'We changed the tax guarantee into specific commitments', but Paxman simply repeated his question (BBC, 2001).[6] By again refusing to give a straight answer, Hague gave credence to the charge that the Conservatives lacked direction, which in turn caused further damage to public perceptions of his leadership competence.

Although the interview was dominated by logos-based arguments about policy, it also featured a number of populist appeals. For example, Hague's statement that 'we're the only party speaking up for the people of this country in this election campaign' is a representative claim, whereby he (maker) offered the Conservatives (subject) as the voice of the British people (object) to television viewers (audience). Indeed, Hague continued, 'we are gaining support on the key issues of tax, crime, asylum and of keeping the pound' (BBC, 2001). While this approach had 'the added advantage of authenticity since it accorded with Hague's instincts' (Bale, 2011: 374), it did not resonate with the electorate, whose primary concern was the state of Britain's public services (Broughton, 2003: 208). Hague's misrepresentation of his target audience, in conjunction with his failure to establish his fitness to speak for 'ordinary people', contributed to a second disastrous general election performance, and he stood down as party leader on 13 September 2001.

(Shadow) Foreign Secretary

Four years after his resignation, Hague returned to the front benches as (Shadow) Foreign Secretary. As we would expect, his parliamentary rhetoric in this period relied heavily on appeals to logos. In the 2008 Debate on the Address, for instance, Hague told MPs that 'it was announced to the press overnight last night: "The withdrawal of the 4,000 British troops in Iraq will be completed by next June, a senior defence source has disclosed" … If it is true, that information should have been given to Parliament in the form of a statement to the House of Commons' (HC Deb., 10 December 2008, col. 579). Hague then cited a newspaper report as proof of New Labour's lack of transparency, before claiming that 'the government deplore leaks by day and live by them by night'. Here, he employed *antithesis* to characterise New Labour's duplicity, heightening the effect through the temporal contrast of day and night. Interestingly, Hague used less humour in the parliamentary debates considered in this section (but see HC Deb., 29 May 2010, col. 175), which may be indicative of an attempt to cultivate gravitas following his return to front-line politics.

It is also worth highlighting that Hague's rhetoric on Europe featured fewer populist appeals during this stage of his career. In 2010, for example, he told MPs that 'the British public have felt that they have had too little democratic control over developments in the EU', before announcing that the Coalition would 'bring forward a Bill … [requiring] that any proposed future EU treaty that transfers areas of power or competence from Britain to the EU will be subject to a referendum. The British people will then have a referendum lock to which only they hold the key' (HC Deb.,

29 May 2010, col. 188). With the lock-and-key metaphor, Hague memorably summarised his message that the people would be able to decide whether to open the door, so to speak, to closer European integration. While this policy is congruent with Conservative thinking on Europe, Hague's more moderate tone may also be attributable to a desire to project a statesmanlike ethos appropriate to his position. As he told the *London Evening Standard* in 2012, 'I've always been clear I came back into frontline politics to do foreign policy and that's what I'm here doing. When I was leader of the party there were always polls showing I was the least popular. Since I took no notice of these things I've become more popular. So I propose to go on taking no notice whatsoever' (Sands and Murphy, 2012).

As part of Cameron's modernising agenda, the Conservatives endorsed a 'liberal conservative' foreign policy. Hague explained that this approach was 'supportive of spreading freedom and humanitarian intervention, but recognising the complexities of human nature and sceptical of grand schemes to remake the world'. The first of these principles is clearly liberal, while the second is conservative and contains an implicit criticism of Blair's policy of democracy promotion. Using the techniques of *anaphora* and *parison* to add emphasis, Hague committed his party to 'the extension and broadening of our alliances. The enhancing of our moral authority. The understanding of other continents. And the much needed reform of our own'. He then urged: 'Let us make this part of our New Direction, and part of the excitement, purpose and resolve of a new Conservative government' (Hague, 2006). With this combination of pathos and a three-part list, Hague sought to inspire party members with the prospect of a return to office, while presenting the Conservatives as a credible alternative government to the wider electorate.

In his conference speeches, Hague regularly attacked the record of the previous Labour governments and emphasised the achievements of his own party. For instance, he argued in 2010 that 'Labour left Britain on a path to decline, with no vision, no coherent decision-making, and no grip over the finances of defence or diplomacy'. This sentence contains *anaphora*, alliteration and a three-part list, while the journey metaphor carries a negative evaluation – namely that Labour had led the country down the wrong track. Hague then utilised *antithesis* and logos to contrast the failings of his predecessors with the Coalition's performance to date:

> On our first day the Prime Minister established the National Security Council so that all relevant ministers consider [the] issues together with all the expert advice available to them. And the Foreign Office is back where it belongs at the centre of Government, able to lead in constructing a foreign policy which runs through the veins of all government departments. (Hague, 2010b)

As Bryan Turner correctly points out, 'the human body is an ancient metaphor of political institutions' (Turner, 2008: 151), and Hague employed it to vivify his claim that, in an interdependent world, Britain must 'build strong bilateral relationships directly with the world's emerging powers' not only in diplomacy, but in such diverse areas as commerce, education and sport (Hague, 2010b).

A key aim of Hague's 2011 conference address was to show that the Conservatives had consistently proved their detractors wrong. He identified Libya as a case in point, and described how the Coalition had secured 'what many said was impossible: an unequivocal UN Security Council resolution authorising military force, strong regional support from Arab nations, and a military operation that was limited, legal, morally right and successful'. Hague was particularly keen to demonstrate his party's prescience on Europe in the light of the ongoing financial crisis, and he reminded his audience that 'Fourteen years ago I predicted that the Eurozone would become a burning building with no exits'. This combination of foresight and consistency contributed to an ethos of authority and competence, though it is worth noting that Hague linked his prediction to the broader populist claim that 'our approach to the European Union is one in tune with the instincts of the British people'. However, he resisted the urge to gloat and went on to say: 'But because the Eurozone countries are our friends and neighbours, and because our prosperity and financial stability is tied with theirs, we must now support them in quenching the flames' (Hague, 2011). Although Hague's warning conferred a negative evaluation of the Eurozone through the use of a destruction metaphor (see Charteris-Black, 2011: 125–7), his subsequent representation of Britain as a rescuer contained no such judgement. This refusal to revel in the misfortune of the Eurozone countries further enhanced Hague's ethos of statesmanship, and thus helped to restore his reputation with the electorate.

The issue of Europe dominated an interview Hague gave to the BBC's *Politics Show* in January 2006. At this time, the Conservatives were seeking to withdraw their MEPs from the European People's Party-European Democrats (EPP-ED) group in the European Parliament, a move that caused tensions between the Eurosceptic Parliamentary Party and pro-European MEPs (Lynch, 2009: 187, 196).[7] Hague justified this decision as follows:

> What it comes down to … it's influencing future ideas, it is moving on from the old Europe. Just tagging along with received wisdom is no longer adequate and there's a real crisis coming in European affairs and we want to build a political grouping that can address that, and advocate a modern, flexible, open Europe, not an ever-more centralised declining Europe. (BBC, 2006a)

Through this rhetoric of crisis, Hague sought to win support for the new grouping by inducing fear in his listeners. Using *antithesis*, he then contrasted the 'old', centralised Europe with the 'modern, flexible, open Europe' that the Conservatives endorsed as a solution to the impending crisis. This vision is, of course, consistent with the Thatcherite hostility towards big government, which has been present in Hague's political philosophy throughout his career. It also contains echoes of his 'in Europe, but not run by Europe' position, according to which member states had to choose between 'an integrationist path leading to a European "superstate" or a flex-ible "network" Europe' (Lynch, 2003: 151).

A further challenge facing the international community is the possibility that Iran might one day acquire nuclear weapons. In an appearance on *The Andrew Marr Show* in 2012, Hague gave the following response to a question about whether Israel would attack Iran:

> Either that will happen and there will be a war, or there would be a Cold War in which Iran for the long-term would be subject to these kinds of very intense economic sanctions and they would find that other nations in their region developed nuclear weapons, so they would be in a permanent standoff with those countries. Like the Cold War, but without many of the safeguards against accidents and misunderstandings that we had in the Cold War. (BBC 2012)

Here, Hague drew an analogy between the Cold War and a hypothetical future scenario in the Middle East. By doing so, he activated an array of negative associations, such as protracted ideological struggle and the ever-present threat of nuclear annihilation, and directed them towards a target, namely Iran (see Charteris-Black, 2011: 13–15). This emotional effect was heightened by Hague's warning about the precariousness of his imaginary situation, an appeal to pathos that was intended to incite fear in his audience and thus persuade them to support the government's position.

Conclusion

It is clear from this discussion that Hague has a strong grasp of the techniques of classical rhetoric and that he is an accomplished speaker. He is particularly effective in Parliament, where he is able to use logos and humour to sometimes devastating effect against his opponents. However, Hague's debating aptitude, which 'would have made him a giant in a 19th century context is less relevant to a mass audience in the age of the sound-bite and the image-conscious television appearance' (Nadler, 2000: 209). Kathleen Hall Jamieson observes that this setting instead requires a 'personal, self-disclosing style that draws public discourse out of a private self and comfortably reduces the complex world to dramatic narratives'. As such, it has rendered obsolete the data-driven, combative, impersonal style of public communication that dominated the pre-television era (Jamieson, 1988: 84, 89). This style was also characteristic of Hague's oratory, which contributed to his image of aloofness and thus hindered his attempts to establish a connection with the electorate.

Contemporary politicians need to prove that they possess the attributes required for good leadership, while demonstrating that they know and share the concerns of ordinary people (Finlayson, 2002: 590). Hague's failure to master this (admittedly difficult) balancing act is partly attributable to the lack of authority that dogged his leadership from the beginning. More important from the point of view of the electorate was his inability to present himself convincingly as 'one of them'. Although his advisers set up several photo opportunities intended to make Hague appear more 'normal' (Fletcher, 2012: 191), their efforts came across as inauthentic; 'neither Hague nor his team had the flair to pull off the art of rehearsed spontaneity' (Nadler, 2000: 211–12) and he was widely mocked as a result. These attempts at image management also raised questions about Hague's judgement, which in turn caused further damage to his leadership credibility.

Hague's lack of a believable ethos of ordinariness gravely undermined the effectiveness of his representative claims. After all, if large sections of the public did not relate to him as an 'ordinary person', they were unlikely to accept him as speaking and acting on their behalf. Equally problematic was Hague's construction of his audience as a silent, small-c conservative majority, on the ground that a substantial part of the electorate rejected this portrayal of themselves. In the words of Philip Lynch and Mark Garnett, Conservative MPs had relied too heavily on 'gut instincts and anecdotal evidence from canvassing in Tory strongholds, rather than opinion polls'. As a result, they 'wrongly assumed that their message accorded with the views of target voters' (2003: 256), a miscalculation that would prove critical in the Conservatives' 2001 defeat.

As (Shadow) Foreign Secretary, Hague was responsible for advancing his party's 'liberal conservative' approach to international affairs. In this role, an ability to connect with the public is less important, which may explain why Hague has avoided making representative claims. Instead, he has relied consistently on logos and *antithesis* to attack Labour's record and to present the Conservatives as a credible party of government. It is worth highlighting that Hague utilises less humour than he did previously, and that he has noticeably moderated his populism. This has enabled him to cultivate an ethos of statesmanship, and thus to restore his reputation with the electorate.

Notes

I am very grateful to the Editors for their insightful comments on an earlier draft of this chapter.

1 According to Hague, the purpose of the all work test was to 'assess the effect of a person's medical condition on his or her ability to carry out work-related functions' (HC Deb., 2 February 1995, col. 1236).

2 These sources include newspaper reports (e.g. HC Deb., 17 November 1999, col. 16), previous parliamentary debates (e.g. HC Deb., 6 December 2000, col. 14) and the views of professional bodies (e.g. HC Deb., 17 November 1999, col. 21).

3 See HC Deb., 20 April 1998, col. 484.

4 The phrase 'trust the people' was first coined by Lord Randolph Churchill in 1884. It was subsequently quoted by party leaders such as Winston Churchill (1945), Edward Heath (1967) and David Cameron (2005), who thus sought to locate themselves within the Conservative tradition.

5 These techniques were also present in Hague's 1999 conference speech, where he asserted that: 'When minor operations are carried out to meet political targets while people die waiting for their heart bypass, Britain needs a Common Sense Revolution. When local councils spend more money looking after bogus asylum seekers than after old people in homes, Britain needs a Common Sense Revolution.'

6 For an analysis of the types of non-replies used in political interviews, see Bull and Mayer (1993).

7 In the event, Conservative MEPs did not leave the EPP-ED until June 2009.

11

The oratory of Boris Johnson

Katharine Dommett

On paper Alexander Boris de Pfeffel Johnson, or Boris as he is widely known and recognised, is largely indistinguishable from his senior Conservative colleagues. Like David Cameron he attended Eton and later Oxford, becoming a member of the exclusive Bullingdon Club alongside George Osborne. Like William Hague he became president of the Oxford Union Society. And like Michael Gove he elected for a career in journalism, working at *The Times*, the *Spectator* and the *Telegraph* (where he retains a column). Accordingly his decision to run as a Conservative candidate for Parliament in 1997 (where he was defeated) and again in 2001 for his Henley seat (where he was successful) was unsurprising. However, to view Boris Johnson as a conventional politician would be a mistake. Far from fitting the mould of his contemporaries Johnson cuts a unique figure within the Conservative Party and indeed, contemporary party politics.

Johnson is a paradoxical individual. Whilst his conservative views on Europe, taxation, immigration, nationalism, bureaucracy and crime are well publicised through his journalistic output and novels, he is better known to the majority of the public for a series of scandals, controversial episodes and misdemeanours. Notably he was forced to travel to Liverpool to apologise for offensive comments in an editorial of the *Spectator* where it was argued that the city was wallowing in 'disproportionate' grief (BBC, 2004). He attracted controversy after asserting that Conservative leadership disputes were like 'Papua New Guinea-style orgies of cannibalism and chief-killing' (BBC, 2006b). And he gained similar censure from Portsmouth after claiming that the city was 'one of the most depressed towns in Southern England, a place that is arguably too full of drugs, obesity, underachievement and Labour MPs' (BBC, 2007b). He received attention for his decision to invite Rupert Murdoch to be his personal guest at the Olympics, and he memorably became stuck on a zip-wire in London's Victoria Park (Chapman, 2012). Such antics have seen Johnson labelled a 'buffoon' and a 'clown prince' and in 2006, journalist Simon Heffer described him as 'a man blessed with high intelligence and great abilities [who] has, through moral failure and self-indulgence, now largely ceased to be taken seriously in public life' (Ferguson, 2007).

Yet despite these misdemeanours, polling has found that Johnson is respected by 58 per cent of the public – a score which far outshines Margaret Thatcher, Cameron and other senior Conservative politicians (Watt and Clark, 2012). Moreover, 51 per cent view Johnson favourably (compared with 29 per cent for Cameron and 11 per cent for Osborne), and the Conservative Party would receive a six-point poll boost if he became party leader (Boffey and Helm, 2012; Newton Dunn, 2012). Accordingly, rather than appearing a figure of fun Johnson has confounded expectations, being seen as authentic, honest and a breath of fresh air. He is held up as a welcome break from micro-managing, image-conscious politicians, succeeding because 'voters – even some Labour voters – want to see more of him. They feel he brightens up their life a little bit' (Dunt, 2012). It is these traits which have led him to achieve phenomenal personal success. Between 2008 and 2010 he was the most senior Conservative politician in office having triumphed in the London mayoral election, and he has subsequently been re-elected despite critiques of his tenure. His platform as London Mayor has allowed him to become a forceful advocator of conservative principles, and whilst other Conservative politicians have subsequently gained power in the Coalition government his status has not diminished.

Accordingly Boris Johnson is a complex and apparently contradictory politician. He has close connections to the elite of the Conservative Party, but has cultivated an image as an outsider; he advances controversial views, yet is seen as a champion of common sense and normality; and he attracts scandal, yet has managed to be elected, twice, as London Mayor. For any other politician, maintaining the balance of these different personas would be an impossibility, yet Johnson does so with apparent ease. In this chapter it is argued that his success can be attributed to his skills as an orator and his understanding of persuasion and performance. To advance this argument Johnson's oratory in front of the party conference and public is examined to demonstrate how a blend of humour, logic and emotion (pathos, logos and ethos) as well as physical theatre is used to create a unique personal appeal and broad support.

However, in casting light on the oratorical secrets of Johnson's success this chapter also sounds a note of caution for those proclaiming his worth as a future Conservative Party leader. Although Johnson's political approach is seen to offer an attractive alternative in the wake of Cameron's (now failed) modernisation project, the combination of plain speaking, humour and controversy is not seen to succeed in every context. By exploring the different facets of his oratory as Mayor and his contributions to Parliament the limits of his appeal are highlighted. On this basis it is argued that whilst Boris Johnson has great strengths as a distinctive outsider figure within the Conservative Party, his appeal has profound limitations within more formal, institutionalised and collegiate contexts. From this perspective Johnson's credentials should be viewed with caution as the party contemplates its future direction and leadership.

Boris and the party conference

Johnson has long been a firm favourite of the party conference and unlike most senior politicians regularly packs out the conference hall and fills fringe meetings. Indeed, his popularity reached such a feverous peak that his appearance at the 2012 party conference was seen to be providing 'a logistical headache for Number 10' where there were worries that Johnson would 'outshine the prime minister and emerge as the unquestioned darling of the conference' (Helm, 2012). Johnson's success is largely built upon his willingness to express controversial, yet popular (amongst the grassroots) opinions and to utilise a range of oratorical and rhetorical skills to win over his audience.

Much has been written about the increasing formalisation of conferences as media events, with messages heavily scripted and trailed in focus groups, and opportunities for manifestations of disagreement and conflict minimised (Kavanagh, 1996; Stanyer, 2001). As attested by the frequently empty conference halls seen in media footage, the vast majority of party conference speeches are formulaic and uninspiring – aimed as much (if not more) at the public as the immediate audience. However, Johnson's interventions do not fit this mould as he refuses to adopt the formalised conventions of party conference speeches, and instead blends humour and controversy to capture the audience's attention. A short extract of his 2007 conference speech is illustrative of this approach:

> I stand before you proud to be your candidate, proud to be given the chance to represent the greatest city on earth, but what gives me the greatest pride of all is that from day one I have provoked such gibbering squeals of denunciation from King Newt and his allies that I know they are scared and they can see all too clearly that we Conservatives are launching a fightback in London that will recapture the capital for common sense government for the first time in a generation. (Johnson, 2007)

A number of different techniques are used here but what is immediately noticeable is Johnson's engagement with the party audience. Rather than speaking to 'the public' he creates a bond between himself and party members, portraying himself as 'your candidate' and adopting the 'we' pronoun to herald Conservative success. In adopting this approach Johnson emphasises his ethos, declaring himself to be 'proud' to be a Conservative candidate and reinforcing bonds of party commonality which most other party elites have a tendency to neglect or downplay in this forum. Such references build (implicitly) upon his reputation for expressing unabashed conservative views, enabling him to forge his position as a party darling who speaks up for the grassroots.

In developing his persona Johnson relies on a distinctive use of humour and intellect. In the above passage, he emphasises his conservative credentials by humorously depicting his opponent Ken Livingstone as 'King Newt' engaged in 'gibbering squeals of denunciation' (Johnson, 2007). This irreverent portrayal stokes partisan attitudes towards his opponent but also strengthens Johnson's own image by drawing a comparison between a hysterical rival and himself as a level-headed, authentic politician. This point is underlined by his subsequent assertion: 'I can think of nothing more serious than the security and prosperity of the powerhouse of the British economy' (Johnson, 2007). Such juxtapositions are used repeatedly by Johnson to underline his credibility, distinctiveness and authenticity, using humour and a nononsense approach to distinguish himself from other politicians.

He also underlines his trustworthiness, using a range of techniques to demonstrate his capacity to govern. Unlike some other Conservative politicians he actively demonstrates his education and intellect, peppering his speeches with references to 'Marie Celeste' floors, 'recidivism' and historical figures and events from Mahatma Ghandi to Mary Tudor (Johnson, 2010b; 2011c). Such references are, however, balanced with humour to minimise critiques of being aloof; hence in 2011 he twisted an 'intellectual' reference into a joke, commenting: 'FD Roosevelt had the new deal, I give you the wheel deal' (Johnson, 2011c). Elsewhere he uses flamboyant language as a counterweight outlining, in 2010, his determination to defeat 'the doomsayers and the gloomadon poppers' (2011c) and asserting his desire to end 'jack-knifing, traffic-blocking, self-combusting, cyclist-crushing bendy buses' (2011c). Whilst listing and vivid language are rhetorical techniques evident in the speeches of other politicians, Johnson's injection of humour creates a distinctive, audibly appealing effect which attracts attention and provokes a response precisely because it defies convention. These devices are used to particular effect when advancing a partisan perspective as evident in his assertion that 'there has been something bizarre about the lip-smacking savagery of the Lib Dems, with Vince Cable morphing into a mad axeman, a transformation as incongruous as the killer rabbit in Monty Python' (Johnson, 2009). This metaphor appears humorous, but it is spiked with a potent political message that is likely to resonate with the grassroots, making it a highly effective oratorical technique.

Johnson also frequently calls upon humour to underline his message. In 2011 he reacted to the London riots by stating: 'I will tell you who did stand up for London – It was the chap who sat on a looter's head. It was the woman who made that great speech in Hackney and scared them off and the restaurant workers who fought them off with rolling pins and saucepans' (Johnson, 2011c). The comical evocation of rolling pins and the colloquial reference to 'chap' neutralise the possibility of Johnson's utterances sounding pious and opportunistic and in turn make his assertions appear more authentic. He also uses humour, specifically self-deprecating humour, to distinguish himself from other politicians. Unlike others Johnson actively embraces his foibles and publicises his scandals, seeking not to avoid controversial occurrences but rather to use them to demonstrate his authenticity in an era of political spin and image consciousness. Whilst other politicians would struggle to use such a tactic Johnson's humorous and irreverent persona allows him to enhance his appeal by evoking scandals. Thus in 2009 Johnson opened his conference speech by asserting '[i]t's wonderful to be here in Manchester, one of the few great British cities I have yet to insult' (Johnson, 2009), a tactic which prompted not condemnation but laughter.

Similarly in 2012 he directly tackled the supposed tensions between himself and Cameron by asserting 'I was pleased to see the other day that you [Cameron] have called me a blond haired mop. A mop. Well if I am a mop then you are a broom. A broom that is cleaning up the mess left by the Labour government and a fantastic job you are doing. I thank you and congratulate you and your colleagues – George Osborne the dustpan, Gove the J cloth' (Johnson, 2012d). In this sense it is the use of humour (pathos) combined with references to his credible conservative credentials (ethos) that makes Johnson such an effective speaker at party conference.

Mannerisms and a theatrical style of delivery are also used to complement these techniques. Unlike other politicians Johnson forsakes the formalised posture of speech-making; instead he often leans on the podium, makes asides to non-existent audience members and waves his hands around. His personal appearance complements his irreverent approach as he often appears dishevelled, with unruly hair and a crumpled suit; an image removed from the manicured appearances of many other politicians. These distinguishing features and his oratorical approach make Johnson an interesting and distinctive figure, a point reflected in the coverage given to his oratory on the television and in newspaper outlets. Whilst most other politicians, beside the party leader, gain limited if any airtime, Johnson's speeches are loved by journalists for their quotable lines, unpredictability and drama. These traits mean that Johnson is able to develop his profile amongst the general public through media coverage, whilst directing his speech to the immediate party conference audience using the techniques discussed above.

In drawing these conclusions it is important not to overlook how Johnson satisfies party members at conference using logos. Unlike other politicians Johnson does not routinely rely on statistics and factual examples to bolster his arguments, but where apparent these techniques are used to enhance perceptions of Johnson's own credibility and capacity to deliver – using logos to persuade the audience that he is an effective leader. For example, references such as: 'the murder rate is down to levels not seen since the 1970s' and 'the poorest 10,000 in the city have had an extra £60m in their pockets' due to the Living Wage, illustrate his record and reinforce perceptions of his effectiveness (Johnson, 2011c).

However, it is important to recognise that logos is not a prevalent part of Johnson's oratorical approach; instead he has a tendency to depict his positions as common sense. This style is exceedingly effective in front of the party audience as it portrays grassroots attitudes as reasonable and attainable, and moreover Johnson as a trustworthy advocate of such principles. Such common-sense depictions are apparent when Johnson asserted, on the issue of housing, that there must be an end to 'rabbit-hutch tower blocks containing some of the smallest rooms in Europe and a blind repetition of the mistakes of the 1960s' (Johnson, 2007). Instead he argued for the necessity of 'homes that will still be loved and valued and conserved in 100 years time so that future generations will look back on our generation with admiration and respect for our foresight, and not blame us for the ghettoes of tomorrow' (2007).

Similarly, he portrayed his view on crime as common sense, asserting that his 'message to London's criminal fraternity is tax and insure your car or you'll get it back for Christmas as a small cube from the crusher with love' (Johnson, 2011c). These examples illustrate Johnson's willingness to present his ideas, and the concerns of party members, with a degree of political honesty – an approach which is often seen to be lacking from politicians attempting to triangulate their positions to attract the most voters. As Melanie Philips argues, he 'goes straight for what they most want to hear, these grass-roots Tories. No pandering to political correctness for Boris' (Philips, 2011). At times this has resulted in controversy as in 2006 he condemned Jamie Oliver's healthy food programme just days after Cameron had praised it, and he called for a European referendum when Cameron was attempting to defuse tension around the issue (for example see Branigan, 2006). Similarly, he has issued challenges to his own party leadership, contending in 2009 that 'if we [the Mayoral team] can cut cost in City Hall, George then you can cut cost in Whitehall as you promise to do. And if we can cut crime in London, then David Cameron can make streets safer across the UK' (Johnson, 2009). This willingness to break the political consensus and invite controversy reinforces rather than undermines his ethos by demonstrating his commitment to conservative ideas.

In assessing Johnson's performances at the party conference it therefore appears that his personal and emotional appeals and his willingness to talk to – and address the concerns of – the immediate audience are integral to his success. Whilst other politicians use this forum to project a public image, addressing the party as a secondary audience, Johnson cultivates an image as an authentic advocate of conservative views. This approach has helped to garner Johnson widespread appeal amongst the party audience, but his willingness to court controversy and throw off the conventions of party conference speeches also allow him to 'cut through' to members of the public, developing a persona as a non-typical politician. It is this combination of traits which allows Johnson to forge such a unique appeal, being remembered as much, if not more, for his style and humour as his views.

Boris and the public

In the public sphere Johnson has held an unusual prominence derived largely from his media presence. On entering Parliament in 2001 he retained his column at the *Telegraph* and has continued to air his political views, weekly, through this medium. As such his ideas have achieved far greater prominence than those of other politicians, helping him to develop a distinctive persona. To appraise his prolific work, Johnson has, in his own words, 'stuck up for foxhunting and bankers and entered a general plea on behalf of all fat, white, male, heterosexual Tories who see nothing much wrong with drinking a bottle of wine at lunch and then having a quiet cigar' (Johnson, 2012c). He has described metal thieves killed on railway lines as getting 'their comeuppance' (Johnson, 2011d), and in reporting on Andy Murray's defeat at Wimbledon he opined on the possibility that countries' tax arrangements impacted upon players' desire 'to run that extra half yard for the ball' (Johnson, 2011a). His views chime with key conservative principles but are often expressed in extreme terms and colourful language, leading to controversy and criticism. Yet when Johnson's name is evoked it is often his civic, mayoral speeches rather than his journalistic outputs which are pre-eminent; hence whilst his views are well established they are often seen to be secondary to his personal appeal.

Johnson's public oratory, like his party utterances, is heavily invested with humorous references and irreverent asides – traits which contribute significantly to his popularity. This use of pathos was evident most explicitly in his appearance on *Have I Got News for You* where Johnson used controversy and self-effacing wit to attract interest and create an affinity with the audience. Through such techniques Johnson has forged an appeal which whilst not disavowing his personal views is distinct from them – allowing him to expand his public support beyond those who simply share his perspective. In this regard in the public, civic realm he appears as an almost non-political politician, a persona particularly evident in his Olympic speeches.

When examining his oratory in this forum Johnson once again is seen to balance illustrations of his education, a willingness to speak his mind (however controversial) and a bumbling, self-effacing humour to attract public interest and create a bond with the audience. For example, in his speech launching the Olympic Clock in July 2011 he stated:

> No sooner had this masterpiece of the Swiss Chronometer's art been installed than it unexpectedly packed up. But with the help of various Swiss chronometers we got it going again didn't we? And then it was attacked by a horde of hooded crusties protesting at something or other. And still that clock ticks on, to remind us that nothing and no one is going to stop us in our work of preparing London for the greatest event that has taken place in this city in the last 50 years. (Johnson, 2011b)

In this passage he entwines educated references to 'chronometers' with the colloquial and highly normative language of 'hooded crusties', using this juxtaposition to comedic effect to prompt a favourable response from his audience. By directly referencing the failure of the clock and using the 'we' pronoun to reveal triumph over adversity Johnson evokes British stereotypes of stoicism and determination, using patriotic sentiments to create a common bond between the audience and himself. This use of pathos, tied into Johnson's personal commitment to the Games (ethos), helps to generate public support which is distinct from his political views – revealing how he is able to cultivate widespread appeal.

Johnson's public utterances are also distinctive because, like his conference speeches, they depart from the conventions of political oratory witnessed in his contemporaries' speeches. Throughout Johnson's orations it is possible to find jokes which other politicians would be cautious of making, and references which sail close to the wind. To give an illustration, in 2012 in his Hyde Park speech he said: 'I hear there's a guy called Mitt Romney who wants to know whether we're ready ... Yes, we are. The venues are ready. The Stadium is ready. The Aquatics Centre is ready. The Velodrome is ready. The security is ready. The police are ready. The transport system is ready. And our Team GB athletes are ready, aren't they?' (Johnson, 2012b). The irreverence shown towards Romney (at this time the Republican candidate for the presidency) with the comment 'I hear there's a guy' differed dramatically from the cautious responses of Cameron and Ed Miliband, suggesting that Johnson's ethos is distinct from most other speakers as he is willing to stand up for London and honestly express his opinion. This difference is further underlined by use of listing and *epiphora*; the repetition of the same words at the end of a clause or sentence (Glover, 2011: 24), a rhetorical technique which compounds his point.

In addition to courting controversy Johnson's oratory also confounds expectations of political speeches by using a range of 'Borisisms' (as they have been termed) such as 'Olympomania' and 'zoink' which signal a deviation from the traditional, formalised approach to public oratory. Additionally jokes such as '[t]here's going to be more gold, silver, bronze medals than you'd need to bail out Greece and Spain together' (Johnson, 2012b) are also a key part of this approach as they allow Johnson to test the bounds of acceptability – creating an outrageous, entertaining persona that is attractive due to its novelty and apparent authenticity. In this sense an audience never quite knows what Johnson may say next, making him far more interesting and engaging than the average politician. Crucial to this interest is the fact that Johnson's utterances are not subject to close scrutiny or challenge in this forum, making it easy for him to get away with controversial utterances which may be challenged if made elsewhere.

Johnson also emphasises his bumbling yet authentic character to maximise his appeal, asserting, for example, at the 2012 Olympic victory parade that 'my God there is a lot of you' and 'I'm not sure judo was invented in London but never mind' (Johnson, 2012c). Such references – especially when made in the wake of David Cameron's formal political speech – distinguish him from 'conventional politicians', marking him out instead as a more authentic individual in touch with the concerns of the people. This impression is emphasised by Johnson's repeated attempts to engage his audience. Throughout his public rhetoric he asks rhetorical questions, uses call-and-response, and references anecdotes to capture attention (Atkins and Finlayson, 2013); techniques which help to reduce the inequality between speaker and audience and allow him to create a more intimate, personal appeal removed from his political views.

Johnson's irreverent and unconventional approach to public, civic oratory therefore allows him to forge a unique public appeal founded on authenticity, humour and a willingness to deviate from the status quo. It is these traits which explain his widespread popularity, as rather than operating within the traditions of political discourse, he builds a relationship with the audience that is divorced from his own political views, yet, significantly, does not disavow or attempt to obscure those views. This approach allows him to simultaneously appear authentic (in his commitment to his ideas) and to attract attention and support from those who frequently do not identify with politics and politicians. Hence, Johnson is able to transcend partisan affiliations to gain at least a hearing from people with differing views to his own, using pathos and ethos to present an inclusive, unexpected and entertaining form of oratory.

Boris and the London Assembly

On the above evidence Johnson's appeal to the Conservative Party is clear as he offers a new model of public engagement which does not belie his conservative beliefs or attempt to obscure them, but rather offers an inclusive persona which attracts voters. In the London Assembly many of the techniques evident above are apparent, yet in this context Johnson's oratory subtly shifts with his own political views and ideas gaining greater prominence. Whilst in front of a public audience Johnson is seen to effectively manage this shift in context, actively embracing the fact that the London Assembly is 'so open, so accessible' (Johnson, 2008: 5), in front of politicians and more formal political scrutiny his oratory is noticeably different. Hence, whilst when viewed in public Johnson thrives, deploying humour and intellect to demonstrate his leadership, authenticity and appeal, when exposed to political scrutiny he often fails to engage, appearing aloof, uninterested and condescending. This juxtaposition is seen to be crucial to understanding the limitations of Johnson's appeal and the need for caution when evaluating his future credentials within the Conservative Party.

At the public level, question and answer sessions and public consultation events have allowed Johnson to cultivate his persona, drawing on techniques apparent in front of both the party and civic public audiences to maximise his appeal. Indeed, humour, irreverence, claims of credibility, authenticity and partisan attacks remain in evidence, yet in this context two other traits come to the fore: a desire to express and defend his personal opinions, and an eagerness to engage with and help the audience. These traits are significant as in addition to provoking a positive response from the audience using pathos (humour), he is able to illustrate his credentials as a strong, decisive leader who remains committed to representing and serving the interests of his constituents.

Whilst Johnson's strong views are, as the previous section detailed, widely publicised through his newspaper column, in his appearances as London Mayor these views also become a prominent aspect of his oratory and are used to underline his personal credibility, authenticity, distinctiveness (from his opposition) and authority. Hence in asserting, in public question and answer sessions, '[l]isten, I am afraid I am a free marketeer. I believe in capitalism' (Johnson, 2008: 21) and arguing that 'the issue of supermarkets reduces the British population to their worst depths of hypocrisy ... We yearn for the old shops but we use Tesco' (2008: 15) he is illustrating his own views but also demonstrating his strength of character in expressing those views. These two examples are particularly illustrative as they were made in response to critical questions, but rather than pacifying questioners Johnson offered a frank answer. Whilst these responses were likely to be unsatisfactory at a normative level for the people asking the question, his willingness to engage directly and openly disagree is novel and hence is likely to inspire (potentially begrudging) respect for Johnson as an authentic politician who stands up for what he believes in.

In offering a distinctive position Johnson also deploys his views to attack political opponents – specifically Labour and Ken Livingstone. To illustrate, in relating his decision to scrap *The Londoner* Johnson asserted that he was removing 'a demented kind of Commie-era free-sheet that used to get bunged through everybody's ... It was sort of Pyongyang-style journalism. We have saved £6 million by getting rid of this thing and we have used it to plant the first of 10,000 trees' (2008: 8). This comment and similar assertions such as the previous administrations' policies being 'absolute codswallop' (2008: 24) use humour, appealing to the audience's emotions to make his condemnation acceptable. By confounding expectations and using such passionate language Johnson is able to temper and deflect the negative impact such attacks may have upon his own character, whilst also aiming to demonstrate his own clear views, decisiveness and superior judgement. This partisan attack therefore serves to advance rather than undermine his own credibility by demonstrating that his credentials and opinions are more common sense and appealing than his opponents.

In balancing these strong views Johnson also emphasises his determination to stand up to opposition in all its forms and hence demonstrates his personal tenacity and authority. Indeed, throughout his public speeches he asserts his determination to 'struggle with anybody that I have to, in the interests of London!' (Johnson, 2010a: 3). At times this places Johnson in direct conflict with other senior figures – situations which are used to demonstrate his own power. Hence in tackling a question from a member of the public on traffic issues around the Blackwall Tunnel he asserted: 'having just seized the reins of the Metropolitan Police Authority ... I intend to make sure that we get this done' (Johnson, 2008: 14). The use of 'we' in this sentence creates an affiliation between his own determination to create change and his audience's desires, reinforcing the impression of himself as a public champion. This commonality is contrasted with his depiction of the Metropolitan Police Authority as an outsider body which he – holding 'the reins' – has the power to direct to his (and the audience's) will. This illustration of his own power and the overt linkage to the audience again strengthens his ethos and personal credibility. At times such comments are linked directly to Johnson's status as an outsider as he asserts that 'I am afraid I have to go now, and to have an audience with the Chancellor of the Exchequer. Now, what do you want me to tell him about London business?' (Johnson, 2010a: 26). In this example he uses Osborne's formal title to portray himself as removed from government and the individuals who compose it. Such oratory works to underline his focus on London not internal party politics, emphasising that rather than maintaining a 'party line' he defends London using conservative principles rather than defending the Conservative Party.

In maintaining this persona as a strong leader Johnson also expresses a willingness to help. At numerous consultation and outreach events he attests that he 'will make sure that we get you a proper answer' (Johnson, 2011e: 35) and will 'certainly take it up on your behalf and see whether I can intercede, but I want you to know that whatever I can do, it will not involve taxpayers' money' (Johnson, 2010a: 17). His eagerness is often highly proactive, asserting 'please, if you are in any confusion about it, get on to our website or make direct contact with my office and with Richard Barnes, the Deputy Mayor' (Johnson, 2011e: 20). Such traits illustrate a clear desire to serve and assist Londoners – underlining his personal authority, credibility and capacity to deliver for his constituents.

In the public forums of the London Assembly Johnson therefore utilises many of the oratorical skills seen to succeed in other forums; however, in front of Assembly politicians Johnson's persuasive appeal is seen to be lacking. Whilst in public his persona as a disarming yet credible politician is crucial to persuading and/or attracting his audience, in front of politicians at Mayor's question and answer sessions his approach differs dramatically. Far from appearing at ease, Johnson's oratory is highly defensive and at times condescending, being devoid of the humorous asides and jokes which lighten his contributions elsewhere. Indeed, when addressing comments to speakers no attempt is made to forge bonds or affiliations between himself and other politicians; rather he adopts a direct approach, making assertions such as 'Darren, as you know ...' (Johnson, 2012a: 1) and '[a]s you know, I am always happy to accept blame for whatever you want to blame me for, Darren' (2012a: 2). Such assertions, far from revealing intimacy and a desire to engage (as apparent when he uses individuals' names in other contexts) convey a sense of irritation because of indications of shared prior knowledge hinted at by the comments 'as you know'. This linguistic shift appears all the more stark when compared to his open desire to assist his public audience, suggesting that he has little patience with, or confidence in Assembly members' capacities.

The shift in approach to his audience is also apparent in the scope of responses, as whilst in public he is willing to opine on issues far beyond his sphere of responsibility as Mayor, when questioned by the Assembly he repeatedly outlines the limits of his remit and powers, deflecting attention and responsibility elsewhere. So, in response to critiques over his apparent failure to uphold the Olympics Living Wage policy in hotels he asserted: '[i]f it is true that there is another hotel group that would have been willing to pay more than the Hilton, as you suggest or as you imply, then let us see it' (2012a: 3). In this regard he refuses to accept responsibility, instead pushing the imperative back on Assembly members. At times his responses to comments from members, such as John Biggs's assertion that '[o]bviously, you could spend the whole morning listing facts', are irreverent and dismissive, as in this instance when he responded 'I could actually, yes' (2012a: 4). Such contributions indicate that far from being ill-equipped to persuade his audience, Johnson actively decides not to engage, suggesting that rather than seeming universally appealing, his persona has limitations, limitations which are specifically apparent in formal institutional contexts. This finding is underlined when examining Johnson's speeches in Parliament.

Boris and Parliament

Johnson held his seat in Henley between 2001 and 2008 but despite his relative longevity in the post, both as a backbench MP and as a minister, his contributions in the House were widely derided, with one commentator arguing that he appeared as 'a lightweight ... echoing parody of himself' (Purnell, 2012). Whilst the oratorical and rhetorical techniques seen to be so successful above were in evidence, three limitations to his approach were apparent. First, Johnson did not appear comfortable in this forum, making numerous mistakes and attracting criticism – traits which are seen to have undermined his ability to persuade others. Second, whilst in other forums he balanced humour and credibility, in Parliament he was vocally derided by other politicians, undermining his status and effectiveness as an orator. And, third, the humorous, irreverent asides and journalistic style which worked so well in front of a public audience are seen to have backfired in this forum, compounding criticism with claims of pomposity. In this regard the strengths of Johnson's individualistic, outsider style of oratory are not seen to be effective in the formalised, more collegiate institution of Parliament where parties and party discipline are more important than individuals.

Despite spending seven years in Parliament Johnson's oratory illustrates an uncomfortable relationship with the institution. In light of his preference for irreverence and his desire to court controversy to create appeal the formalised structures of Parliament are understandably out of kilter with his oratorical style. Throughout his contributions friction is evident, with Johnson receiving numerous rebukes such as a reprimand from the Deputy Speaker of the House for not using 'correct terminology' when referring to Members of the House (Deputy Speaker, 2002: Column 666), and censure from Menzies Campbell for an impatient approach to interventions (Campbell, 2005: Column 301). His inability to operate in accordance with the rules of Parliament led to widespread derision from opposition MPs and fostered a reputation for incompetence and laziness. Such attitudes are evident in John Healey's comment:

> I welcome the hon. Gentleman to the debate. We missed his contribution and his presence in earlier debates. May I tell him that he was in fact speaking to the next group of amendments? We are talking about housing strategy and health, but we will come to planning next. I hope that he will stay and contribute to that debate as well. (Healey, 2007: Column 502)

Similarly in an exchange with Hazel Blears attention was drawn to that fact that 'he has not been in Committee for the whole debate', continuing, '[i]t is important to develop arguments in Committee, so I will be disappointed if he does not make a serious point' (Blears, 2005: Column 870–1). Such condemnation, dismissed by Johnson as 'most unfair' (Blears, 2005: Column 870–1), reveals the contempt in which he was held by MPs, a position which lessened his personal capital and thus his ability to effectively convince his audience. This trait was in turn compounded by frequent failures to accurately present his argument. For example, in outlining his position on EU extradition law he made factual errors, leading him to thank 'the Minister for clearing up the point about unanimity and majority voting, and I am sorry to have got that wrong just now' (Johnson, 2003a: Column 202). He also lacked clarity of argument, as Tom Harris MP and George Howarth MP respectively highlighted in their assertions that Johnson was 'in danger of misrepresenting the case' and that 'the logic of his argument was muddled' (Johnson, 2003a: Column 202–3). Such occurrences suggest Johnson's lack of familiarity and comfort with the conventions and rules of Parliament, attributes which served to undermine his persuasive appeal and accordingly significantly lessened the impact of his oratory.

Turning to Johnson's credibility there are numerous examples which suggest that, far from using humour to disarm and attract his audience, in Parliament his attempts to use humour often backfired. As witnessed above, Johnson utilises self-effacing wit, irreverence and humorous language in combination with intellectual references and evidence of his successes to carefully manage perceptions of his ethos, yet in Parliament the balancing act did not succeed. In part this was due to parliamentarians' apparent contempt for his popular appeal, a trait which led his character and popularity to be readily mocked, as was done by George Howarth MP who scorned his 'iconic status among the young people of Liverpool' (Howarth, 2003: Column 202–3). Yet more fundamentally it derived from a negative reaction to his comedic devices and a direct challenge to his portrayal of himself.

In relation to the first point it is easy to find contributions from Johnson which displayed the Borisisms and flamboyant language apparent elsewhere. For example, he asserted:

> I am grateful to the Minister for interrupting his hymn of praise to the hon. Member for Croydon, Central (Geraint Davies). Will he break off from his glutinous complacency about everything that Labour has done and explain to the House why, if things

are so much better, violent crime has gone up in the Thames Valley area by 38 per cent? (Johnson, 2002a: Column 852)

Whilst in other circumstances language such as 'glutinous' and 'hymn of praise' would be used to provoke laughter, due to its apparent incongruity with his background, in the parliamentary context it appears highly partisan and attacking. This impression is evident throughout his oratory where comments such as 'I will not take sedentary interventions from a chap of whose identity I have no knowledge' did not evoke humour but rather conveyed an aloof, condescending persona (Johnson, 2002b: Column 211). Context therefore has a significant impact on Johnson's ability to garner an advantage from his oratorical approach, with the parliamentary environment having a negative effect on his persuasive appeal. This perception is apparent in the numerous demonstrations of contempt for Johnson such as the MP David Taylor's quip that he thanked 'the hon. Member for Pomposity on Thames for giving way' (D. Taylor, 2002: Column 210).

This impression is further compounded by the discursive context of Parliament as in this forum Johnson's claims were subject to scrutiny and re-articulation – a process which limited his ability to cultivate a specific impression of his persona. To illustrate, in advancing the case for his local brewery Johnson's comments were addressed by Taylor, who asserted:

> I have heard the heartfelt pleas of the hon. Member for Henley (Mr. Johnson), who opined about the imminent demise of a brewery that served his alma mater. I would hate to go down in history as the Financial Secretary responsible for depriving the boys of Eton college of their favourite brew. Deprived and underprivileged as they are, to deprive them of their beer would really be the last straw. (2002: Column 170)

In the other forums examined Johnson is largely given a free hand to present a specific ethos to the audience, yet in Parliament other voices are influential and serve to undermine his carefully balanced persona. Whilst alone this factor could be countered, taken with his unfamiliarity with Parliament this served to undermine his effectiveness as an orator.

Finally, Johnson's approach to parliamentary debate is also seen to have contributed to his apparent failures, as rather than complying with conventions, as seen above, his interventions are ill-informed, journalistic and often not serious. To illustrate this point it is useful to consider two different passages. In the first Johnson's journalistic style was directly commented upon when he asserted:

> **Mr. Johnson:** The scheme was expected to have 1.1 million subscribers; it eventually had 2.5 million. It went 30 per cent over budget and those who have reason to know say that the total cost was in excess of £550 million, half of which was defrauded from the Government by Mickey Mouse, Donald Duck, Del Boy Trotter and assorted other alleged purveyors.
>
> **Mr. Taylor:** And the Boris Johnson school of journalism? (Johnson, 2002b: Column 211).

His use of logos here, apparent in the statistics referenced, marked an attempt to discredit the government's message, yet his opponent's quip about his journalistic style implicitly suggested a lack of credibility and thus undermined the impact of his contribution. In this regard his extra-parliamentary persona is seen to directly inhibit his persuasive appeal. Yet this is not the only factor shaping perceptions of his credibility; his conduct in the House with his colleagues was also influential, as rather than cutting an authoritative figure he often engaged in irreverent banter rather than debate. For example, in 2003, in discussing changes to airline rules he commented:

> **Mr. Johnson:** Many people frankly find it difficult to put up with the rigours of a long
>   flight without the sustenance and reassurance of a smoke. Indeed, one cannot even
>   get peanuts nowadays on aeroplanes, because they have been banned. They will
>   not serve me peanuts at all.
> **Mr. Osborne:** Really?
> **Mr. Johnson:** It is because of nut allergies. One cannot smoke, and one is now not
>   to be allowed to be drunk, without there being any definition of drunkenness in
>   the Bill.
> **Mr. Osborne:** An infringement of our civil liberties! (Johnson, 2003b: Column 663)

This exchange appears to defy the conventions of parliamentary debate and scrutiny and accordingly contributed towards perceptions of Johnson as an irreverent, clownish figure – a perception which was not balanced by the claims of credibility and authenticity used in other forums. Accordingly, Johnson's own approach within and beyond Parliament is seen to have compounded the above impressions – once again lessening his effectiveness in this context.

Conclusion

From the above it appears that Johnson has varying degrees of success in different forums, but this variation seems as much to do with his personal disposition and attitude as with the oratorical techniques he uses. As analysis of his conference speeches and public oratory has demonstrated, Johnson has a masterful command of his self-image and utilises humour and a willingness to court controversy to cultivate support which other politicians would find exceedingly difficult to gain. In this regard, he plays upon the idea of himself as an unconventional politician, freeing himself from many of the entrenched negative attitudes recorded in polling towards politicians. This approach defines his success, but when appearing in more formal political environments such as the London Assembly and Parliament these techniques do not work as they are out of kilter with the formalised context.

However, in judging Johnson it is important to remain cognisant of whom he is trying to appeal Whilst most members of the political classes are entwined within the hierarchical structures of the Parliamentary Party where patronage, loyalty and discipline are the key to individual success, Johnson has forged his reputation as an outsider, campaigning as Mayor of London for the interests of the city's residents rather than the interests of the Conservative Party. In so doing he has not rejected his conservative beliefs, but neither has he been forced to present the party line (as many MPs and London Assembly members are). The individualistic nature of the position of Mayor therefore frees Johnson from the conventions of contemporary politics, allowing him to use humour, controversy and straight talking to cultivate appeal away from Parliament.

Taken in this context his irreverence to London Assembly members and his ineffectiveness in Parliament appear less significant, as whilst he by no means thrives in these arenas, success there is not necessary for his personal and political capital. Indeed, arguably, it could be seen as an advantage as it allows him to develop alternative ideas and campaigns which, although informed by conservative beliefs, are not synonymous with the Conservative Party. Hence, Johnson has led a debate over the party's aviation policy, arguing for a 'Boris Island' rather than an expansion of Heathrow. Similarly, he defended bankers in the wake of the financial crisis whilst many other politicians were condemning the profession. This outsider status and often critical voice fosters debate within the Conservative Party and, whilst it may not always be welcomed by the parliamentary leadership, helps to present the public with a multifaceted picture of conservatism.

These findings suggest that Johnson's success as an orator is unlikely to be replicated. Unlike most other politicians he is not skilled in the use of logos, but rather relies on pathos and ethos to cultivate appeal. In so doing he portrays his conservative principles as common sense, neglecting detailed policy arguments in favour of grand visions and plans which often range far beyond his remit. In relying on his personal credibility and authenticity, and his ability to draw a response from an audience through humour, Johnson is able to glean diverse support – but this strategy works because it is alien from the political norm and defies convention. If his irreverent attitude and maverick approach was widely replicated, its novelty would quickly subside as would the political capital which Johnson is able to draw from this approach. Accordingly, whilst Johnson is an asset to the Conservatives in electoral terms, his oratorical style should not be seen as a playbook to be copied. Furthermore, his success should not be seen to be invulnerable as there is no guarantee that his approach – built as it is on irreverence, scandal and eccentricity – would thrive in Parliament where party discipline and collective responsibility are paramount. Such possibilities should be contemplated when discussing Johnson returning to Parliament, entering the Conservative Cabinet, or even becoming party leader.

12

The oratory of David Cameron

Tim Bale

Even David Cameron's detractors would acknowledge that he possesses excellent presentational skills and that he performs effectively across the range of speaking opportunities that the twenty-first century offers its top politicians. Certainly, at PMQs in the Commons, Cameron gives as good as he gets and has done so right from his very first day in the job (YouTube, 2010a). He is also capable of delivering pitch-perfect speeches in the House on other occasions, particularly when they call for a bipartisan approach, as with his parliamentary apology for the killing of unarmed demonstrators by British troops on Bloody Sunday back in 1972 (YouTube, 2011a). Cameron is likewise an accomplished performer in televised party political broadcasts: indeed, his hastily re-arranged straight-to-camera piece at the height of the parliamentary expenses scandal in 2009 (YouTube, 2009) arguably ensured that it was the then prime minister, Gordon Brown, who took the bigger hit. Cameron bested Brown, too, in the UK's first TV leadership debates and, although he badly underestimated his other opponent, Nick Clegg, in the first encounter (YouTube, 2010b), he clearly had the measure of him in the second and third (see Pattie and Johnston, 2011). Cameron was also the first British party leader to appear in an ongoing series of 'professionally amateur' clips designed for YouTube, with the first offering from 'WebCameron' appearing in the autumn of 2006 (YouTube, 2006). True, he is perhaps less at ease in the potentially more dangerous (because less controllable) chat-show environment – a format on which he has occasionally come a cropper both at home and abroad: his appearances on shows hosted by Jonathan Ross and David Letterman spring quickly (and excruciatingly) to mind (YouTube, 2011b; 2012). But Cameron's handling of more formal formats like the extended political interview certainly ranks up there with the best of his predecessors in the job.

To many, Cameron's presentational skills are all of a piece with his background – a combination of 'that bottomless self-assurance than characterises Old Etonians at Oxford' (Young, 2010) and seven years spent in PR at Carlton Communications. They are also widely believed, by helping him to make his 'Look, no notes' pitch to the Tory party conference in Blackpool in 2005 (YouTube, 2010c), to have played a big part in winning him the Conservative leadership in the first place. Given this, it seems particularly appropriate to analyse his oratory by analysing his speeches as leader to that same body.

Confining ourselves to just seven annual speeches, running from 2006 to 2012, has its downsides of course. After all, part of what makes the current Conservative leader such a stand-out politician is his ability to perform well in a range of oratorical environments. On the other hand, limiting ourselves to conference speeches still allows us to consider the three main audiences – parliamentarians, ordinary party members and the electorate. Conference speeches routinely contain 'something for everyone' and, by the same token, they also employ all three of Aristotle's primary modes of persuasive appeal – ethos, pathos, and logos – although rarely, of course, in equal measure. Concentrating on conference speeches has its upsides, too. It ensures that we are able to say something satisfyingly concrete rather than overly abstract and that we stay helpfully focused on one part of the leader's repertoire rather than flitting from one instance to another in an inherently impossible attempt to capture the whole. Just as importantly, it allows us to track whether there is much change over time and to consider the impact of Cameron's transformation from Leader of the Opposition to prime minister – a role that, notwithstanding all the other things he or she has to do, still requires the incumbent to spend time and effort on rhetorical persuasion (Toye, 2011). It turns out, in fact, that, though there is change – for instance, once in Number 10 Cameron seemed more concerned with making reasoned or at least evidence-based arguments than he was in establishing his *bona fides* – there is much that stays the same and can therefore be assumed to be 'characteristically Cameron'.

Ethos

Almost all Conservative party leaders' conference speeches (and certainly every one of David Cameron's) begin with what classical scholars would have referred to as the *exordium* (see Leith, 2011) – in this case anyway, a fairly transparent attempt not just to set the tone but, right from start, to remind the audience in the hall that they should feel good about themselves, that he is both their champion and one of them and, of course, that he is up to the job. As a new leader, this is especially important, which is why Cameron, delivering the first of two speeches in that capacity in October 2006, attempted to lend himself additional weight by reminding his audience right from the start that he had already seen off not just the Liberal Democrats' Menzies Campbell but their one-time nemesis, Tony Blair. It is also why he moved swiftly on to associate himself with popular figures in the party whom he had taken on as lieutenants – a move which allowed him symbolically to heal the breach with his main rival for the leadership, David Davis, at the same time as putting him firmly in his place by thanking him for his 'fantastic support'. And it is why, after some knockabout attacks on Labour, he attempted to establish a sense of momentum, first by referring to the party's relatively successful showing in the spring local elections and, second, by pointing to an influx of new members (albeit one that later turned out to be far more apparent than real).

Cameron sought, too, to dovetail that momentum with rather more controversial changes to policy and candidate selection processes, short-circuiting continuing concern about those changes in the parliamentary and wider party by asserting that delivering them was what they had elected him to do. In his second speech to that first conference, Cameron switched from the second to the first person, and the audience that he had addressed earlier in the week mainly as 'you' became 'we' – presumably in an effort to isolate those who were ambivalent about or even opposed to reform. The latter, even though many of them would have been in the audience, were pointedly referred to in the third person as he staked his claim to speak on behalf of all by suggesting that 'when some people talk about substance [which he was accused by internal critics of lacking], what they mean is they want the old policies back. Well', he continued, 'they're not coming back. We're not going back'.

Cameron – partly because he was so obviously something of a smooth operator – was chronically concerned about being characterised, whether by Labour or by Tory critics, as insubstantial and inauthentic. By the time of his second conference as party leader in October 2007, however, that concern had become acute. When he spoke in Blackpool – the scene of his triumph two years earlier in the leadership contest – the stakes could not have been higher. The year had promised so much but had swiftly gone from bad to worse as Gordon Brown, who had finally achieved his ambition to replace Blair as prime minister, enjoyed a surprising bounce in popularity while the Tories had begun tearing lumps out of each other over grammar schools and disappointing by-election results. By the autumn, Brown was clearly considering a snap election – one which, if the headline figures in the opinion polls were anything to go by, Labour stood a pretty good chance of winning. The Tory leader, therefore, had to do his utmost to convince Brown and his advisors, as well as the country as a whole, that he was not some superficial, spin-obsessed lightweight but a serious prospect with guts and a mind of his own.

Establishing ethos, in these circumstances, demanded not so much that Cameron emphasise his authority but that he stress his authenticity – something he did by repeating the trick he had pulled off in 2005, namely the supposedly off-the-cuff speech: 'it might be a bit messy', he appeared to confess, 'but it will be me'. He also moved swiftly – and not unusually these days (see Pettitt, 2012) – into the first-person singular, both in his opening and in this, his peroration:

> I've told you what I believe, I've told you about the changes I want to make to our economy, to politics, to health, housing, education, the environment … But I've said something else, it's about me. People want to know: are you really up for it? Do you have what it takes? Are you tough enough and strong enough to make those decisions? And I answer unreservedly: yes … So, Mr Brown, what's it going to be? Why don't you go ahead and call that election?

Cameron's fighting talk, combined with some discouraging news from the marginals, was enough to push Brown into 'bottling' the election and in so doing virtually guaranteeing that the contest would not be called until the Parliament had run its full five-year term. The task for Cameron was therefore to extend what had been a fairly fragile Tory lead into the sort of double-digit cushion that would see the party through what was bound to be a tough campaign in 2010. And since polling continued to suggest that he was running some way ahead of his party in the public's estimation, it made sense for him to continue to focus on his qualifications for the top job. Since, as a relatively young politician with no executive and little parliamentary experience, he could hardly claim to be a Whitehall (or even for that matter a Westminster) veteran, he had to rely for ethos mainly on claims about his personal credo and character rather than his record or even his judgement – indeed, the latter had on several recent occasions been called into question by his (and George Osborne's) initially uncertain reaction to the global financial crisis. Hence, in his next conference speech in Birmingham in 2008, made just days after Brown had claimed that the crisis meant that this was 'no time for a novice', he claimed that:

> In the end, [it's] not really about your policies and your plans … [P]eople want to know what values you bring to big situations and big decisions that can crop up on your watch. And people want to know about your character: the way you make decisions; the way that you operate … You can't prove you're ready to be Prime Minister – and it would be arrogant to pretend you can. The best you can do is tell people who you are and the way you work; how you make decisions and then live with them.

He then reminded his audience that he was 'a forty-one year old father of three who thinks that family is the most important thing there is', that he was 'deeply patriotic about this country', and that he was 'not an ideologue' but that he held 'to some simple principles' ('strong defence, the rule of law and sound money'). So far, so conventionally Conservative. But – in keeping with what has been called 'the politics of and' (the idea that the Tories had to stress that tough and tender were compatible not zero sum) – he switched into modernising mode, insisting that he was also 'a child of [his] time' who wanted 'a clean environment as well as a safe one', who knew that 'quality of life matters as much as quantity of money', and who recognised 'that we'll never be truly rich while so much of the world is so poor'. He also, rather more conventionally, drew a none-too-implicit contrast between himself and Labour's current and former leader:

> I believe in building a strong team – and really trusting them. Their success is to be celebrated – not seen as some kind of threat. Thinking before deciding is good. Not deciding because you don't like the consequences of a decision is bad. Trust your principles, your judgment and your colleagues. Go with your conviction, not calculation. The popular thing may look good for a while. The right thing will be right all the time.

Certainly, all this was rather more convincing than his reminding his audience during the same speech that 'I've studied economics at a great university. I've worked in business alongside great entrepreneurs. And … I've been inside the Treasury during a crisis' – not so impressive perhaps when one recalls that economics constituted only one-third of his undergraduate degree, that he worked in the PR rather than the operational or financial side of things at Carlton, and that he was special advisor to Norman Lamont when the UK fell out of the European Exchange Rate Mechanism after blowing billions of pounds in just one day in a doomed attempt to prop up sterling.

By the same time the next year, Cameron was addressing what was bound to be the last Tory conference before the 2010 election – one in which he knew he was still going to have to fend off charges from Labour (and quell widespread concerns among voters and even some in his own party) that he was little more than a slick, metropolitan posh boy. Dreadful as it must have been, the death of his six-year-old son earlier in the year (which he referred to only briefly in order to stress that he was sure of his calling) meant that he could hardly be accused of not knowing adversity. But again, he chose to root his ethos in his traditional values and in his character, this time using changes made to the party both to demonstrate that he was capable of combining tradition and modernity and to urge Tory members (not for the first time) to accept and even to own those changes. And once again, he began by reminding them of the high-wire act that helped him win the leadership:

> We could have come to Manchester this week and played it safe. But that's not what this party is about and it's certainly not what I'm about. When I stood on that stage in Blackpool four years ago it wasn't just to head up this party, sit around and wait for the tide to turn. It was to lead this party and change it, so together we could turn the tide. Look what we've done together.

And then, both before and after yet more mentions of his role as a parent (something many of us can identify with) rather than as a politician (who, as a class, many of us despise):

> I am not a complicated person … This is my DNA: family, community, country. These are the things I care about. They are what made me. They are what I'm in public service to protect, promote and defend.

When Cameron next addressed his party he had been in Number 10 for nearly half a year, and – just as importantly – it was generally agreed, even by opponents, that he looked and sounded the part. As a result, and inasmuch as it derives from status as much as character, ethos was not really a problem – especially after Cameron's first line: 'It is an honour and a privilege to stand here, before the party I lead, before the country I love, as the Conservative prime minister of the United Kingdom.' However, although that was still more than enough to help him through his speech in 2011, it could not last forever. In the run up to the party gathering in Birmingham in 2012,

Cameron was having to cope with a stuttering economy, with a Labour leader who was beginning to do better than many had predicted, and with rumours that, unless things improved, he might sooner or later be challenged for the leadership by Boris Johnson, the mercurial Mayor of London. Accordingly, back came character – this time a clever attempt to persuade people that his comfortable upbringing made him not only a secure, family-centred individual but also provided him with access to a first-class education that he was now apparently determined to give every child. In contrast to his years in opposition, however, Cameron could also associate himself with popular policies and with a successful Olympic games. And what he could also do – like Tory prime ministers before him – was assert his credentials as a leader prepared to stand up for the national interest in the face of an all-too-familiar foe:

> Last December I was at a European Council in Brussels. It was three in the morning, there was a treaty on the table that was not in Britain's interests[,] and twenty five people around that table were telling me to sign it. But I did something that no other British leader has ever done before[.] I said no – Britain comes first – and I vetoed that EU treaty.

Understandable? Perhaps. Predictable? To some, depressingly so. Effective? Probably – though for how long was anyone's guess.

Pathos

From the very start, references to his children served not just to establish Cameron's values and character but to forge an emotional connection with his immediate and wider audience: 'There is nothing', he said in the first of the two leader's speeches he gave in Bournemouth in 2006, 'that matters more to me than the safety and happiness of my family'. Six years later, at the 2012 conference in Birmingham which followed the UK's successful summer of sport, Cameron recalled his father's triumph over disability – something which, like the love shown to him by his parents, mattered more, he seemed to be signalling, than all the privileges which flowed to him from the considerable wealth that his opponents like to harp on. And earlier on in the speech, Cameron literally brought tears to his own and many of his listeners' eyes by confessing:

> I am so grateful for what all those Paralympians did. When I used to push my son Ivan around in his wheelchair, I always thought that some people saw the wheelchair, not the boy. Today more people would see the boy and not the wheelchair – and that's because of what happened here this summer.

An emotional connection, however, can be achieved by laughter as well as tears. Only a minute or so into his very first leader's speech, Cameron was joking about Blair trying to suggest that he was 'all style and no substance': 'In fact,' he confided 'he wrote me a letter about it. Dear Kettle … You're black. Signed, Pot'. Not long afterwards, exploiting the very obvious tensions between Blair's wife, Cherie, and Gordon Brown, who had finally succeeded in winkling her husband out of the top job, he noted that 'a member of the Cabinet said "it would be an absolute effing disaster" if Gordon got to No.10', then, after pausing for comic effect, reminded his audience that 'That was just the husbands'. But the humour could be self-deprecating, too: talking about the possibilities opened up by the Internet in 2007, he noted that

> There is a network on Facebook called 'David Cameron is a hottie.' It's got 74 members. And I looked a little further and there is another network called 'Am I the only person who doesn't like David Cameron?' and it's got 379 members – I am sure there is nobody here today.

Cameron's use of humour could even involve some gentle teasing of the traditionalists: during the same speech he raised the possibility of an across-the-board scheme to encourage school-leavers to get actively involved in their communities, but warned his audience that he wasn't 'about to suggest a return to national service. Sorry to disappoint you'. And sometimes it could even be a touch risqué (or what passes as such in polite Conservative company): talking to his audience in Birmingham in 2008, he observed 'I admire entrepreneurs. I should do – I go to bed with one every night'. In 2009, when the emphasis had to be on his credentials as a potential prime minister, there was no room for jokes, unlike back in 2010, when, safely ensconced in Downing Street, he could afford to relax a little. Whether this did much for the quality of the jokes, of course is a moot point: his opener was one involving his having to watch the England football team getting thrashed by Germany in the company of Chancellor Angela Merkel – something which, he claimed, had 'brought a whole new element to Anglo-German diplomatic relations: whatever you do, don't mention the score'. His reference to a six-year-old girl sending in a pound coin given to her by the tooth-fairy in order to help restore the nation's finances ('There we are, George – nearly there') was a little better, but only just. More pointed, and almost certainly more successful, was what began as a joke but ended in a list that allowed Cameron both to show his party that he shared their anger at what Labour had done to the country and to remind voters why they had thrown it out of office:

> The mess this country is in – it's not all because of Labour. Of course, they must take some of the blame. Alright – they need to take a lot of the blame. Let me just get this off my chest. They left us with massive debts, the highest deficit, overstretched armed forces, demoralised public services, endless ridiculous rules and regulations and quangos and bureaucracy and nonsense. They left us a legacy of spinning, smearing, briefing, back-biting, half-truths and cover-ups, patronising, old-fashioned, top-down, wasteful, centralising, inefficient, ineffective, unaccountable politics, 10p tax and 90 days detention, an election bottled and a referendum denied, gold sold at half price and council tax doubled, bad news buried and Mandelson resurrected, pension funds destroyed and foreign prisoners not deported, Gurkhas kept out and extremist preachers allowed in. Yes, they deserve some blame, and we'll never let them forget it.

Cameron's 2012 speech also saw Cameron paint a mental picture for his audience – done on that occasion not only to convey the human cost of the credit crunch but to counter internal resistance to changes to planning legislation:

> there are those who say 'yes of course we need more housing' … but 'no' to every development – and not in my backyard. Look – it's OK for my generation. Many of us have got on the ladder. But you know the average age that someone buys their first home today, without any help from their parents? 33 years old. We are the party of home ownership – we cannot let this carry on … [W]e need to build more houses in Britain. There are young people who work hard year after year but are still living at home. They sit in their childhood bedroom, looking out of the window dreaming of a place of their own. I want us to say to them – you are our people, we are on your side, we will help you reach your dreams.

This use of imagery was actually rather unusual for Cameron, and in any case insufficiently melodramatic to qualify as what scholars of rhetoric call *enargia*. It may, though, have reflected the fact that, following journalist Julian Glover's less-than-successful stint as the prime minister's main speech-writer, the role had been handed to Claire Foges, an English graduate in her early thirties who had been on the team under Glover's predecessor, Ameet Gill. The switch did not, however, mean that Cameron stopped using the well-worn technique of evoking understanding and sympathy by recalling letters from or meetings with 'ordinary people' – often named individuals, be they pensioners, small businessmen, young couples, benefits claimants, cancer patients whose personal plights and experiences 'cut through' statistics and more abstract arguments (see Atkins and Finlayson, 2013). More often than not, they were constituents, but occasionally Cameron brought in someone he'd met on his travels. Most powerfully, perhaps, was his recalling in 2008 – during one of the encomiums to the bravery of the UK's armed forces that seem to be an obligatory feature of Cameron's speeches – of a conversation in Afghanistan with eighteen-year-old Blaine Miller: 'He's not much more than a boy and he's there in the forty-five degree heat, fighting a ferocious enemy on the other side of the world. I told him that what he was doing was exceptional. He told me he was just doing his job.'

Cameron's most persistent effort to establish an emotional connection, however, revolved around his appeal to optimism. This was perhaps most obvious in his conference speech in 2008, whose peroration is a good example of the blurring not just of second and first person but party, voters and nation:

> I know we are living in difficult times but I am still optimistic because I have faith in human nature … in our remarkable capacity to innovate, to experiment, to overcome obstacles and to find a way through difficulties … whether those problems are created by man or nature. We can and will come through. We always do. Not because of our government. But because of the people of Britain. Because of what you do – because of the work you do, the families you raise, the jobs you create … because of your attitude, your confidence and your determination. So because we are united … Because we have had the courage to change … Because we have the fresh answers to the challenges

of our age. I believe we now have the opportunity, and more than that the responsibility, to bring our country together. Together in the face of this financial crisis. Together in determination that we will come through it. Together in the hope, the belief that better times will lie ahead.

Optimism was also a big part of his pre-election conference speech in 2009, whose peroration neatly summed up the balance of individualism and collective endeavour that Cameron had been developing throughout his leadership but also illustrates his use of classic rhetorical ploys, such as *anaphora* and the journey metaphor so beloved of leaders all over the world (Charteris-Black, 2011: 66–71, 178–80, 211–17):

> So if we cut big government back. If we move society forward. And if we rebuild responsibility, then we can put Britain back on her feet. I know that today there aren't many reasons to be cheerful. But there are reasons to believe. Yes it will be a steep climb. But the view from the summit will be worth it. Let me tell you what I can see. I see a country where more children grow up with security and love because family life comes first. I see a country where you choose the most important things in life ... I see a country where communities govern themselves ... I see a country with entrepreneurs everywhere, bringing their ideas to life – and life to our great towns and cities. I see a country where it's not just about the quantity of money, but the quality of life ... I see a country where you're not so afraid to walk home alone, where you're safe in the knowledge that right and wrong is restored to law and order. I see a country where the poorest children go to the best schools not the worst, where birth is never a barrier. No, we will not make it if we pull in different directions, follow our own interests, take care of only ourselves. But if we pull together, come together, work together – we will get through this together.

Two years later, having earlier called on his audience to 'reject the pessimism' and to 'bring on the can-do optimism', Cameron ended his speech in almost exactly the same terms:

> Let's turn this time of challenge into a time of opportunity. Not sitting around, watching things happen and wondering why. But standing up, making things happen and asking why not. We have the people, we have the ideas, and now we have a government that's freeing those people, backing those ideas. So let's see an optimistic future. Let's show the world some fight. Let's pull together, work together. And together lead Britain to better days.

Cameron's appeal to the emotions through optimism, of course, went all the way back to his pitch for the leadership in 2005, which centred on his ability to turn around a party that had lost three general elections in a row. Optimism, too, had been the central theme of his very first conference speech as leader in October 2006 when, perhaps rather too obviously channelling Ronald Reagan, he told his audience that 'In a few years' time, Britain could wake up to a bright new morning' and then, risking pastiche perhaps, called on them to 'Let sunshine win the day'. And he was back the next year in Blackpool, doing the very same thing he had done in

Bournemouth, attempting to invert the traditional association of conservatism with pessimism about human nature, arguing that it was its optimism that individuals could be trusted with responsibility, power and control which distinguished it from a Labour Party whose gloomy view of civil society meant its default solution for any problem was the state. He was also, of course, trying to mobilise activists for the snap general election that he believed Brown might be about to call:

> And do you know the greatest service that this party can do to our public today, it is to get out and fight for what we believe in and the changes we want to make. Because you know, people in this country after 10 years of Labour really despair that they can get the sort of change they want. They don't believe it is possible any more and we've got to inspire them, we've got to say to them, it doesn't have to be like this. You don't have to put up with this, you can get it if you really want.

If the last phrase reminded some (though one would have thought very few Tory members actually sitting in the hall) of a song, that was quite deliberate, since Cameron used a ploy he had foisted on Michael Howard when he was leader and was to use himself again, namely a conference theme tune which was played over the PA system at the beginning and end of speeches. Howard had been accompanied in 2004 by a remix of Elvis Presley's 'A Little Less Conversation' and in 2012, Cameron received the by now compulsory standing ovation to the strains of the Jam's cover of Curtis Mayfield's 'Move on Up', having used another Motown hit, 'It Takes Two' by Marvin Gaye and Kim Weston in 2010. In 2007, however, Cameron chose 'You Can Get it if You Really Want' by reggae legend, Jimmy Cliff.

Which of Cameron's more or less illustrious predecessors were turning in their graves we shall never know. One who might not have been, however, was Harold Macmillan, who, for all his classical education and references, was desperately keen to keep up with the times. Nor was he averse to dropping into the demotic – something that distinguishes Cameron's speeches too. In 2006, he mocked Labour's promise that the transfer of power from Blair to Brown would be a 'stable and orderly transition' – 'Yeah, right'. In 2007, talking about the so-called 'couples penalty' imposed by the benefit system, Cameron spoke of meeting a young man who 'had recently been in prison and he was trying to go straight, he had got a job. He's got a kid already and he's got another on the way'; he also spoke, in a passage about the over-bureaucratisation of the criminal justice system, about being told of a mother whose 'son was nicking money out of her wallet'. He also talked about a benefit claimant who'd been advised to go on incapacity benefit after a minor injury who told the benefits agency 'you're having a laugh'. The year after, in 2008, he was clearly trying to connect with those in poverty by using the language he assumed they spoke – 'the call centre worker whose mortgage has gone up by four hundred quid a month' and 'the hairdresser who's a single mum doing another job on the side to try and make ends meet'. Interestingly the use of such vocabulary dropped away as Cameron was on the verge of, and then in, power. The exception was his continued use of the word 'mum' – a universal connector, if you like, even when employed by a man from a social milieu that tends to use the term 'mummy' in private.

Logos

More than most Conservative leaders, David Cameron wanted to communicate the impression to the electorate that his party realised that it had made mistakes, had moved too far (and too obsessively) to the right, and was going to have to make changes. Moreover, all this was bound to involve doing things that directly contradicted some of the policies and processes that many Tory members, both in the constituencies and at Westminster, had got used to taking as read. Had Cameron truly been 'the heir to Blair' then he might have more ruthlessly exploited this internal resistance (as long as he could overcome it) to send a message to voters about how much the Tories were changing. But Cameron wasn't Blair. Except when it came to 'social issues' like achieving greater representation for women and ethnic minorities or more rights for gay people, he – like most Conservative 'modernisers' – didn't actually believe there was much fundamentally wrong with the party's stances on the economy and public services, with the exception of its damagingly ambivalent position on the NHS, which he changed immediately and without discussion, referring again and again to 'our NHS' and to the Tories as 'the party of the NHS'. The aim, then, was to do enough to persuade the electorate that the party had learned its lessons and was heading back to the mainstream without either throwing Thatcherism overboard or provoking an uncontrollable backlash on the part of grassroots and Parliamentary Party members – and, of course, the 'party in the media' (the columnists and commentators whose views play just as big a role as those of paid-up members and MPs).

It is noticeable that, right throughout his time in opposition (but decreasingly in government), Cameron, beginning in 2006, stressed repeatedly that Labour (and Blair in particular) had 'good intentions' rather than a malign purpose and that its problem was a) that it had not worked out how to deliver on those intentions and b) that it was too wedded to solutions that involved 'the state'/'government' rather than (like the Conservatives) 'society' – terms that, interestingly, were not only continually counterposed but counterposed in such a manner as to suggest (in orthodox, Thatcherite fashion) that there was a zero sum game between them. This *concessio* was to take the ideological heat out of Tory opposition and communicate to voters that it was reasonable – indeed, expressed more in sorrow than in anger. This was part and parcel of an explicit commitment to fighting on 'the centre ground' – not simply because that was where the votes were but because (as he put it in Bournemouth in 2006) it was 'where you find the concerns, the hopes and the dreams of most people and families in this country'. This was coupled with a historical argument that allowed him to praise Thatcher but also (before the economic crash in 2007/8) to argue that things had moved on, that the agenda was now different: in 1978 most people wanted a government to tame the unions, rescue our economy and restore Britain's pride. Margaret Thatcher offered precisely that alternative. And this Party can forever take pride in her magnificent achievements. Today, people want different things. The priorities are different. Safer streets. Schools that teach. A better quality of life. Better treatment for carers. That's what people are talking about today. But for too long, we were having a different conversation. Instead of talking about the things that most people care about, we talked about what we cared about most … For years, this country wanted – desperately needed – a sensible centre-right party to sort things out in a sensible way. Well, that's what we are today. In these past ten months we have moved back to the ground on which this Party's success has always been built. The centre ground of British politics. And that is where we will stay.

The argument for social change based on reason rather than emotion was perhaps most evident in his handling of immigration. In fact, his speeches rarely touched upon the issue in any detail, so toxic had it become, but when they did, as in 2007, there was a clear attempt both to remind voters and the party that it would continue to take a tough line at the same time as recommending that it was an issue which it had to 'approach sensibly':

> I think this country has benefited immeasurably from immigration. People who want to come here and work hard and contribute to our country. I think our diverse and multi-racial society is a huge benefit for Britain, but we do have recognise the pressures that can be put on public services, schools and hospitals and housing if immigration is unlimited … I want our party, a modern Conservative party, to talk about this issue in a reasonable, humane and sensible way and to take the very sensible measures that are necessary. What I always find with the government is that you get the exact opposite. You get a whole lot of language, often quite inflammatory but they don't take steps that Britain needs. So let us be the ones that handle this issue in the way that it needs to be for the good of our country and our public services.

Cameron also used sound-bites that gave the impression that the Tories were moving away from their traditional positions and allies but which made it reassuringly clear that those positions and allies were still important. For example, in 2006 he claimed (and was much quoted to the effect) that 'we must stand up to big business when it's in the interests of Britain and the wider world' but then went straight on to talk about the need for deregulation and the fact that (reflecting the influence on his speeches at that stage of Steve Hilton) 'We want companies to create their own solutions to social and environmental challenges, because those are the solutions most likely to last'. Likewise, a year later, he talked about the need for business to be more family friendly, but was careful to offer to employees with children 'the right to ask for flexible working', not the right to flexible working itself.

That said, Cameron was not averse to adopting an explicitly pedagogic tone, telling his audience in 2007, for instance, that 'the argument I want to make today' was about the need to adapt to the challenges of the modern world and informing them that 'I want to tell you what's wrong with our country and I want to explain what I am going to do to put it right'. And in 2008, he embarked on a very (some critics would no doubt say overly) ambitious attempt to explain the origins of, and then the Tory solution to, the global financial crisis. Indeed, it was on the economy that Cameron most often appealed to logic and reason, although always of course in such a way as to privilege his own preferred solution. In 2009, for example, he suggested there were essentially three ways to handle the debt crisis, the only two options other than the immediate move to pay off government borrowing which he was advocating being default and the deliberate stoking of inflation.

Often, of course, the arguments against Labour policies and for Conservative alternatives were made from what was supposedly common sense, the resort to which is a common rhetorical technique (Leith, 2011: 65). Hence, in 2007, Cameron argued that 'We must be crazy in this country to be using the benefits system to drive people apart rather than bring them together', while in true populist fashion, it was often enough to make the argument for traditional techniques in school (such as setting, synthetic phonics, exclusion) by reminding his audience that such things were apparently opposed by the 'educational establishment' (Cameron, 2007a). Likewise, 'everyone' apparently wanted, he said, borrowing from the standard tabloid lexicon, 'beat-based, zero-tolerance policing' (2007b) and an end to 'top-down targets' in the NHS. Similarly in 2008, a fairly sophisticated, albeit brief, historical argument about how the welfare state when it was first founded may have been right to offer unconditional benefits since most people were in and wanted to work but now had to change because of the perverse incentives that system had created, culminated in criticism of 'the something for nothing culture' (Cameron, 2008). In other words, Cameron's conference speeches – even when making a supposedly reasoned argument – often relied more on self-evidence than on evidence itself.

Cameron's speeches also relied on reason in the sense of presenting voters with a more or less explicit contract, the contents of which neatly summed up the Tory message by making it clear who the party was appealing to – and by implication who would be left out (and by implication condemned to harsher treatment). In his pre-election conference speech of 2009, for example, which inevitably focused on the Conservative offer to voters, Cameron, once again employing the time-honoured rhetorical trick, *anaphora*, although combining it on this occasion with *hypophora* (the asking and answering of questions to develop an argument or position), promised:

> If you put in the effort to bring in a wage, you will be better off. If you save money your whole life, you'll be rewarded. If you start your own business, we'll be right behind you. If you want to raise a family, we'll support you. If you're frightened, we'll protect you. If you risk your safety to stop a crime, we'll stand by you. If you risk your life to fight for your country, we will honour you. Ask me what a Conservative government

stands for and the answer is this, we will reward those who take responsibility, and care for those who can't. (Cameron, 2009a)

Once in power, with the ability to deliver rather than simply plan and promise, Cameron also made more use – when appealing to voters and party members – of the tangible, the particular rather than the general. In 2010, for instance, he had notably more recourse to detailed figures than in most of his previous speeches, noting 'We spend £41,000 a year on each prisoner – and within a year of leaving, half of them reoffend. There are 150,000 people in Britain today who get their heroin substitutes on the state, their addictions maintained by the taxpayer' (Cameron, 2010a). And, after a section in the same speech which aimed to explain the logic behind his choosing to head up a Coalition government (something many in his party would nevertheless continue to fail to grasp), he imported a technique – *isocolon* – from the floor of the House of Commons where supportive MPs are encouraged to join the prime minister in vocal affirmation as a list of statistics is read and achievements ticked off:

> People wondered what a coalition could achieve. But just look at what we are achieving already – together, in the national interest. Conservative policies, policies you campaigned on, policies we are delivering. Two hundred new academies. Ten thousand university places. Fifty thousand apprenticeships. Corporation tax – cut. The jobs tax – axed. Police targets – smashed. Immigration – capped. The third runway – stopped. Home Information Packs – dropped. Fat cat salaries – revealed. ID Cards – abolished. The NHS – protected. Our aid promise – kept. Quangos – closing down. Ministers' pay – coming down. A bank levy – coming up. A cancer drugs fund – up and running. £6bn of spending saved this year. An emergency budget to balance the books in five years. An EU referendum lock to protect our sovereign powers every year. For our pensioners – the earnings link restored. For our new entrepreneurs – employees' tax reduced. And for our brave armed forces – the operational allowance doubled. Look what we've done in five months. Just imagine what we can do in five years.

In this case an attempt to separate logos from pathos risks seeming artificial. In 2011, in the wake of continuing criticism about his decision to 'ring-fence' the UK's overseas development spending, Cameron talked about visiting a clinic in Nigeria:

> It was very hot, pretty basic and the lights kept going off. But to the rows of women, cuddling their babies, this place was a godsend. One of the nurses told me that if it wasn't for British aid, many of those beautiful babies would be dead. In four years' time, this country will have helped vaccinate more of the world's poorest children than there are people in the whole of England. Of course, we'll make sure your money goes to the people who need it most, and we'll do it in a way that's transparent and accountable. But I really believe, despite all our difficulties, that this is the right thing to do. (Cameron, 2011)

Whether the combination worked or not is a moot point: Cameron had to return to the argument in 2012. And he had to do the same on the relaxation of planning laws in spite of a seemingly no-ifs-no-buts resort to statistics and cold hard logic in 2011, when he reminded opponents that '[t]he proportion of land in England that is currently built up is 9 per cent' and had told them: 'Take your arguments down to the job centre. We've got to get Britain back to work' (2011). On other issues in 2011, he tried a more mixed approach. 'Do you know' he asked, 'how many children there are in care under the age of one? 3,660. And how many children under the age of one were adopted in our country last year? Sixty. This may not seem like the biggest issue facing our country, but it is the biggest issue for these children' (2011). He also reminded his audience:

> I once stood before a Conservative conference and said it shouldn't matter whether commitment was between a man and a woman, a woman and a woman, or a man and another man. You applauded me for that. Five years on, we're consulting on legalising gay marriage. And to anyone who has reservations, I say: Yes, it's about equality, but it's also about something else: commitment. Conservatives believe in the ties that bind us; that society is stronger when we make vows to each other and support each other. So I don't support gay marriage despite being a Conservative. I support gay marriage because I'm a Conservative. (Cameron, 2011)

Conclusion

The oratorical difference between Cameron as prime minister and Cameron as Leader of the Opposition was perhaps most pronounced in his speech to the Tory conference in Birmingham in 2012. In it, Cameron conducted what amounted to a sustained argument, supported by statistics, that his government's determination to stick to its debt and deficit-reduction plan and to its planning, civil service, welfare and education reforms. This was about making what could still be 'the most enterprising, buccaneering, creative, dynamic nation on earth' capable of competing in 'a global race', and that it was 'an hour of reckoning for countries like ours'. Values and character hadn't completely disappeared, nor had emotions. But the primary focus was on argument, on explanation and on examples.

That said, while logos was to the fore in the 'narrative' (Grube, 2012) woven by Cameron in 2012, there was still room for pathos and ethos, and for many of the techniques and tropes that he had been employing since he made his first conference speech in 2006: indeed, the references to his family and to Britain's history, the use of 'ordinary people', the admiring nod to the armed forces, the appeal to optimism, and even the use of suitably-themed pop music to accompany him off stage could be said to be characteristically Cameron. Gone, however, were the jokes and his early willingness to give Labour a little credit rather than write it off as at best incompetent and at worst hypocritical. To the orator, *decorum* (appropriateness) and *kairos* (timeliness) are crucial considerations. With thoughts turning to the 2015 election, Cameron – if the media's largely positive reaction to the speech was anything to go by – could feel reasonably confident that, once again, he had pitched it right. How much difference it made to his chances of winning the election, however, was anyone's guess.

Acknowledgement

I would like to thank Martin Shovel and Peter Hoskin for their help and advice on this chapter.

Conclusion

Oratory and rhetoric in Conservative Party politics

Richard Hayton and Andrew S. Crines

The contributors to this book have each analysed the oratory and rhetoric of a significant figure from Conservative Party history, ranging from the 1920s to the present day. Each chapter has considered how the individual subject utilised their oratorical skills in three important arenas that relate to three key audiences, namely: (i) Parliament and the Parliamentary Party; (ii) the party conference and the wider party membership; and (iii) the electoral arena (i.e. public and media engagement). As each chapter has reached its own specific conclusions about the orator it features, these will not be repeated here. However, the analysis of each orator utilised the analytical prism of the three modes of persuasion identified by Aristotle, namely ethos, pathos and logos. This concluding essay will therefore ask whether we can generalise in any way about Conservative oratory in relation to these key elements of effective rhetoric.

Is there a particular style of oratory that characterises successful Conservative speakers? The short answer to this question is clearly no. As we have seen in the previous twelve chapters, so much depends on the personality and style of each individual orator, and cultivating a credible ethos involves fashioning a way of communicating that is a convincing extension of a speaker's image and persona. Boris Johnson for example, as Katharine Dommett (Chapter 11) discussed, has developed an idiosyncratic manner that is unlikely to be effectively or plausibly replicated. Nonetheless, there are some observations that can be made about how leading Conservative politicians seek to persuade people with their arguments, which relate to their party's ideological outlook and electoral strategy. These are discussed below in relation to ethos, pathos and logos.

Ethos

The introduction to this volume suggested that the British Conservative Party has always been a relatively centralised, top-down organisation, with the party leadership therefore occupying a pivotal role. This has been reflected in Conservative historiography which has often focused on the role played by leading individuals, while political scientists have analysed the statecraft strategies of the party leadership (Bulpitt,

1986). Considering the appeals to ethos (character) utilised by Conservative orators therefore seems like an appropriate starting point for these concluding remarks. The statecraft model deployed by Bulpitt (1986) to explain the electoral success the Conservatives enjoyed under Thatcher stressed the importance of an image of governing competence, and while this goes beyond simply the reputation of a single individual, personal credibility is vital for any orator. As one leading analyst of political rhetoric has noted:

> Politics is about building trust, and because of an increasing awareness of manipulation of public opinion through media presentation and the 'massaging' of consent, trust has become a rare commodity in democracies. Orators need to convince followers that they and their policies can be trusted. (Charteris-Black, 2014: 9)

Conservative orators have sought to win the trust of their fellow politicians, party members and supporters, and the wider electorate, by conveying various forms of political character. Some such as Macmillan had a patrician style, exuding the sense that they and their fellow Conservatives were the 'natural' party of government (Bale, 2011: 4). This style of leadership was particularly associated with the One Nation tradition, and retreated with it. In their analysis of the decline of One Nation conservatism, Dorey and Garnett (2014) stress how the social composition of the party elite changed, noting that: 'In a sense, One Nation politicians had conspired in their own downfall by urging that the post-war Conservative Party should broaden its field of parliamentary candidates' (2014: 8). They quote one Conservative MP with a One Nation outlook, Julian Critchley, bemoaning the fact that by the late 1970s his party had undergone a 'process of petit-embourgeoisement' and 'become less patrician, less grand' (quoted in Dorey and Garnett, 2014: 8). The waning of the One Nation tradition, and the commensurate emergence of Thatcherism, can thus be partly understood in terms of a shift towards a more meritocratic Conservative Party which naturally fostered a greater sense of energetic individualism, 'personified' by the grammar school-educated, lower-middle-class Margaret Thatcher (Dorey and Garnett, 2014: 8).

As Peter Dorey discusses in relation to Thatcher in Chapter 7 of this volume, the ethos cultivated by many of her generation of Conservative MPs was very different to that of leading One Nation figure Macmillan, who sought to present himself as an aristocratic gentleman, with an air of superiority and distance from the average voter (Chapter 3). Thatcher by contrast made frequent reference to her more humble origins, and sought to present herself as an ordinary housewife and therefore able to relate to commonplace concerns. John Major pursued a similar approach, and his modest background was seen as a virtue during the 1990 leadership contest and during the 1992 election (Chapter 9).

As the first leader of the Conservative Party to have attended Eton (indeed the first to be privately educated) since Alec Douglas-Home, David Cameron marked something of a break from this trend. In the 2005 leadership election, which is remembered by many as a 'tale of two speeches', Cameron's oratorical prowess was crucial in his triumph over a candidate of working-class origins, David Davis (Denham and Dorey, 2006). As Tim Bale discusses in Chapter 12, Cameron has appeared at ease in a leadership role, but he has still been vulnerable to the charge that he is emblematic of an out-of-touch political elite. There are some signs that amongst the new generation of Conservative MPs (the sizable 2010 intake) there may be a desire to offer a post-Cameron version of conservatism with a more explicitly blue-collar ethos (Lakin, 2014). However, the embedding of meritocracy as a core value in the party, displacing the patrician tradition, may mean that the background of the leader is regarded as largely irrelevant. Future Conservative leaders will, however, still need to project an authentic character which voters respond to positively, even if many do not relate to it directly.

Therefore it can be discerned that leading Conservatives use their character in their wider efforts to project an image of governing competence in an effort to secure the electorate's trust. More often than not this ethos is juxtaposed with a negative portrayal of the party's political opponents as not to be trusted with the business of governing the country. This relates in substantial part, but not exclusively, to economic management. For example, Margaret Thatcher exploited her ethos to highlight her 'awareness of the [economic] issues faced by the electorate. Indeed, this apparent "closeness" to the electorate was a significant element of the rhetorical ethos because it enabled her to claim a wider constituency of support' (Crines, 2014: 6). The loss of the electorate's trust on the economy following 'Black Wednesday' in September 1992 was highly damaging to the party's reputation, and was something that successive leaders would struggle to recapture in opposition (Hayton, 2012a). As such, we can see the electoral value to a party of effective orators with a credible and engaging ethos.

Pathos

As we have seen throughout this volume, there are countless examples of politicians seeking to appeal to the emotions of an audience. According to Charteris-Black, 'Aristotle's definition of emotion was that it was characterized by pleasure (for example, happiness) and by pain (for example, anger and fear)' (2014: 14). Using this straightforward distinction between what we might consider positive and negative emotional appeals, we can identify two recurring currents in Conservative oratory. The first is a positive appeal centred around patriotism. The Conservative Party has traditionally promoted a patriotic appeal to a sense of Britishness, linked to its defence of traditional British institutions (the monarchy, the Union and so on). This has been an important feature of the party's efforts to build an electoral coalition that includes a substantial element of working-class support, and is linked to the Conservative claim to represent the whole country (or One Nation) and not merely a sectional interest (a charge they have often levelled at Labour in relation to the trade union movement). As we have seen in this volume, patriotism has been a fea-ture of the pathos of Baldwin, Churchill, Macmillan, Thatcher, Major and Cameron, amongst others. At times patriotism has also acted as a useful substitute for more overtly ideological appeals. The unifying theme of conservatism as an ideology is its espousal of a limited form of politics (O'Sullivan, 2013), meaning that unlike socialism it does not have a utopian vision of the ideal it is striving for. Instead, a patriotic sense of attachment to the nation can be used as an optimistic enticement to voters.

The negative pathos in Conservative oratory has primarily been about elicit-ing the emotional reaction of fear. This can be a potent tool, and at different times has been used in rhetoric in relation to a range of policy areas, for example wel-fare (see Hayton and McEnhill, 2014). Most frequently and powerfully, however, Conservative orators have invoked the language of fear in relation to immigration. In the run-up to the 1979 general election Thatcher famously, and quite deliberately, referred in a television interview to fears that Britain would be 'swamped' by immi-grants. It is worth quoting her comments at length:

> [T]here was a committee which looked at it and said that if we went on as we are then by the end of the century there would be four million people of the new Commonwealth or Pakistan here. Now, that is an awful lot and I think it means that people are really rather afraid that this country might be rather swamped by people with a different cul-ture and, you know, the British character has done so much for democracy, for law and done so much throughout the world that if there is any fear that it might be swamped people are going to react and be rather hostile to those coming in. (Thatcher, 1978c)

The most notorious and inflammatory attempt to incite fear of immigrants by a Conservative Party politician is of course the 'rivers of blood' speech by Enoch Powell, which led to his dismissal by Heath from the Shadow Cabinet (Chapter 5). Powell's claim that 'in this country, in fifteen or twenty years' time, the black man will have the whip hand over the white man' and his infamous premonition of 'the River Tiber foaming with much blood' were just two of the most widely quoted lines of a speech crafted to provoke a fearful response. To his credit, Heath moved quickly to distance the party from Powell and condemned his views as extreme and his lan-guage as inflammatory. Powell would never return to the Conservative mainstream and eventually departed to sit as an Ulster Unionist. Since the 1968 speech, such overtly racist language and views have not been expressed by a leading Conservative Party politician. Negative pathos has though continued to feature in much of the rhetoric around immigration, for example fear of asylum seekers, or in more recent times migrant welfare claimants from within the European Union. Such language clearly continues to have resonance with a significant chunk of the electorate, with immigration continuing to feature high on the list of the electorate's concerns.

Fear of Labour's economic imprudence is also a significant driver of Conservative rhetoric. For example prior to the 2010 general election Cameron argued: 'If we win the election, we will have to confront Labour's debt crisis, deal with it, and take the country with us. I want everyone to understand the *gravity of our situation*' (Cameron, 2009). Here Cameron is striving to create a sense of overt fear by catastrophising Labour's economic performance. He went on by 'using fear to argue Britain's economic situation was more perilous than that faced by the Conservatives in 1979' (Crines, 2014), which was used by the Thatcher government to legitimise her neo-liberal economic experiment during the 1980s. Pathos is used to legitimate neo-liberalism (Crines, 2014) whilst simultaneously using negative emotions to attack Labour's economic record and arguments. Consequently, emotional rhetoric tends to use fear to imply the dangers of another (collectivist) course of action, encapsulated by Thatcher's mantra that 'there is no alternative' (Chapter 7).

Logos

All politicians like to claim that 'the facts' are on their side, and that their arguments are grounded in 'reality' (or at least a version of it). Indeed, the construction of reality can depend upon what Foucault called a 'regime of truth'. These represent 'the types of discourse which it accepts and makes function as true; the mechanisms and instances which enable one to distinguish true and false statements, the means by which each is sanctioned; the techniques and procedures accorded value in the acquisition of truth; the status of those who are charged with saying what counts as true' (Foucault, 1980: 131). For the orators considered in this volume an essentially sceptical view of the state represents the bread and butter of Conservative Party rhetoric. This is because, essentially, conservatism makes a claim to be an empirically grounded form of pragmatism that eschews romanticised utopian ideals or societies driven by non-pragmatic idealism. Thus conservatism takes its starting point as being where we are, and sometimes where we have been (or think we have been) and does not, like most ideologies, have an abstracted vision of an idealised future. As Oakeshott noted, 'to be conservative, then, is to prefer the familiar to the unknown, to prefer the tried to the untried, fact to mystery, the actual to the possible, the limited to the unbounded, the near to the distant, the sufficient to the superabundant, the convenient to the perfect, present laughter to utopian bliss'. This drives the conservative need to preserve rather than idealise as seen through the rhetorical arguments used by Conservative orators.

Consequently instances of logos tend to be used to provide an empirical basis to legitimise specific economic strategies. In simple terms, for most Conservatives such economic arguments centre around the need to maintain a grip on state spending and a preference for lower taxation, which is seen as beneficial for the private sector. Since 1979 Conservative economic strategy has largely been communicated through a Thatcherite discourse (Hayton, 2012a: 119–36). As a justification for neo-liberal policies, both Thatcher and Cameron used the size of the public sector debt to attack Labour. For example in 1979 Thatcher used logos rooted in her 'regime of truth' to argue 'the total amount of debt held outside the public sector when we left office – the Prime Minister was talking about an inheritance – was some £3000 million. One would have thought that that was sufficient. This year the estimate is some £8000 million interest on borrowings alone' (Thatcher, 1979d). In more recent years Cameron uses logos in a similar manner to legitimise reductions in spending by arguing 'I promise you this: that if we pull together to deal with these debts today, just a few years down the line the rewards will be felt by everyone in our country' (Cameron, 2009). We can see the presentation of such 'facts' at the heart of justifications for efforts to reduce the size and scope of the state, most notably in the 2010–15 Parliament in relation to the austerity agenda. Conservative politicians have consistently identified the central purpose of the Coalition government as to 'clean up Labour's mess'. Establishing the need to tackle the public sector deficit and debt as the overriding priority of the Coalition has also helped the Conservatives retain dominance over the government's agenda, sidelining the Liberal Democrats (Hayton, 2014).

As such, economic arguments are more often than not at the heart of Conservative logos. At present such arguments may have a particular appeal to the electorate because of how they are rhetorically framed around the notion of the national interest. 'As a legitimising narrative, the national interest goes beyond politics, seemingly elevating them to a higher plane than Labour, paradoxically gaining political benefit' (Crines, 2013). For the Conservatives in Coalition this narrative 'revolves around fiscal austerity' which ensures 'they are able to implement free market reforms' in the public sector (Crines, 2013). The logos of this strategy relates to the notion of an 'effective statecraft strategy' which 'enables the Conservatives to define the political terrain over which political arguments occur' (Heppell and Seawright, 2012). In sum, Conservative orators tend to use logos to present their governing programme as being economically sound and in the national interest rather than ideologically driven, and to try to support their ethos as competent and trustworthy. Without this reputation for governing competence the Conservatives are all at sea, as they were for a decade under New Labour.

Conclusion

The book argues that powerful oratory and persuasive rhetoric have been key features of Conservative politics in the modern era, and vital to the political success of many of the party's leading politicians. Along with its sister volume on Labour orators, this book makes a contribution to the growing literature on oratory and rhetoric in British politics. The various contributors have demonstrated how debates within Conservative Party politics have been shaped and driven by leading orators and rhetoricians. Those debates have touched upon the emergence of a 'new conservatism' under Baldwin, the dominance and the decline of the One Nation tradition in the post-war era, and the emergence and transformative effect of Thatcherism.

Following 1997 the process of renewal was lengthy and difficult; however, the party retained its economic liberalism whilst seemingly becoming more socially liberal under Cameron.

Throughout the volume we have seen how orators have tried to appeal, with varying degrees of success, to a number of different audiences – whether that be their party colleagues, wider membership and supporters, or the electorate more broadly. While the perceived importance of different oratorical arenas such as the Commons and the conference chamber has varied over time, it remains the case that leading British politicians are expected to be able to adapt their delivery style to suit often quite contrasting demands, while also maintaining a coherent and authentic identity as a speaker. For future Conservative politicians, particularly those that aspire to the leadership, the ability to inspire the party conference, dominate the Commons and connect with the electorate remain as vital as ever. As such, the art of oratory will no doubt continue to fascinate politicians and political observers for many generations to come.

Appendix

The following gives the definition for each node, the number of *sources* (speeches) in which it appears and the number of times the *node* is referred to in those sources.

Node	Sources	References
New social and industrial order The impact of mass industrial society and its destabilising effects on the deferential, old family capitalist-industrial structure and culture is working itself out but change accelerated because of the war. Old structures may have decayed but basic attitudes and preferences are unchanged, giving a sound base on which to build the new.	7	34
Englishness This is the collective category in which all individual characteristics and the rural myth combine to produce the definitive English genius. This identifies a conception of an unchanging England persisting across generations that is resistant to the social and economic change of the previous 150 years. A powerful foundational myth. It is transcendental not in terms of time but also in terms of space (the Empire and social class).	9	28
Role of the Conservative Party Conservative Party should be a force for unity and not division in the new mass industrial society – and motivated by a spirit of self-sacrifice in the national interest even at the expense of party interest.	6	25

Node	Sources	References
Mass democracy	6	25

This refers to the creation of (virtually) universal suffrage with
the 1918 act. This is a fundamental transformation of pre-1914
limited democracy, which creates a political process (vulnerable
to demagogues) and an electorate that is 'uneducated' and
must be 'educated' in the ways of democracy to avoid being
attracted to dangerous and radical solutions to the post-war
political, social, economic and cultural dislocation.

Node	Sources	References
Change in industrial society	6	24

Industrialisation has produced dramatic social change
that often outstrips the understanding of society and
individuals; change is, however, inevitable and does
bring welcome progress if carefully managed.

Node	Sources	References
Impact of war	7	23

The war falls across British society and politics and nothing
will ever be the same again. A profoundly destabilising event
that transforms the nature and conduct of politics.

Node	Sources	References
Industrial conflict	5	18

Industrial conflict is endemic in mass industrial society and no
section of society can be isolated from its effects.

Node	Sources	References
New attitudes needed	5	18

As the growth of mass industrial society, and all that implies,
cannot be halted and as conflict, misunderstanding and
individual interest predominates, these must be controlled
in the common good by drawing deeply on that which unites.

Node	Sources	References
Rejection of foreign models	7	14

Avoid being attracted by seemingly more 'sophisticated' and
superficially attractive, 'modern' attitudes and behaviours
that appear 'smart' and proffer immediate (and therefore
illusory) solutions to deep-seated problems.

Node	Sources	References
Baldwin's 'remembered world'	3	13

Baldwin lays claim to a special knowledge of social and
industrial questions and intuitive grasp of Englishness,
giving him authority and legitimacy to speak on these issues
with credibility. As party leader Baldwin's intention was to makes
his personal experience the strategy of the Conservative Party.
This is part of, but separate from, the Conservative Party node.

Node	Sources	References
Traditional industrial culture Small, family owned and managed enterprises that owed more to rural patterns and mutualism than either the individualism or collectivism of contemporary industrial society. This is a short-hand term for 'the world we have lost' as a result of socio-economic change and the dislocation caused by the war.	4	11
Diversified individualism A nation of individuals, of diverse character (cf. Dickens) but this diversity is a source of strength and not division.	4	6
Anti-intellectualism Suspicion of foreign or theoretical models not grounded in the nation; dislike of the currently fashionable.	2	5
Grumble but remain cheerful A behavioural characteristic that testifies to the soundness and stability of the nation; and indicator of political maturity and common sense.	2	5
Emotional stability in crisis This is the result of grumbling (not worrying) and anti-intellectualism; a deep reservoir of cultural capital on which to draw.	3	5
Efficiency not supreme virtue A trade-off existed between efficiency and social stability. Willing to bear costs of inefficiency for other non-economic benefits.	1	4
The image of England 'England' constructed as a series of sensory impressions (sight, sound, smell) that have material consequences for attitudes and conduct. The section of 'England' which sets this out is sometimes presented as quintessentially Baldwin; Wright's 'ur-text'.	1	3
Produces geniuses Despite their anti-intellectualism the English contributed a large number of geniuses in all fields, and demonstrate a more empirical temperament.	1	2
Kindness, sympathy for underdog This is a universal characteristic that applies to all classes and can be seen in the work of, for example, George Orwell and J. B. Priestley that is perhaps best expressed by Orwell's notion of 'decency'.	1	1

Bibliography

Addison, P. (1992) *Churchill on the Home Front 1900–1955*, London: Pimlico.

Addison, P. (1999) 'The British Conservative Party from Churchill to Heath: Doctrine or Men?', *Contemporary European History*, 8(2): 289–98.

Adonis, A. (2011) 'The Left's Favourite Tories: Michael Heseltine', *New Statesman*, 6 October 2011.

Aldgate, A. and Richards, J. (1994) *Britain Can Take It: British Cinema in the Second World War*, 2nd edition, Edinburgh: Edinburgh University Press.

Aldous, R. (1996) 'A Family Affair: Macmillan and the Art of Diplomacy', in *Harold Macmillan and Britain's World Role*, Basingstoke: Macmillan, 9–36.

Aldous, R. and Lee, S. (1999) *Aspects of Political Life*, Basingstoke: Macmillan.

Allen, G.W. (1958) *The Reluctant Politician: Derick Heathcoat-Amory*, London: Christopher Johnson.

Aristotle (2004a) *The Art of Rhetoric Translated with an Introduction and Notes by H.C. Lawson-Tancred*, London: Penguin Books.

Aristotle (2004b) *Rhetoric: Book I*, Chapter 2. Available at: http://rhetoric.eserver.org/aristotle/rhet1-2.html. Accessed 7 February 2014.

Atkins, J. (2011) *Justifying New Labour Policy*, Basingstoke: Palgrave Macmillan.

Atkins, J. and Finlayson, A. (2010) '"As Shakespeare so Memorably Said …": The Rhetoric of Quotation in British Political Speech'. Paper presented at the 60th Annual Conference of the Political Studies Association, 31 March.

Atkins, J. and Finlayson, A. (2013) '"… A 40-Year-Old Black Man Made the Point to Me": Anecdotes, Everyday Knowledge and the Performance of Leadership in British Politics', *Political Studies*, 61: 161–77.

Atkins, J., Finlayson, A., Martin, J. and Turnbull, N. (eds) (2014) *Rhetoric in British Politics and Society*, Basingstoke: Palgrave Macmillan.

Atkinson, M. (1984) *Our Masters Voices: The Language and Body Language of Politics*, London: Routledge.

Atkinson, M. (2004) *Lend Me Your Ears*, London: Vermillion.

Baker, D., Gamble, A. and Ludlam, S. (1994) 'The Parliamentary Siege of Maastricht 1993: Conservative Divisions and British Ratification', *Parliamentary Affairs*, 47(1): 37–60.

Baldwin, A.W. (1955) *My Father: The True Story*, London: George Allen & Unwin.

Baldwin, S. (1926) *On England and Other Addresses*, London: Philip Allan.

Baldwin, S. (1935a) *G. Lloyd to Baldwin, 8 November*. Baldwin MSS 203/57–8 Cambridge: Cambridge University Library.

Baldwin, S. (1935b) *P. Gower to Baldwin, 2 November*. Baldwin MSS 203/40 Cambridge: Cambridge University Library.

Baldwin, S. (1937) *This Torch of Freedom*, 4th edition, London: Hodder & Stoughton.

Bale, T. (2011) *The Conservative Party from Thatcher to Cameron*, Cambridge: Polity Press.

Bale, T. (2012) *The Conservative Party Since 1945: The Drivers of Party Change*, Basingstoke: Palgrave.

Bale, T. and Sanders, K. (2001) 'Playing by the Book: Success and Failure in John Major's Approach to Prime Ministerial Media Management', *Contemporary British History*, 15(4): 93–110.

Ball, S. (1998) *The Conservative Party since 1945*, Manchester: Manchester University Press.

Ball, S. (ed.) (1999) *Parliament and Politics in the Age of Churchill and Attlee: The Headlam Diaries 1935–1951*, London: Royal Historical Society/Cambridge University Press.

Ball, S. (2013) *Portrait of a Party: The Conservative Party in Britain, 1918–1945*, Oxford: Oxford University Press.

Barnes, J. and Nicholson, D. (eds) (1980) *The Leo Amery Diaries Volume 1: 1896–1929*, London: Hutchinson.

Barnes, J. and Nicholson, D. (eds) (1988) *The Empire at Bay: The Leo Amery Diaries Volume 2: 1929–1945*, London: Hutchinson.

Bates, S., Kerr, P., Byrne, C. and Stanley, L. (2014) 'Questions to the Prime Minister: A Comparative Study of PMQs from Thatcher to Cameron', *Parliamentary Affairs*, 67, 253–80.

Bazeley, P. (2007) *Qualitative Data Analysis with NVivo*, 2nd edition, London: Sage Publications.

BBC (1987) *Panorama*, broadcast 8 June. Available at: www.margaretthatcher.org/document/106647.

BBC (1997) 'William Hague Interview', *On the Record*, 1 June. Available at: www.bbc.co.uk/otr/intext/Hague1.6.97.html.

BBC (2001) 'Interview with William Hague', *Newsnight*, 31 May. Available at: http://news.bbc.co.uk/1/hi/events/newsnight/1362843.stm.

BBC (2004) '"Sorry" Johnson Sent to Liverpool', 16 October. Available at: http://news.bbc.co.uk/1/hi/uk_politics/3749548.stm.

BBC (2006a) 'Interview with William Hague', *Politics Show*, 29 January. Available at: http://news.bbc.co.uk/1/hi/programmes/politics_show/4659840.stm.

BBC (2006b) 'Boris Apology to Papua New Guinea', 8 September. Available at: http://news.bbc.co.uk/1/hi/uk_politics/5327984.stm.

BBC (2007a) 'Your Favourite Conference Clips', *Daily Politics*, 3 October. Available at: http://news.bbc.co.uk/1/hi/programmes/the_daily_politics/6967366.stm.

BBC (2007b) 'MP Slammed over "Fat City" Slur', 3 April. Available at: http://news.bbc.co.uk/1/hi/england/hampshire/6521603.stm.

BBC (2010) 'Westland Cabinet Minutes Released', 12 October. Available at: http://www.bbc.co.uk/blogs/opensecrets/2010/10/westland_cabinet_minutes_relea.html.

BBC (2012) 'Interview with William Hague', *The Andrew Marr Show*, 19 February. Available at: http://news.bbc.co.uk/1/hi/programmes/andrew_marr_show/9697684.stm.

BBC News Online (1998) 'Politicians say Farewell to Enoch Powell', *BBC News Online*, 18 February.

BBC Radio 4 (1978) *Desert Island Discs*, broadcast 1 February. Available at: http://www.margaretthatcher.org/document/103509.

Becket, F. (2006) *Macmillan*, London: Haus.

Beer, S. (1982) *Britain Against Itself*, London: Faber & Faber.

Blake, R. (1970) *The Conservative Party from Peel to Churchill*, London: Eyre & Spottiswoode.

Blake, R. (1980) 'Grand Old Man', *London Review of Books*, 2: 8.

Blake, R. (1985) *The Conservative Party from Peel to Thatcher*, London: Methuen.

Blake, R. (1998) *The Conservative Party from Peel to Major*, London: Arrow Books.

Blears, H. (2005) *Debate on Terrorism Bill*, 2 November. Available at: www.publications.parliament.uk/pa/cm200506/cmhansrd/vo051102/debtext/51102-17.htm.

Body, R. (2001) *England for the English*, London: New European Publications.

Boffey, D. and Helm, T. (2012) 'While Cameron Struggles, in the Shires they Talk of Boris', *Guardian*, 7 October.

Bower, T. (2012) 'Immigration', in Lord Howard of Rising (ed.), *Enoch at 100*, London: Biteback Publishing, 147–71.

Boyd-Carpenter, J. (1980) *Way of Life: The Memoirs of John Boyd-Carpenter*, London: Sidgwick and Jackson.

Branigan, T. (2006) 'Johnson makes Gaffes on all Fronts', *Guardian*, 4 October. Available at: www.guardian.co.uk/politics/2006/oct/04/uk.conservatives20061.

Broughton, D. (1999) 'The Limitations of Likeability: The Major Premiership and Public Opinion', in P. Dorey (ed.), *The Major Premiership: Politics and Policies Under John Major, 1990–97*, Basingstoke: Macmillan, 199–217.

Broughton, D. (2003) 'The 2001 General Election: So, No Change There Then', in M. Garnett and P. Lynch (eds), *The Conservatives in Crisis*, Manchester: Manchester University Press, 198–216.

Brown, H. (1966) *Prose Styles: Five Primary Types*, Minneapolis: University of Minnesota Press.

Brunson, M. (2000) *A Ringside Seat*, London: Hodder & Stoughton.

Bryant, C. (1997) *Stafford Cripps: The First Modern Chancellor*, London: Hodder & Stoughton.

Bull, P. and Mayer, K. (1993) 'How Not to Answer Questions in Political Interviews', *Political Psychology*, 14: 651–66.

Bulpitt, J. (1986) 'The Discipline of the New Democracy: Mrs Thatcher's Domestic Statecraft', *Political Studies*, 34(1): 19–39.

Burnham, J., Jones, G. and Elgie, R. (1995) 'The Parliamentary Activity of John Major, 1990–94', *British Journal of Political Science*, 25(4): 551–63.

Butler, D. and King, A. (1966) *The British General Election of 1966*, London: Macmillan.

Butler, D. and Pinto-Duschinsky, M. (1971) *The British General Election of 1970*, London: Macmillan.

Butler, D. and Rose, R. (1960) *The British General Election of 1960*, Basingstoke: Macmillan.

Butler, Lord (1970) *The Art of the Possible*, Harmondsworth: Penguin Books.

Cameron, D. (2005) *Leadership Acceptance Speech*, 6 December.

Cameron, D. (2007a) 'David Cameron Pledges Return to Family', *Daily Telegraph*, 7 October. Available at: www.telegraph.co.uk/news/uknews/1565089/David-Cameron-pledges-return-to-family.html?mobile=basic.

Cameron, D. (2007b) 'Let the People Decide', *BBC News*, 3 October. Available at: http://news.bbc.co.uk/1/hi/7024919.stm.

Cameron, D. (2008) 'Jobless Must Work for Benefits says Cameron', *Daily Express*, 8 January. Available at: www.express.co.uk/news/uk/30774/Jobless-must-work-for-benefits-says-Cameron.

Cameron, D. (2009) 'Speech to the Conservative Party Conference', *Guardian*, 8 October. Available at: www.theguardian.com/politics/2009/oct/08/david-cameron-speech-in-full. Accessed 22 June 2014.

Cameron, D. (2009a) 'David Cameron: We'll Put Britain Back On Her Feet', *Guardian*, 8 October. Available at: www.theguardian.com/politics/2009/oct/08/cameron-conference-speech.

Cameron, D. (2010) 'Our Big Society Plan', *Conservative Party Website*.

Cameron, D. (2010a) 'David Cameron's Speech to the Tory Conference in Full', *Guardian*, 6 October. Available at: www.theguardian.com/politics/2010/oct/06/david-cameron-speech-tory-conference.

Cameron, D. (2011) 'David Cameron's Conservative Conference Speech', *BBC News*, 5 October. Available at: www.bbc.co.uk/news/mobile/uk-politics-15189614.

Campbell, A. (2007) 'Wit, Oratory – and Evasion: A Master Debater at Work', *Observer*, 24 June. Available at: www.guardian.co.uk/books/2007/jun/24/politics.houseofcommons.

Campbell, J. (1997) *Nye Bevan: A Biography*, London: Richard Cohen Books.

Campbell, J. (2000) *Margaret Thatcher, Vol. 1: The Grocer's Daughter*, London: Jonathan Cape.

Campbell, J. (2009) *Pistols at Dawn: Two Hundred Years of Political Rivalry*, London: Jonathan Cape.

Campbell, M. (2005) *Debate on European Affairs*, 15 June. Available at: www.publications.parliament.uk/pa/cm200506/cmhansrd/vo050615/debtext/50615–16.htm.

Cannadine, D. (2002) *In Churchill's Shadow: Confronting the Past in Modern Britain*, London: Allen Lane/The Penguin Press.

Catterall, P. (2003) *The Macmillan Diaries: The Cabinet Years 1950–1957*, London: Macmillan.

Chandos, Lord (1962) *The Memoirs of Lord Chandos*, London: Bodley Head.

Chapman, J. (1998) *The British At War: Cinema, State and Propaganda, 1939–1945*, London: I.B. Tauris.

Chapman, J. (2012) 'I'll Take Murdoch as My Guest to the Games: Boris Johnson Accused of "Appalling Judgment"', *Daily Mail*, 31 July. Available at: www.dailymail.co.uk/news/article-2181724/Boris-Johnson-courts-controversy-inviting-Rupert-Murdoch-Olympics-event-personal-guest.html#ixzz269kYtVV0.

Charteris-Black, J. (2011) *Politicians and Rhetoric: The Persuasive Power of Metaphor*, Basingstoke: Palgrave Macmillan.

Charteris-Black, J. (2012) 'Comparative Keyword Analysis and Leadership Communication: Tony Blair – A Study of Rhetorical Style', in L. Helms (ed.), *Comparative Political Leadership*, Basingstoke: Palgrave, 142–64.

Charteris-Black, J. (2014) *Analysing Political Speeches: Rhetoric, Discourse and Metaphor*, Basingstoke: Palgrave Macmillan.

Chilton, P. (2004) *The Analysis of Political Discourse: Theory and Practice*, London and New York: Routledge.

Churchill, W. (1945) *Here is the Course We Steer*, London: National Union of Conservative and Unionist Associations.

Clark, A. (1998) *The Tories: Conservatives and the Nation State, 1922–1997*, London: Weidenfeld & Nicolson.

Collings, D. and Seldon, A. (2001) 'Conservatives in Opposition', *Parliamentary Affairs*, 54: 624–37.

Collins, R. (1991) *Reflections of a Statesman: The Writings and Speeches of Enoch Powell*, London: Bellew Publishing.

Commonwealth Tour papers (1958) *The Right Honourable Harold Macmillan, January–February 1958*, Texts of Speeches.

Coote, C. (1965) *Editorial*, London: Eyre and Spottiswoode.

Cosgrave, P. (1989) *The Lives of Enoch Powell*, London: Bodley Head.

Cosgrave, P. (1998) 'Enoch Powell', *The Independent*, 9 February.

Cowley, P. and Bailey, M. (2000) 'Peasants Uprising or Religious War? Re-examining the 1975 Conservative Leadership Contest', *British Journal of Political Science*, 30(4): 599–629.

Cowling, M. (1970) 'Mr Powell, Mr Heath, and the Future', in J. Wood (ed.), *Powell and the 1970 Election*, Kingswood: Elliot Right Ways Books, 8–18.

Cowling, M. (1971) *The Impact of Labour 1920–1924: The Beginning of Modern British Politics*, Cambridge: Cambridge University Press.

Crick, M. (1997) *Michael Heseltine: A Biography*, London: Penguin.

Criddle, B. (1994) 'Members of Parliament', in A. Seldon and S. Ball (eds), *Conservative Century: The Conservative Party since 1900*, Oxford: Oxford University Press, 145–68.

Crines, A. (2013) 'The Rhetoric of the Coalition: Governing in the National Interest?', *Representation*, 49(2): 207–18.

Crines, A. (2014) 'The Rhetoric of Neoliberalism in the Politics of Crisis', *Global Discourse*, Early View. http://dx.doi.org/10.1080/23269995.2014.922360.

Crines, A.S. and Hayton, R. (2014) *Labour Orators from Bevan to Miliband*, Manchester: Manchester University Press.

Critchley, J. (1978) 'How to get on in the Conservative Party', *The Political Quarterly*, 44(4): 467–73.

Critchley, J. (1987) *Heseltine: An Unauthorised Biography*, London: Coronet Books.

Critchley, J. (1992) *Some of Us: People Who Did Well Under Thatcher*, London: John Murray.

Critchley, J. (1994) *A Bag of Boiled Sweets*, London: Faber & Faber.

CUL (1938) *Robertson Scott Memorandum, 28 January*. Add.8770, Cambridge: Cambridge University Library.

Dale, I. (2010) 'Foreword', in I. Dale (ed.), *Margaret Thatcher: In Her Own Words*, London: Biteback, 9–18.

Davies, A.J. (1995) *We, The Nation*, London: Little, Brown.

Deedes, W. (1973) 'Review of Nigel Fisher, *Iain Macleod*', *Daily Telegraph*, 10 May.

Denham, A. and Dorey, P. (2006) 'A Tale of Two Speeches? The Conservative Leadership Election of 2005', *Political Quarterly*, 77(1): 35–42.

Denham, A. and Garnett, M. (2001) *Keith Joseph: A Life*, Chesham: Acumen.

Department of Business, Innovation and Skills (2012) *Lord Heseltine Review: No Stone Unturned in the Search for Growth.*

Deputy Speaker (2002) *Debate on Budget Resolutions*, 17 April. Available at: www.publications.parliament.uk/pa/cm200102/cmhansrd/vo020417/debtext/20417-24.htm.

Dorey, P. and Garnett, M. (2014) '"The Weaker-Willed, the Craven-Hearted": The Decline of One Nation Conservatism', *Global Discourse*, DOI: 10.1080/23269995.2014.914823.

Dorey, P., Garnett, M. and Denham, A. (2011) *From Crisis to Coalition: The Conservative Party 1997–2010*, Basingstoke: Palgrave.

Dowding, K. (2013) 'The Prime Ministerialisation of the British Prime Minister', *Parliamentary Affairs*, 66: 617–35.

Dunt, I. (2012) 'Profile Boris Johnson', www.politics.co.uk, 30 April. Available at: www.politics.co.uk/comment-analysis/2012/04/30/profile-boris-johnson.

Evans, B. and Taylor, A. (1996) *From Salisbury to Major: Continuity and Change in Conservative Politics*, Manchester: Manchester University Press.

Evans, H. (1981) *Downing Street Diary: The Macmillan Years 1957–63*, London: Hodder & Stoughton.

Fairlie, H. (1953) 'The Art of Churchill', *The Spectator*, 10 July, 63–4.

Ferguson, E. (2007) 'A Bumbler with High Ambition', *Guardian*, 16 September. Available at: www.guardian.co.uk/politics/2007/sep/16/london.media.

Field, F. (2012) 'Enoch Powell as a Parliamentarian', in Lord Howard of Rising (ed.), *Enoch at 100*, London: Biteback Publishing, 47–53.

Finlayson, A. (2002) 'Elements of the Blairite Image of Leadership', *Parliamentary Affairs*, 55: 586–99.

Finlayson, A. (2003) *Making Sense of New Labour*, London: Lawrence & Wishart.

Finlayson, A. (2004) 'Political Science, Political Ideas and Rhetoric', *Economy and Society*, 33(4): 528–49.

Finlayson, A. (2006) '"What's the Problem?": Political Theory, Rhetoric and Problem-Setting', *Critical Review of International Social and Political Philosophy*, 9(4): 541–57.

Finlayson, A. (2007) 'From Beliefs to Arguments: Interpretative Methodology and Rhetorical Political Analysis', *British Journal of Politics and International Relations*, 9(4): 545–63.

Finlayson, A. (2012) 'Rhetoric and the Political Theory of Ideologies', *Political Studies*, 60(4): 751–67.

Finlayson, A. and Martin, J. (2008) '"It Ain't What You Say...": British Political Studies and the Analysis of Speech and Rhetoric', *British Politics*, 3: 445–64.

Fisher, N. (1973) *Iain Macleod*, London: Andre Deutsch.

Fletcher, N. (2012) 'William Hague, 1997–2001', in T. Heppell (ed.), *Leaders of the Opposition: From Churchill to Cameron*, Basingstoke: Palgrave Macmillan, 184–95.

Foley, M. (2000) *The British Presidency*, Manchester: Manchester University Press.

Foley, M. (2002) *John Major, Tony Blair and the Conflict of Leadership: Collision Course*, Manchester: Manchester University Press.

Foot, M. (1984) *Another Heart and Other Pulses*, London: Collins.

Foot, M. (1986) *Loyalists and Loners*, London: Collins.

Foucault, M. (1980) *Power/Knowledge: Selected Interviews and Writings 1972–1977*, New York: Pantheon Books.

Fowler, N. (1991) *Ministers Decide: A Personal Memoir of the Thatcher Years*, London: Chapman's Publisher.

Freeden, M. (1996) *Ideology and Political Theory*, Oxford: Clarendon Press.

Gaffney, J. and Lahel, A. (2013) 'Political Performance and Leadership Persona: The UK Labour Party Conference of 2012', *Government and Opposition*, 48(4): 481–505.

Gale, G. (1970) 'The 1970 Election Campaign', in J. Wood (ed.), *Powell and the 1970 Election*, Kingswood: Elliot Right Ways Books, 50–82.

Gamble, A. (1988) *The Free Economy and the Strong State*, London: Macmillan Press.

Gamble, A. (1994) *The Free Economy and the Strong State*, 2nd edition, Basingstoke: Macmillan.

Garnett, M. (2003) 'Win or Bust: The Leadership Gamble of William Hague', in M. Garnett and P. Lynch (eds), *The Conservatives in Crisis*, Manchester: Manchester University Press, 49–66.

Garnett, M. (2013) 'The Conservative Party, David Cameron and Lady Thatcher's Legacy', *Contemporary British History*, 27(4): 514–24.

Garnett, M. and Lynch, P. (2003) 'Introduction', in M. Garnett and P. Lynch (eds), *The Conservatives in Crisis*, Manchester: Manchester University Press, 1–6.

Gilbert, M. (1988) *Winston S. Churchill, Vol. VIII: Never Despair*, London: Heinemann.

Gilmour, I. (1992) *Dancing with Dogma: Britain under Thatcherism*, London: Simon & Schuster.

Glover, D. (2011) *The Art of Great Speeches and Why We Remember Them*, Cambridge: Cambridge University Press.

Granada TV (1975) *World in Action*, 31 January.

Griffiths, P. (1969) *Empire into Commonwealth*, London: Benn.

Grigg, J. (1977) 'Churchill, the Crippled Giant', *Encounter*, April, 9–16.

Grube, D. (2012) 'Prime Ministers and Political Narratives for Policy Change: Towards a Heuristic', *Policy and Politics*, 40(4): 569–86.

Hague, W. (1977) *Speech to the Conservative Party Conference*. Available at: www.britishpoliticalspeech.org/speech-archive.htm?speech=325.

Hague, W. (1994) *Pensions and Benefits*, HC Deb 16 February, vol. 237 cols 1023–28.

Hague, W. (1995) *Social Security*, HC Deb 2 February, vol. 253 cols 1233–41.

Hague, W. (1996) *Welsh Affairs*, HC Deb 29 February, vol. 272 cols 1024–40.

Hague, W. (1997) *Welsh Affairs*, HC Deb 27 February vol. 291 cols 457–68.

Hague, W. (1998) *Speech to the Conservative Party Conference*, 8 October.

Hague, W. (1999a) *Debate on the Address*, HC Deb 17 November, vol. 339 cols 14–23.

Hague, W. (1999b) *Speech to the Conservative Party Conference*, 7 October.

Hague, W. (2000a) *Debate on the Address*, HC Deb 6 December, vol. 359 cols 6–30.

Hague, W. (2000b) *Speech to the Conservative Party Conference*, 5 October.

Hague, W. (2006) *Speech to the Conservative Party Conference*, 3 October.

Hague, W. (2008) *Debate on the Address*, HC Deb 10 December, vol. 485 cols 574–84.

Hague, W. (2010a) *Debate on the Address*, HC Deb 26 May, vol. 510 cols 174–89.

Hague, W. (2010b) *Speech to the Conservative Party Conference*, 6 October.

Hague, W. (2011) *Speech to the Conservative Party Conference*, 5 October.

Hailsham, Lord (1947) *The Case for Conservatism*, London: Penguin.

Hailsham, Lord (1990) *A Sparrow's Flight*, London: Collins.

Halcrow, M. (1989) *Keith Joseph: A Single Mind*, London: Macmillan.

Hall, S. and Jacques, M. (eds) (1983) *The Politics of Thatcherism*, London: Lawrence & Wishart, in association with Marxism Today.

Hargrove, E. (1998) *Presidential Leadership: Appealing to the Better Angels of Our Nature*, Lawrence: University Press of Kansas.

Harris, R. (1997) 'Introduction', in R. Harris (ed.), *Margaret Thatcher: The Collected Speeches*, London: HarperCollins.

Harris, R. (2011) *The Conservatives: A History*, London: Bantam Press.

Hattenstone, S. (2001) 'The Mane Man', *Guardian*, 2 April.

Hayton, R. (2012a) *Reconstructing conservatism? The Conservative Party in Opposition, 1997–2010*, Manchester: Manchester University Press.

Hayton, R. (2012b) 'Iain Duncan Smith', in T. Heppell (ed.), *Leaders of the Opposition: From Churchill to Cameron*, Basingstoke: Palgrave Macmillan.

Hayton, R. (2014) 'Conservative Party Statecraft and the Politics of Coalition', *Parliamentary Affairs*, 67: 6–24.

Hayton, R. and McEnhill, L. (2014) 'Rhetoric and Morality in Coalition Welfare Policy', in J. Atkins, A. Finlayson, J. Martin and N. Turnbull (eds), *Rhetoric in British Politics and Society*, Basingstoke: Palgrave Macmillan, 101–18.

Healey, J. (2007). *Debate on the Health Inequalities Strategy*, 11 October. Available at: www. publications.parliament.uk/pa/cm200607/cmhansrd/cm071011/debtext/71011-0012. htm#07101129000993.

Heath, E. (1967) *Speech to the Conservative Party Conference*. Available at: http://www.brit-ishpoliticalspeech.org/speech-archive.htm?speech=114.

Heath, E. (1998) *The Course of My Life*, London: Hodder & Stoughton.

Heffer, S. (1999) *Like the Roman*, London: Phoenix.

Heffer, S. (2007) *Great British Speeches*, London: Quercus.

Helm, T. (2012) 'Boris Johnson to Take "How to Win" Message to Tory Party Conference', *Guardian*, 15 September. Available at: www.guardian.co.uk/politics/2012/sep/15/boris-johnson-conservative-party-conference.

Hennessy, P. (1992) *Never Again: Britain 1945–1951*, London: Cape.

Heppell, T. (2007) 'Weak and Ineffective? Reassessing the Party Political Leadership of John Major', *Political Quarterly*, 78(3): 382–91.

Heppell, T. (2008a) *Choosing the Tory Leader: Conservative Party Leadership Elections from Wilson to Brown*, London: I.B. Tauris.

Heppell, T. (2008b) 'No More than Another Major: How William Hague became Leader of the Conservative Party', *Conservative History Journal*, 7: 22–8.

Heppell, T. (2012) *Leaders of the Opposition: From Churchill to Cameron*, Basingstoke: Palgrave Macmillan.

Heppell, T. (2013) 'The Conservative Party Leadership of David Cameron: Heresthetics and the Realignment of British Politics', *British Politics*, 8: 260–84.

Heppell, T. (2014) *The Tories: From Winston Churchill to David Cameron*, London: Bloomsbury.

Heppell, T. and Seawright, D. (2012) *Cameron and the Conservatives*, Basingstoke: Palgrave Macmillan.

Herbert, A.P. (1953) 'Churchill's Humour', in C. Eade (ed.), *Churchill By His Contemporaries*, London: Hutchinson, 295–302.

Heritage, J. and Greatbatch, D. (1986) 'Generating Applause: A Study of Rhetoric and Response at Party Political Conferences', *American Journal of Sociology*, 92(1): 110–57.

Heseltine, M. (1981) *Conservative Party Conference Speech*, 15 October.

Heseltine, M. (1982) *Conservative Party Conference Speech*, 7 October.

Heseltine, M (1985) 'Sinking of the Belgrano', HC Deb 18 February, vol. 73 cols 733–826.

Heseltine, M. (1986) *Conservative Party Conference Speech to Tory Reform Group*, 9 October.

Heseltine, M. (1991) 'Speech to the Conservative Party Conference', *BBC News*. Available at: http://news.bbc.co.uk/1/hi/programmes/the_daily_politics/6967366.stm. Accessed 2 April 2013.

Heseltine, M. (1992) *Conservative Party Conference Speech*, 7 October.

Heseltine, M. (1995) *Conservative Party Conference Speech*, 11 October.

Heseltine, M. (2000) *Life in the Jungle*, London: Hodder & Stoughton.

Hirschman, A. (1991) *The Rhetoric of Reaction: Perversity, Futility, Jeopardy*, Cambridge, MA: Harvard University Press.

HLRO (1926) *J.C.C. Davidson to Edward Halifax*, 14 June, Davidson Papers, London: House of Lords Record Office.

HLRO (1928) *J.C.C. Davidson to Stanley Baldwin*, 14 January, Davidson Papers, London: House of Lords Record Office.

HLRO (1939) *David Kirkwood to Stanley Baldwin*, 18 September, Davidson Papers, London: House of Lords Record Office.

Hoffman, J.D. (1964) *The Conservative Party in Opposition 1945–51*, London: MacGibbon and Kee.

Hoggart, S. (1997) 'Hobnobbing, Review of *Michael Heseltine: A Biography* by Michael Crick', *London Review of Books*, 19(8): 25–6.

Hore-Belisha, L. (1953) 'How Churchill Influences and Persuades', in C. Eade (ed.), *Churchill By His Contemporaries*, London: Hutchinson, 269–75.

Horne, A. (1989) *Macmillan 1957–1986*, London: Macmillan.

Horne, A. (2008) *Macmillan: The Official Biography*, London: Macmillan.

Howard, A. (1987) *RAB*, London: Cape.

Howarth, G. (2003) *Debate on New Clause 11: Passage of Time*, 25 March. Available at: www.publications.parliament.uk/pa/cm200203/cmhansrd/vo030325/debtext/30325-17.htm.

Hughes, E, (1962) *Macmillan: Portrait of a Politician*, London: Allen & Unwin.

Humes, J. (1980) *Churchill: Speaker of the Century*, New York: Stein and Day.

Humes, J. (1991) *The Sir Winston Method: The Five Secrets of Speaking the Language of Leadership*, New York: Morrow.

Hurd, D. (2003) *Memoirs*, London: Little, Brown.

Hutber, P. (1977) *The Decline and Fall of the Middle Class and How it Can Fight Back*, London: Penguin.

Hutchinson, G. (1970) *Edward Heath: A Personal and Political Biography*, London: Longman.

Hutchinson, G. (1980) *The Last Edwardian at No.10*, London: Quartet.

Jamieson, K. (1988) *Eloquence in an Electronic Age: The Transformation of Political Speechmaking*, Oxford and New York: Oxford University Press.

Jeffrey, T. (1989) 'Suburban Nation: Politics and Class in Lewisham', in D. Feldman and G. Stedman-Jones (eds), *Metropolis*, London: Routledge, 189–219.

Jenkins, R. (1993) *Portraits and Miniatures*, London: Macmillan.

Jenkins, R. (1994) 'Churchill: The Government of 1951–1955', in R. Blake and W.R. Louis (eds.), *Churchill*, Oxford: Oxford University Press, 491–503.

Jenkins, R. (2001) *Churchill*, London: Macmillan.

Johnson, B. (2002a) *Debate on London and the South East*, 12 March. Available at: www.publications.parliament.uk/pa/cm200102/cmhansrd/vo020312/debtext/20312–33.htm.

Johnson, B. (2002b) *Debate on Education and Skills Training*, 19 March. Available at: www.publications.parliament.uk/pa/cm200102/cmhansrd/vo020319/debtext/20319-17.htm.

Johnson, B. (2003a) *Debate on New Clause 11: Passage of Time*, 25 March. Available at: www.publications.parliament.uk/pa/cm200203/cmhansrd/vo030325/debtext/30325-17.htm.

Johnson, B. (2003b) *Debate on Aviation (Offences) Bill*, 16 May. Available at: www.publications.parliament.uk/pa/cm200203/cmhansrd/vo030516/debtext/30516-14.htm.

Johnson, B. (2007) 'Our Nation's Capital Deserves More', *Speech to the Conservative Party Conference*, 30 September. Available at: www.conservatives.com/News/Speeches/2007/09/Boris_Johnson_Our_nations_capital_deserves_more.aspx.

Johnson, B. (2008) *Transcript: People's Question Time*, The Bromley Civic Centre, 6 November.

Johnson, B. (2009) 'The Future of the Conservatives', *Speech to the Conservative Party Conference*, 5 October. Available at: www.epolitix.com/latestnews/article-detail/newsarticle/boris-johnson-speech-on-the-future-of-the-conservatives/.

Johnson, B. (2010a) *Transcript: Small Business is Big Business: Supporting Local Businesses*, 24 May.

Johnson, B. (2010b) 'Keep the UK Motor Going', *Speech to Conservative Party Conference*, 4 October. Available at: www.conservatives.com/News/Speeches/2010/10/Boris_Johnson_Keep_the_UK_motor_going.aspx.

Johnson, B. (2011a) 'Wimbledon 2011: Game, Set and Tax – Why Andy Murray Will Always Get Clobbered', 4 July. Available at: www.telegraph.co.uk/comment/columnists/boris-johnson/8614808/Wimbledon-2011-Game-set-and-tax-why-Andy-Murray-will-always-get-clobbered.html.

Johnson, B. (2011b) *Speech given to Trafalgar Square to launch the Olympic Clock*, 27 July.

Johnson, B. (2011c) *Speech to the Conservative Party Conference*, 4 October. Available at: www.newstatesman.com/uk-politics/2011/10/london-city-police-crime-help.

Johnson, B. (2011d) 'Metal Thieves Dishonour the War Dead with their Vandalism', *The Telegraph*, 7 November. Available at: www.telegraph.co.uk/comment/columnists/borisjohnson/8873488/Metal-thieves-dishonour-the-war-dead-with-their-vandalism.html.

Johnson, B. (2011e) *Transcript: People's Question Time*, The Queen's Theatre, Hornchurch, 7 November.

Johnson, B. (2012a) *Transcript: Mayor's Question Time*, 22 February.

Johnson, B. (2012b) *Speech given to Torch Relay Day 69 Evening Celebration Event in Hyde Park*, 26 July.

Johnson, B. (2012c) 'British Businesses are Taking an Unfair Whacking from America', *Telegraph*, 17 September. Available at: www.telegraph.co.uk/comment/columnists/boris-johnson/9547195/British-businesses-are-taking-an-unfair-whacking-from-America.html.

Johnsons, B. (2012d) *Speech to the Conservative Party Conference*, 9 October. Available at: www.cpc12.org.uk/Speeches/Boris_Johnson.aspx.

Johnson, B. (2012e) *Olympic Victory Parade Speech*, London, 10 September.

Jones, T. (1954) *A Diary with Letters 1931–1950*, London: Oxford University Press.

Jones, T. (1969a) *Whitehall Diary Volume I, 1916–1925*, ed. K. Middlemas, London: Oxford University Press.

Jones, T. (1969b) *Whitehall Diary Volume II, 1926–1930*, ed. K. Middlemas, London: Oxford University Press.

Jones, P. and Hudson, J. (1996) 'The Quality of Political Leadership: A Case Study of John Major', *British Journal of Political Science*, 26(2): 229–44.

Joseph, K. (1970) *Speech to Young Conservative National Advisory Committee*, 7 March, London: Conservative Central Office.

Joseph, K. (1974a) *Speech at Farley Hill*, Luton, 3 October, London: Conservative Central Office.

Joseph, K. (1974b) *Speech at Grand Hotel*, Birmingham, 19 October, London: Conservative Central Office.

Kavanagh, D. (1996) 'New Campaign Communication Consequences for British Political Parties', *The International Journal of Press Politics*, 1(3): 60–76.

Kelly, R. (2001) 'Conservatism Under Hague: The Fatal Dilemma', *Political Quarterly*, 72: 197–203.

King, A. (1985) 'Margaret Thatcher: The Style of a Prime Minister', in A. King (ed.), *The British Prime Minister*, Basingstoke: Macmillan, 96–140.

Kingdom, J. (1984) *Agendas, Alternatives and Public Policy*, Boston: Little Brown.

Laing, M. (1972) *Edward Heath: Prime Minister*, London: Sidgwick and Jackson.

Lakin, M. (2014) 'After Cameron: The New New Right and the Unchaining of Britannia', *Global Discourse*, 4(1): 71–89.

Lamont, N. (1999) *In Office*, London: Little, Brown.

Lanham, R.A. (1991) *A Handlist of Rhetorical Terms*, 2nd edition, London: University of California Press.

Lawrence, J. (2009) *Electing Our Masters: The Hustings in British Politics from Hogarth to Blair*, Oxford: Oxford University Press.

Lawson, N. (1992) *The View From No.11: Memoirs of a Tory Radical*, London: Corgi.

Lee, S. (1996) 'Staying the Game', in *Harold Macmillan and Britain's World Role*, Basingstoke: Macmillan, 123–48.

Leith, S. (2011) *You Talking to Me? Rhetoric from Aristotle to Obama*, London: Profile Books.

LeMahieu, D.L. (1988) *A Culture for Democracy: Mass Communication and the Cultivated Mind in Britain Between the Wars*, Oxford: Clarendon Press.

Letwin, S. (1992) *The Anatomy of Thatcherism*, London: Fontana.

Lewis, R. (1979) *Enoch Powell: Principles in Politics*, London: Cassell.

Lord Carrington (1989) 'Preface', in A. Horne, *Macmillan 1957–1968*, London: Macmillan.

Lord Egremont (1968) *Women and Children First*, London: Macmillan.

Lynch, P. (2003) 'The Conservatives and Europe, 1997–2001', in M. Garnett and P. Lynch (eds), *The Conservatives in Crisis*, Manchester: Manchester University Press, 146–63.

Lynch, P. (2009) 'The Conservatives and the European Union: The Lull Before the Storm?', in S. Lee and M. Beech (eds), *The Conservatives under David Cameron: Built to Last?*, Basingstoke: Palgrave Macmillan, 187–207.

Lynch, P. and Garnett, M. (2003) 'Conclusions: The Conservatives in Crisis', in M. Garnett and P. Lynch (eds), *The Conservatives in Crisis*, Manchester: Manchester University Press, 248–68.

Macleod, I. (1958) *Speech to the Conservative Party Conference*, Blackpool.

Macleod, I. (1961) *Speech to the Conservative Party Conference*, Brighton.

Macmillan, H. (1968) *Tides of Fortune*, Basingstoke: Macmillan.

Macmillan, H. (1971) *Riding the Storm 1956–1959*, Basingstoke: Macmillan.

Macmillan, H. (1973) *At the End of the Day 1961–63*, Basingstoke: Macmillan.

Macmillan Papers (C794, Paper 10, 10/08/1960).

Macmillan Papers (C335, Paper 15, 27/04/1963).

Major, J. (1990) *Speech on becoming Prime Minister*, 28 November. Available at: http://www.johnmajor.co.uk/0003.html.

Major, J. (1992a) *Speech to the Central Council*, 14 March. Available at: http://www.johnmajor.co.uk/page877.html.

Major, J. (1992b) *Speech at Conservative Party Rally*, 5 April. Available at: http://www.johnmajor.co.uk/page2437.html.

Major, J. (1993) *Speech to the Conservative Group for Europe*, 22 April. Available at: http://www.johnmajor.co.uk/page1086.html.

Major, J. (1993a) *Speech to the Conservative Party Women's Conference*, 4 June. Available at: http://www.johnmajor.co.uk/page1309.html.

Major, J. (1993b) *Speech to the Conservative Party Annual Conference*, 8 October. Available at: http://www.johnmajor.co.uk/page1096.html.

Major, J. (1994) *Speech to the Conservative Annual Party Conference*, 14 October. Available at: http://www.johnmajor.co.uk/page1147.html.

Major, J. (1995) *Speech to the Conservative Party Annual Conference*, 13 October. Available at: http://www.johnmajor.co.uk/page1269.html.

Major, J. (1996) *Speech to the Conservative Party Annual Conference*, 11 October. Available at: http://www.johnmajor.co.uk/page849.html.

Major, J. (1997a) *Speech to the Central Council*, 15 March. Available at: http://www.johnmajor.co.uk/page1306.html.

Major, J. (1997b) *Comments on the European Union*, 22 April. Available at: http://www.johnmajor.co.uk/page1999.html.

Major, J. (1999) *The Autobiography*, London: HarperCollins.

Margach, James (1970) 'Iain Macleod', in T. Stacey (ed.), *Here Come the Tories*, London: Tom Stacey Ltd, 41–50.

Martin, J. (2013) 'A Feeling for Democracy? Rhetoric, Power and the Emotions', *Journal of Political Power*, 6(3): 461–76.

Martin, J. (2014) *Politics and Rhetoric: A Critical Introduction*, London: Routledge.

Maudling, R. (1978) *Memoirs*, London: Sidgwick & Jackson.

McAnulla, S. (1999) 'The Post-Thatcher Era', in D. Marsh, J. Buller and C. Hay (eds), *Postwar British Politics in Perspective*, Cambridge: Polity, 189–207.

McKibbin, R. (1998) *Classes and Cultures: England 1918–1951*, Oxford: Oxford University Press.

Millar, R. (1993) *A View from the Wings: West End, West Coast, Westminster*, London: Weidenfeld & Nicolson.

MO (1941) *What Britain Means To Me*. File Report 904, 8 October, Brighton: University of Sussex, Mass Observation Archive.

Montague Browne, A. (1995) *Long Sunset: Memoirs of Winston Churchill's Last Private Secretary*, London: Cassell.

Montalbo, T. (1990) 'Churchill: A Study in Oratory', *Finest Hour*, 69: 10–13.

Montgomerie, T. (2012) 'Boris Johnson Emerges as Grassroots' Early Favourite to be Next Tory Leader', *ConservativeHome*, 30 July. Available at: http://conservativehome.blogs.com/thetorydiary/2012/07/boris-johnson-emerges-as-grassroots-early-favourite-to-be-next-tory-leader.html.

Moran, Lord (1968) *Winston Churchill: The Struggle for Survival 1940–1965*, London: Sphere Books.

Morgan, J. (1975) *The House of Lords and the Labour Government, 1964–1970*, Oxford: Clarendon Press.

Morgan, K. (2001) *Britain since 1945: The People's Peace*, 3rd edition, Oxford: Oxford University Press.

Mount, F. (2009) *Cold Cream: My Early Life and Other Mistakes*, London: Bloomsbury.

Mountford, M. (2012) 'Enoch Powell as a Classicist', in Lord Howard of Rising (ed.), *Enoch at 100*, London: Biteback Publishing, 237–50.

Myers, F. (2000) 'Harold Macmillan's Wind of Change Speech: A Case Study in the Rhetoric of Political Change', in *Rhetoric and Public Affairs*, 3(4): 555–75.

Nabarro, G. (1969) *NAB 1: Portrait of a Politician*, Oxford: Robert Maxwell.

Nabarro, G. (1973) *Exploits of a Politician*, London: Arthur Barker.

Nadler, J. (2000) *William Hague: In His Own Right*, London: Politico's.

Newton Dunn, T. (2012) 'Boris Jonson in Charge would Destroy Labour Lead', *The Sun*, 12 September. Available at: www.thesun.co.uk/sol/homepage/news/politics/4533522/Boris-Johnson-in-charge-would-destroy-Labour-lead.html.

Nicolson, H. (1966) *Diaries and Letters 1930–1939*, ed. Nigel Nicolson, London: Collins.

Nicolson, N. (1968) *Harold Nicolson: Diaries and Letters 1945–1962*, vol. 3, London: Collins.

Norton, P. (1975) *Dissension in the House of Commons 1945–74*, London: Macmillan.

Norton, P. (1978) *Conservative Dissidents*, London: Temple Smith.

Norton, P. (1998) 'In Office but Not in Power', in A. King, I. McLean and P. Norton (eds), *New Labour Triumphs: Britain at the Polls*, London: Chatham House, 75–112.

Norton, P. (2012) 'Enoch Powell', in P. Norton (ed.), *Eminent Parliamentarians*, London: Biteback, 129–58.

Nutting, A. (1967) *No End of a Lesson*, London: Constable.

Ogden, C. (1990) *Maggie*, New York: Simon & Schuster.

Olmstead, W. (2006) *Rhetoric: An Historical Introduction*, Oxford: Blackwell.

Orwell, J. (1982) *The Lion and the Unicorn. Socialism and the English Genius*, introduction by B. Crick, first published 1941, Harmondsworth: Penguin.

O'Sullivan, N. (2013) 'Conservatism', in M. Freeden, L.T. Sargent and M. Stears (eds), *The Oxford Handbook of Political Ideologies*, Oxford: Oxford University Press, 293–311.

Pattie, C., and Johnston, R. (2011) 'A Tale of Sound and Fury, Signifying Something? The Impact of the Leaders' Debates in the 2010 UK General Election', *Journal of Elections, Public Opinion and Parties*, 21(2): 147–77.

Pauley, G.E. (2007) *LBJ's American Promise: The 1965 Voting Right Address*, College Station: Texas A&M University Press.

Pettitt, R. (2012) 'Me, Myself and I: "Self-referencing" in Labour Party Conference Leaders' Speeches', *British Politics*, 7: 111–34.

Philips, M. (2011) 'Pure Political Viagra', *Daily Mail*, 4 October. Available at: www.dailymail. co.uk/debate/article-2045108/Conservative-Party-Conference-2011-Boris-Johnson-pure-political-Viagra.html#ixzz26ifUnmpB.

Portillo, M. (2005) 'Life inside the Commons Club', *The Sunday Times*, 10 April.

Portillo, M. (2009) 'Relentlessly Factual and Logical Delivery Force the House to Hang on Every Word' in I. Church (ed.), *Official Report [Hansard] House of Commons: Centenary Volume 1909–2009 Great Speeches from 100 Years*, London: The Stationery Office, 425–38.

Powell, J.E. (1964) 'Is it Politically Practicable?', in *The Rebirth of Britain: A Symposium of Essays by Eighteen Writers*, London: Pan, 257–68.

Powell, E. (1968) 'Enoch Powell's "Rivers of Blood" Speech – Full Text'. Available at: www. telegraph.co.uk/comment/3643826/Enoch-Powells-Rivers-of-Blood-speech.html.

Powell, E. (1973) 'Review of Nigel Fisher, *Iain Macleod*', *The Times*, 10 May.

Powell, E. (1977) *Joseph Chamberlain*, London: Thames & Hudson.

Purnell, S. (2012) 'So, Bumbling Boris Johnson is Lovable and Funny? Well, Have I Got News For You', *Guardian*, 5 August. Available at: www.guardian.co.uk/commentisfree/2012/aug/05/sonia-purnell-boris-johnson-not-prime-minister-material.

Prior, J. (1986) *A Balance of Power*, London: Hamish Hamilton.

Pugh, M. (1985) *The Tories and the People 1880–1935*, Oxford: Blackwell.

Raban, J. (1989) *God, Man & Mrs Thatcher*, London: Chatto & Windus.

Ramsden, J. (1978) *A History of the Conservative Party: The Age of Balfour and Baldwin, 1902–1940*, London: Longman.

Ramsden, J. (1995) 'Winston Churchill and the Leadership of the Conservative Party, 1940–51', *Contemporary Record*, 9(1): 99–119.

Ramsden, J. (1996) *The Winds of Change: Macmillan to Heath 1957–1975*, London: Longman.

Ramsden, J. (1998) *An Appetite for Power: The History of the Conservative Party*, London: HarperCollins.

Rawlinson, P. (1989) *A Price Too High*, London: Weidenfeld & Nicolson.

Reid, C. (2004) 'Margaret Thatcher and the Gendering of Political Oratory', in Michael Edwards and Christopher Reid (eds), *Oratory in Action*, Manchester: Manchester University Press, 164–85.

Rhodes James, R. (1967) *Chips: The Diaries of Sir Henry Chips Channon*, London: Weidenfeld & Nicolson.

Rhodes James, R. (1969) *Memoirs of a Conservative: J.C.C. Davidson's Memoirs and Papers 1910–1937*, London: Weidenfeld & Nicolson.

Rhodes James, R. (1974a) *Winston S. Churchill: His Complete Speeches 1897–1963: Volume VII 1943–1949*, London: Chelsea House Publishers.

Rhodes James, R. (1974b) *Winston S. Churchill: His Complete Speeches 1897–1963: Volume VIII 1950–1963*, London: Chelsea House Publishers.

Rhodes James, R. (1993) 'Churchill the Parliamentarian, Orator and Statesman', in R. Blake and W.R. Louis (eds), *Churchill*, Oxford: Oxford University Press, 503–18.

Riddell, P. (1985) *The Thatcher Government*, Oxford: Blackwell.

Riddell, P. (1991) *The Thatcher Era and its Legacy*, Blackwell: Oxford.

Ridley, N. (1991) *My Style of Government: The Thatcher Years*, London: Hutchinson.

Roberts, A. (1994) *Eminent Churchillians*, London: Weidenfeld & Nicolson.

Roth, A. (1970) *Enoch Powell*, London: Macdonald.

Rubin, G. (2003) *Forty Ways to Look at Winston Churchill*, New York: Random House.

Sampson, A. (1962) *The Anatomy of Britain*, London: Hodder & Stoughton.

Sampson, A. (1967) *Macmillan*, London: Allen Lane.

Sands, S. and Murphy, J. (2012) 'William Hague: I Came Back to be the Foreign Secretary … That's What I'm Doing', *Evening Standard*, 31 August. Available at: http://www.standard.co.uk/news/politics/william-hague-i-came-back-to-be-the-foreign-secretarythats-what-im-doing-8099138.html.

Saward, M. (2006) 'The Representative Claim', *Contemporary Political Theory*, 5(3): 297–318.

Saward, M. (2010) *The Representative Claim*, Oxford: Oxford University Press.

Scammell, M. (1996) 'The Odd Couple: Marketing and Maggie', *European Journal of Marketing*, 30: 114–26.

Scruton, R. (2012) 'The Language on Enoch Powell', in Lord Howard of Rising (ed.), *Enoch at 100*, London: Biteback Publishing, 114–22.

Seawright, D. (2011) *The British Conservative Party and One Nation Conservatism*, New York: Continuum.

Seldon, A. (1981) *Churchill's Indian Summer: The Conservative Government 1951–55*, London: Hodder & Stoughton.

Seldon, A. (1987) 'Escaping the Crysalis of Statism', *Contemporary Record*, 1(1): 26–31.

Seldon, A. (1997) *Major: A Political Life*, London: Weidenfeld & Nicolson.

Self, R. (ed.) (2000) *The Neville Chamberlain Diary Letters. Volume Two: The Reform Years, 1921–1927*, Aldershot: Ashgate.

Seliger, M. (1976) *Ideology and Politics*, New York: HarperCollins.

Shannon, R. (1992) *The Age of Disraeli, 1868–81*, London: Longman.

Shannon, R. (1996) *The Age of Salisbury, 1881–1902*, London: Longman.

Shepherd, R. (1994) *Iain Macleod: A Biography*, London: Hutchinson.

Shepherd, R. (1996) *Enoch Powell*, London: Hutchinson.

Shrapnel, N. (1978) *The Performers: Politics As Theatre*, London: Constable.

Shrapnel, N. (1998) 'Enoch Powell', *Guardian*, 9 February.

Siedentop, L. (1970) 'Mr. Macmillan and the Edwardian Style', in V. Bogdanor and R. Skidelsky (eds) *The Age of Affluence*, Basingstoke: Macmillan.

Siedentop, L. (1979) 'Two Liberal Traditions', in A. Ryan (ed.) *The Idea of Freedom*, Oxford: Oxford University Press.

Snowdon, P. (2010) *Back from the Brink: The Inside Story of the Tory Resurrection*, London: HarperPress.

Stannage. T. (1980) *Baldwin Thwarts the Opposition: The British General Election of 1935*, London: Croom Helm.

Stanyer, J. (2001) *The Creation of Political News: Television and British Political Party Conferences*, Sussex: Sussex Academic Press.

Taylor, A.J. (2002) 'Speaking to Democracy: The Conservative Party and Mass Opinion from the 1920s to the 1950s', in S. Ball and I. Holliday (eds), *Mass Conservatism: The Conservatives and the Public since the 1880s*, London: Cass, 78–99.

Taylor, A.J. (2005) 'Stanley Baldwin, Heresthetics and the Realignment of British Politics', *British Journal of Political Science*, 35(3): 429–63.

Taylor, D. (2002) *Debate on Finance Bill*, 8 May. Available at: www.publications.parliament. uk/pa/cm200102/cmhansrd/vo020508/debtext/20508-08.htm.

Thatcher, M. (1975a) 'Let Our Children Grow Tall', *Speech to the Institute of SocioEconomic Studies*, 15 September. Available at: www.margaretthatcher.org/document/102769.

Thatcher, M. (1975b) *Speech at Glasgow City Hall*, 21 February. Available at: www.margaret-thatcher.org/document/102633.

Thatcher, M. (1976) *Speech to the Conservative Party Conference*, 8 October.

Thatcher, M. (1977) 'Iain Macleod Memorial Lecture – Dimensions of Conservatism', *Speech to Greater London Young Conservatives*, 4 July. Available at: www.margaretthatcher.org/document/103411.

Thatcher, M. (1978a) 'I Believe – a Speech on Christianity and Politics', *Speech to St Lawrence Jewry*, London, 30 March. Available at: www.margaretthatcher.org/document/103522.

Thatcher, M. (1978b) 'The Ideals of an Open Society', *Speech to the Bow Group*, 6 May. Available at: www.margaretthatcher.org/document/103674.

Thatcher, M. (1978c) 'TV Interview for Granada *World in Action*'. Available at: www.marga-retthatcher.org/document/103485

Thatcher, M. (1979a) *Speech to Conservative Rally in Cardiff*, 16 April. Available at: www. margaretthatcher.org/document/104011.

Thatcher, M. (1979b) *Speech at Lord Mayor's Banquet*, 12 November. Available at: www.mar-garetthatcher.org/document/104167.

Thatcher, M. (1979c) 'The Renewal of Britain', *Speech to the Conservative Political Centre Summer School*, 6 July. Available at: www.margaretthatcher.org/document/104107.

Thatcher, M. (1979d) 'Speech to the General Election Press Conference', *Margaret Thatcher Foundation*, 25 April. Available at: www.margaretthatcher.org/document/104042. Accessed 22 June 2014.

Thatcher, M. (1980) Interview on *Weekend World*, London Weekend Television, 6 January. Available at: www.margaretthatcher.org/document/104210.

Thatcher, M. (1984) 'Why Democracy will Last', *The Second Carlton [Club] Lecture*, 26 November. Available at: www.margaretthatcher.org/document/105799.

Thatcher, M. (1985a) *Speech to the Scottish Party Conference*, 10 May. Available at: www. margaretthatcher.org/document/106046. Accessed 1 March 2013.Thatcher, M. (1985b) *Interview on Woman to Woman*, Yorkshire Television, 2 October. Available at: www.marga-retthatcher.org/document/105830.

Thatcher, M. (1988) *Speech to General Assembly of the Church of Scotland*, 21 May. Available at: www.margaretthatcher.org/document/107246.

Thatcher, M. (1992) 'Don't Undo My Work', *Margaret Thatcher Foundation*, 27 April. Available at: www.margaretthatcher.org/commentary/displaydocument.asp?docid=111359

Thatcher, M. (1993) *The Downing Street Years*, London: HarperCollins.

Thatcher, M. (1995) *The Path to Power*, London: HarperCollins.

Theakston, K. (2007) 'What Makes for an Effective British Prime Minister', *Quaderni Di Scienza Politica*, 14(2): 227–49.

Theakston, K. (2012) 'Winston Churchill, 1945–51', in T. Heppell (ed.), *Leaders of the Opposition: from Churchill to Cameron*, Basingstoke: Palgrave Macmillan, 7–19.

Thorpe, D. (2010) *Supermac: The Life of Harold Macmillan*, London: Chatto & Windus.

The Times (1953a) 'Prime Minister's Return', 12 October, 8.

The Times (1953b) 'In Search of Peace', 12 October, 9.

Toye, R. (2010) 'Winston Churchill's "Crazy Broadcast": Party, Nation and the 1945 Gestapo Speech', *Journal of British Studies*, 49(3): 655–80.

Toye, R. (2011) 'The Rhetorical Premiership: A New Perspective on Prime Ministerial Power since 1946', *Parliamentary History*, 30(2): 175–92.

Toye, R. (2013a) *Rhetoric: A Very Short Introduction*, Oxford: Oxford University Press.

Toye, R. (2013b) *The Roar of the Lion: The Untold Story of Churchill's World War II Speeches*, Oxford: Oxford University Press.

True, N. (2012) 'European Union', in Lord Howard of Rising (ed.), *Enoch at 100*, London: Biteback Publishing, 1–34.

Turner, B.S. (2008) *The Body and Society: Explorations in Social Theory*, 3rd edition, London: SAGE Publications Ltd.

Turner, J. (1994) *Macmillan*, London: Longman.

Urban, G. (1996) *Diplomacy and Disillusion at the Court of Margaret Thatcher*, London: I.B. Tauris.

Wade, R. (2013) *Conservative Party Economic Policy: from Heath in Opposition to Cameron in Coalition*, Basingstoke: Palgrave Macmillan.

Wapshott, N. and Brock, G. (1983) *Thatcher*, London: Futura.

Watkins, A. (1982) *Brief Lives*, London: Hamish Hamilton.

Watt, N. and Clark, T. (2012) 'Boris Johnson is Britain's Most Respected Politician, Poll Shows', *Guardian*, 14 September. Available at: www.guardian.co.uk/politics/2012/sep/14/boris-johnson-most-respected-politician.

Webb, P. and Poguntke, T. (2013) 'The Presidentialisation of Politics Thesis Defended', *Parliamentary Affairs*, 66: 646–54.

Weidhorn, M. (1974) *Sword and Pen: A Survey of the Writings of Sir Winston Churchill*, Albuquerque: University of New Mexico Press.

Weidhorn, M. (1987) *Churchill's Rhetoric and Political Discourse*, London: University Press of America.

Welshman, J. (2005) 'Ideology, Social Science, and Public Policy: The Debate Over Deprivation', *20th Century British History*, 16(3): 306–41.

White, M. (2012) 'Michael "Del Boy" Heseltine Launches Plan H', *Guardian Blog*. Available at: www.guardian.co.uk/global/2012/oct/31/michael-heseltine-plan-h.

Whittingdale, J. (2012) 'Margaret Thatcher', in P. Norton (ed.), *Eminent Parliamentarians*, London: Biteback, 227–54.

Williams, P. (1979) *Hugh Gaitskell*, London: Cape.

Williams, C. (2009) *Harold Macmillan*, London: Weidenfeld & Nicolson.

Williamson, P. (1999) *Stanley Baldwin. Conservative Leadership and National Character*, Cambridge: Cambridge University Press.

Wills, G. (1992) *Lincoln at Gettysburg. The Words That Remade America*, New York: Simon & Schuster.

Wood, J. (1970) 'Introduction', in J. Wood (ed.), *Powell and the 1970 Election*, Kingswood: Elliot Right Ways Books, 7–9.

Wright, P. (1985) *On Living in an Old Country: The National Past in Contemporary Britain*, London: Verso.

Wyatt, W. (1958) *Distinguished For Talent*, London: Hutchinson.

Young, H. (1989) *One of Us*, London: Pan.

Young, H. (1991) 'Surprising Egotist Proves He is More Equal than Others', *Guardian*, 12 October.

Young, H. and Sloman, A. (1986) *The Thatcher Phenomenon*, BBC Television.

Young, T. (2010) 'Cameron: The Brasenose Years', *Daily Telegraph*, 12 May.

YouTube (2006) 'David Cameron Introduces His New Video Blog Site', www.youtube.com/watch?v=gTd3j31PIPo&feature=plcp, uploaded 31 October 2006.

YouTube (2009) 'Conservative Party Election Broadcast – 15 May 2009', www.youtube.com/watch?v=0bIZLfdEbkc&feature=plcp, uploaded 15 May 2009.

YouTube (2010a) 'David Cameron's First Ever PMQs', www.youtube.com/watch?v=pfUtkdM4wPI, uploaded 27 August 2010.

YouTube (2010b) 'The First Election Debate on ITV1: 15th April 2010', www.youtube.com/watch?v=rk5HvJmy_yg, uploaded 15 April 2010

YouTube (2010c) 'David Cameron: The Big Speech at the Tory Conference', www.youtube.com/watch?v=ZempWzlCctc, uploaded 26 August 2010.

YouTube (2011a) 'David Cameron Apologizes for Bloody Sunday', www.youtube.com/watch?v=I8DSTOGtEkg, uploaded 31 May 2011.

YouTube (2011b) 'That Interview in Full', www.youtube.com/watch?v=u2kerzNLTIY, uploaded 22 July 2011.

YouTube (2012a) 'David Cameron on Letterman', www.youtube.com/watch?v=WcdpMxkyk38, uploaded 27 September 2012.

Index